Table of Contents

Introduction

Is it possible to cook some amazing dishes with only one kitchen appliance? Can you use only one tool to impress everyone with unique flavors and textures? Can you cook some of the best dishes of the life in a new and very attractive way?

We are here to tell you that now all these are possible. You just need one simple tool – an air fryer.

You will discover something totally new and impressive. You will learn that you can cook all the favorite foods in a much healthier way.

You will use less oil and fat and be able to cook the dishes in no time. All the dishes will be completely cooked on the inside and on the outside.

You can forget about the oven, the stove, and deep fryer. An air fryer will roast, steam, bake and grill all of the food for you and the family.

Your family, friends, and dinner guests will be impressed with this new way of cooking. Everything is done much faster and tastes delicious. It's as simple as that. It's efficient, effective, and easy.

The things that affect the day-to-day life, such as your job, taking care of your family, and getting your errands done can sometimes make it impossible for you to find the time cook to cook a good meal. An air fryer and a cookbook loaded with delicious recipes can help you make that a thing of the past.

Purchase the own air fryer and get started today. Look at our simple yet appetizing and satisfying collection of recipes and get ready to field the praises of everyone tasting the food. What more could you ask for? It's time to make a change in the way you cook. It's time for an air fryer and amazing dishes. Get started today!

Breakfast

Cheese Toast

Prep time: 10 minutes
Cooking time: 15 minutes
Servings: 2

Ingredients:
- 4 slices baguette sandwich bread
- 2 slices Swiss cheese
- ¼ cup butter, melted

Directions:

Brush the butter on each side of bread. Put the cheese on one side of bread. Cover the cheese with another slice of bread and add to the cooking basket. Cook at 360 degrees Fahrenheit for 5 minutes or until the cheese has melted.

Porridge with Spiced Fruit and Nuts

Prep time: 5 minutes
Cooking time: 10 minutes
Servings: 2

Ingredients:
- 2 cups water
- 4 ounces steel-cut oats
- 2 tablespoons of any fruit, such as raspberry, gooseberry, or currant
- 1 tablespoon sugar
- 2 ounces sour cream or half and half
- Spices like cinnamon or cardamom
- Hazelnuts or almonds

Directions:

Rinse oats and fruit. Put them into the baking pan with a cup of water. Cook at 260°F for 5 minutes and let sit for 5 minutes until the water has been absorbed. Remove the pan and add sour cream until you reach the desired consistency. Garnish with the nuts and spices.

Italian Pasta with Cheese

Prep time: 5 minutes
Cooking time: 20 minutes
Servings: 4

Ingredients:
- 2 cups pasta
- 1 cup water
- 2 cups thick sour cream
- 2 cups Mozzarella cheese
- 1 teaspoon potato starch

Directions:

Grate the cheese. Place pasta and cheese in separate bowls. Take 1½ cup of the cheese and mix it with the starch. Pour the water into the baking pan, add all ingredients and cover with aluminum foil. Hit the power button and set the temperature to 310°F. Cook for 15 minutes, the open and remove the foil. Sprinkle the rest of the cheese on top. Cool before serving.

Toast Strips

Prep time: 5 minutes
Cooking time: 15 minutes
Servings: 2

Ingredients:

- 4 slices
- 2 tablespoons butter
- 1 egg
- Salt
- Cardamom
- Turmeric
- Ground caraway seeds

Directions:

Beat an egg in a bowl, and then add salt and spices. Butter the bread slices and cut into strips. Preheat the air fryer to 360°F. Dip the each strip into the spiced egg mixture and place them on the pan. After 2 minutes, turn slices of bread on the other side. As soon as slices of bread are golden brown, remove them from air fryer.

English Sandwich

Prep time: 5 minutes
Cooking time: 5 minutes
Servings: 2

Ingredients:

- 1 egg
- 1 English rindless backwash
- 1 breakfast roll
- Salt
- Ground black pepper

Directions:

Beat an egg into a bowl, and then add salt and pepper. Cut the roll in half and the egg and bacon between the halves. Preheat the air fryer to 390°F. Place the roll into the air fryer and cook for 6 minutes.

Spicy German Sandwich

Prep time: 5 minutes
Cooking time: 5 minutes
Servings: 2

Ingredients:

- 125 ounces breakfast sausage
- 2 slices bread
- 125 ounces Cheddar cheese
- 1 egg
- 2 tablespoons milk
- Ground black pepper
- Mustard

Directions:

Cut the sausage in small pieces. Grate the cheese. Beat an egg in a separate bowl and add the milk and pepper. Place all the ingredients in a large bowl. Preheat the air fryer to 310°F. Spread the desired amount of mixture on the bread. Place into the air fryer and grill for 2 minutes. When the time is up, garnish with the mustard.

Eggs en Cocotte

Prep time: 15 minutes
Cooking time: 15 minutes
Servings: 4

Ingredients:
- 500 ounces leaf spinach
- 200 ounces of ham, sliced
- 4 eggs
- 1 tablespoon sunflower oil
- 4 teaspoons milk
- 1 teaspoons butter
- Ground black pepper
- Sea salt

Directions:

Preheat the air fryer to 350°F. Use 4 cocottes or ramekins and butter them with the butter. Wilt the spinach with the oil on the oven. Divide the ham and wilted spinach into the cocottes. Crack an egg in each one and add milk. Add salt and pepper. Cook for 15 minutes or until the eggs reach the texture you desire.

Air-fried Pizza

Prep time: 15 minutes
Cooking time: 20 minutes
Servings: 4

Ingredients:
- 1 sheet puff pastry
- 4 eggs
- 1 teaspoon water
- 3 ounces sour cream
- 2 ounces Parmesan cheese, shredded
- Sea salt
- 4 peppercorns, grounded
- 200 ounces ham, sliced
- 10 green onions

Directions:

Thaw out the dough according to the package instructions. Preheat the air fryer to 420°F. Place parchment paper onto the baking sheet and flour the surface. Roll out the pastry to ¼-inch thick. Beat 1 egg lightly with 1 teaspoon water. Brush the surface of dough with the egg wash, and then refrigerate for 10 minutes. Mix the sour cream and cheese in a bowl, and add salt and pepper. Cover the pastry with the mixture and then add the ham. Beat the remaining eggs in a bowl and add them to the top of the tart, spacing them evenly over the pastry. Cook for about 20 minutes. Mince the onion and garnish the top of the pizza.

Breakfast Omelet

Prep time: 15 minutes
Cooking time: 20 minutes
Servings: 4

Ingredients:

- 4 eggs
- 2 sausages
- 3 tomatoes
- 1 tablespoon sunflower oil
- Dill weed or parsley
- Green onions, minced
- 2 tablespoons cheddar cheese, grated Sea salt
- Ground black pepper

Directions:

Preheat the air fryer to 360°F. Put the tomatoes and sausages in the baking pan and cook for 5 minutes. Mix the remaining ingredients in a small bowl. Take out the baking pan and add the mixture. Cook for 5 minutes.

Potato Casserole

Prep time: 15 minutes
Cooking time: 20 minutes
Servings: 4

Ingredients:

- ½ cheese, grated
- 2 egg
- ½ teaspoon garlic, minced
- ¼ teaspoon cayenne pepper
- ½ teaspoon turmeric
- Sea salt
- Ground black pepper
- 2 tablespoons sunflower oil
- 1½ pounds potatoes
- Dill weed or parsley
- Green onion, minced
- 2 tablespoons cream

Directions:

Preheat the air fryer to 400°F. Beat the eggs and mix them with the grated cheese, garlic, salt, and species. Pour oil into baking dish. Cut potatoes into small strips and place in the baking pan. Add the egg and cheese mixture. Cook for 20 minutes until the potatoes are soft. Serve with the cream and sprinkle it with dill or parsley and onion.

Italian Focaccia with Ham

Prep time: 15 minutes
Cooking time: 20 minutes
Servings: 4

Ingredients:

- 1 teaspoon active dry yeast
- 200 ounces flour
- 1 cup milk
- 1 tablespoon sunflower oil
- Sea salt
- 1 teaspoon cardamom
- ½ tablespoon garlic, minced
- 200 ounces cooked ham.

Directions:

Preheat the air fryer to 350°F. Mix the dry yeast with warm water and leave for 5 minutes until foamy. Cut the ham into small pieces. Add the milk, flour, salt, oil, cardamom, garlic, ham and knead the dough until no longer sticky. Leave the dough for 1 hour or until it doubles in size. Pour the oil into the baking dish. Roll out the dough and place it in the baking pan. Cook for 20 minutes until brown.

Air-fried Potatoes with Spicy Greens

Prep time: 5 minutes
Cooking time: 40 minutes
Servings: 4

Ingredients:

- 4 potatoes
- 1 tablespoon sunflower oil
- Sea salt
- 1 teaspoon shallots,
- ½ tablespoon garlic, minced
- 1 teaspoon basil,
- 1 teaspoon celery
- 1 teaspoon parsley

Directions:

Preheat the air fryer to 390°F. Dice the shallots, garlic, basil, celery, and parsley and place in a bowl. Wash the potatoes and cut them into quarters. Place the potatoes in the baking pan. Drizzle with oil and sprinkle with remaining ingredients and add salt. Cook for 40 minutes until brown. Serve with sour cream.

Noodle Casserole

Prep time: 15 minutes
Cooking time: 20 minutes
Servings: 4

Ingredients:

- 4 sheets lasagna
- ½ cup cherry tomatoes
- ¼ cup milk
- ½ cup mozzarella cheese
- Sea salt
- Ground black pepper

Directions:

Preheat the air fryer to 360°F. Pour the water into the bowl with lasagna and boil until soft. Drain the noodles and set aside. Warm the milk. Cut the cherry tomatoes into quarters. Mix the milk with cheese and add to the pasta and tomatoes. Toss to combine. Sprinkle with salt and pepper. Bake for 15 minutes and let rest. Serve with grated Parmesan cheese.

Sardines in Ramekins

Prep time: 15 minutes
Cooking time: 15 minutes
Servings: 1

Ingredients:

- 1 tablespoon olive oil
- 100 ounces leaf spinach
- 2 whole sardines
- 1 egg

- 2 teaspoons cheddar cheese, grated
- Sea salt
- Black peppercorns, cracked
- Dried Italian herbs

Directions:

Oil the ovenproof ramekin. Lay the spinach leaves on the bottom of it. Beat an egg in a bowl and add the sardines. Sprinkle with cheese, sea salt, cracked pepper and dried Italian herbs. Cook at 350° F for 7 minutes until the egg is white.

Scrambled Eggs with Cheese an Bell Peppers

Prep time: 2 minutes
Cooking time: 2 minutes
Servings: 4

Ingredients:

- 5 eggs
- 1 cup of milk
- ½ large bell pepper
- 1 tablespoon sunflower oil

- 2 tablespoons dried Italian herbs
- 2 tablespoons cheese, shredded
- Sea salt
- Ground black pepper

Directions:

Preheat the air fryer to 360°F. Spread oil on the bottom of the baking pan. Whisk the eggs in a bowl and add milk. Season with salt and pepper. Cut the bell pepper into thin slices and cook in the air fryer for 5 minutes. Pour the eggs mixture and milk onto the peppers and stir well. Cook for 5 minutes or until the eggs set. Serve with the grated cheese and herbs on top.

Air-fried Figs

Prep time: 2 minutes
Cooking time: 5 minutes
Servings: 4

Ingredients:

- 4 figs
- 4 slices bread

- 1 teaspoon tangerine zest
- 2 tablespoons fig preserves

Directions:

Preheat the air fryer to 360°F. Put the bread on the baking pan and air fry for 3 minutes until crispy. Cut figs and place into the baking pan and air fry for 2 minutes. Spread fig preserve on the bread and top with figs. Sprinkle with tangerine zest.

Sushi Rolls

Prep time: 15 minutes
Cooking time: 20 minutes
Servings: 4

Ingredients:
- 1 tofu skin
- 1 seaweed sheet
- 2 ounces salmon or 1 pack of crab sticks
- 1 tablespoon olive oil
- Spicy sauce
- Lettuce leaf

Directions:
Place crab stick or fish onto seaweed sheet. Add the tofu skin and sprinkle with oil. Cook in the air fryer for 5 minutes under 350°F. Serve with leaf lettuce and spicy sauce.

Toast with Button Mushrooms

Prep time: 5 minutes
Cooking time: 10 minutes
Servings: 2

Ingredients:
- 4 slices bread
- 2 tablespoons olive oil
- 1 onion, peeled
- 2 large button mushrooms, trimmed
- Salt
- 1 teaspoon sesame seeds

Directions:
Spread oil on the bread. Cut the onion into rings and the mushrooms into slices. Put an onion ring on each of the bread slices, and then top with a few mushroom slices. Sprinkle with salt and sesame seeds. Cook at 350°F for 7 minutes until the mushrooms are soft.

Scrambled Eggs on Toast with Lettuce

Prep time: 5 minutes
Cooking time: 10 minutes
Servings: 2

Ingredients:
- 2 slices bread
- 2 tablespoons olive oil
- 1 egg
- Salt
- Cayenne pepper
- 2 lettuce leaves
- 1 cherry tomato
- 1 tablespoon Parmesan cheese

Directions:
Beat an egg in a bowl and whisk it, and then cut the tomato in half and season the halves with Salt and spices. Spread oil on the pan. Pour the egg mixture on the pan and cook at 280°F for 10 minutes. Stir until the eggs are scrambled. Air fry 2 slices of bread until crispy. Place leaves of lettuce on bread. Top with the scrambled eggs. Sprinkle with cheese and serve.

Cottage Cheese Casserole

Prep time: 10 minutes
Cooking time: 25 minutes
Servings: 6

Ingredients:

- 2 eggs
- 2 tablespoons olive oil
- 2 cups small curd cottage cheese
- ¼ cup sugar
- 1,8 ounces manna groats½ cup barley
- 1 cup wheat flour
- Salt
- Vanilla extract

Directions:

Preheat the air fryer to 330°F. Mash the cottage cheese with the eggs and sugar. Add the barley and flour. Sprinkle with salt and vanilla extract. Mix until smooth. Spread oil on the pan and pour the mixture into the pan. Cook at 280°F for 25 minutes.

Egg Breakfast

Prep time: 10 minutes
Cooking time: 10 minutes
Servings: 3

Ingredients:

- 3 eggs
- ½ cup bacon
- 1 teaspoon butter
- 1 teaspoon salt
- ½ teaspoon paprika
- 1 onion
- 1 teaspoon fresh basil, chopped
- 1 tablespoon grated Parmesan cheese

Directions:

In a mixing bowl, beat the eggs in a mixing bowl. Peel the onion and chop it. Combine the onion and eggs together and stir well. After this, sprinkle the mixture with salt and paprika. Melt the butter and transfer it to the air fryer basket. Pour the egg mixture into the air fryer and add bacon, close the lid. Cook it for 10 minutes. Remove the eggs from the air fryer and sprinkle the dish with the chopped basil and Parmesan cheese and serve it immediately.

Sweet Milk Quinoa

Prep time: 10 minutes
Cooking time: 20 minutes
Servings: 3

Ingredients:

- 2 cup quinoa
- 1 tablespoon brown sugar
- 1 /2 cup dried fruit
- ⅓ teaspoon salt
- 1 teaspoon vanilla sugar
- 1 teaspoon maple syrup
- 4 cups milk

Directions:

Add the quinoa to a mixing bowl. Add half of the milk and sprinkle with salt. Stir the mixture until salt is dissolved. Add the brown sugar and vanilla sugar. Stir well again. Chop the dried fruit and add them to the quinoa mixture. Open the air fryer lid and transfer the quinoa mixture. Add the syrup and stir well. Close the lid and cook for 20 minutes or until all the water is absorbed. Remove the quinoa from the air fryer and let it cool briefly before serving.

Parsley Muffins

Prep time: 10 minutes
Cooking time: 10 minutes
Servings: 3

Ingredients:

- 1 egg
- 1 cup parsley
- 1 cup flour
- ⅓ cup heavy cream
- 1 teaspoon salt
- ½ teaspoon baking soda
- 1 teaspoon lemon juice
- ½ teaspoon olive oil

Directions:

In a mixing bowl, beat the egg in a mixing bowl. Add the salt and baking soda and whisk the mixture until smooth. Add the lemon juice and olive oil and s and stir. Sift the flour into the mixture and add the cream. Wash the parsley and mince it. Add the parsley to the flour mixture and stir well. Take the muffin form and fill every form halfway with the muffin batter. Transfer the muffins in the air fryer, close the lid and cook for 10 minutes. Remove the muffins from the air fryer and let them cool before serving.

Chicken Rissole

Prep time: 10 minutes
Cooking time: 10 minutes
Servings: 3

Ingredients:

- 1 teaspoon starch
- 1 tablespoon bread crumbs
- 1 egg
- 1 garlic clove
- 10 ounces minced chicken fillet
- 1 teaspoon salt
- 1 teaspoon ginger
- ½ teaspoon nutmeg

Directions:

In a mixing bowl, combine the starch, salt, ginger, and nutmeg together in a mixing bowl and stir well. Add the egg and whisk everything together. Add the minced chicken fillet and combine everything together. Peel the garlic clove and mince it. Add the garlic to the meat mixture and stir well. Make medium-sized balls from the mixture and sprinkle the meatballs with bread crumbs. Open the air fryer lid and transfer the rissoles in the air fryer basket. Close the lid and cook for 10 minutes. Remove the rissoles from the air fryer and serve.

Savory Pancakes

Prep time: 10 minutes
Cooking time: 7 minutes
Servings: 3

Ingredients:

- 1 teaspoon baking soda
- 1 teaspoon salt
- 1 tablespoon apple cider vinegar
- 1 cup flour
- ⅓ cup skim milk
- 1 teaspoon sugar

Directions:

Combine the salt, baking soda, sugar, and apple cider vinegar in a mixing bowl and stir well. Add the skim milk and stir again. Sift the flour into the skim milk mixture and blend using a hand mixer until a smooth batter forms. Add more skim milk, if necessary. Take the pancake form and pour the dough into the form. Open the air fryer lid and place the form into the air fryer and close the lid. Cook for 7 minutes, and then remove the pancakes from the air fryer. Serve warm.

Dill Omelet

Prep time: 5 minutes
Cooking time: 7 minutes
Servings: 3

Ingredients:
- 4 eggs
- ½ cup sour cream
- ½ cup dill
- 1 teaspoon salt
- 1 teaspoon ground black pepper
- 1 teaspoon nutmeg

Directions:

Beat the eggs in a mixing bowl. Add the sour cream and stir well. Sprinkle with the salt, ground black pepper, and nutmeg and stir again. Mince the dill and sprinkle the mixture with it. Open the air fryer lid and pour the egg mixture into the air fryer basket. Close the lid and cook the omelet for 7 minutes. Serve it warm.

Oatmeal with Blueberries

Prep time: 10 minutes
Cooking time: 15 minutes
Servings: 4

Ingredients:
- 2 cups rolled oats
- 3 cups water
- 1 teaspoon maple syrup
- 1 tablespoon brown sugar
- 1 cup blueberry
- 1 tablespoon butter

Directions:

Add the oats to a mixing bowl. Add the brown sugar and butter and stir well. Open the air fryer lid and transfer the oatmeal mixture into it. Add the water and stir well. Close the lid and cook for 15 minutes. Combine the blueberries with the maple syrup and stir well. When the oatmeal is cooked, remove it from the air fryer. Sprinkle the oatmeal with blueberry mixture, mix well and serve.

Cabbage Cutlets

Prep time: 15 minutes
Cooking time: 10 minutes
Servings: 4

Ingredients:
- 13 ounces cabbage
- 1 egg
- 1 teaspoon salt
- ⅓ cup oatmeal flour
- 1 teaspoon sour cream
- 1 tablespoon olive oil
- 1 teaspoon ground black pepper
- 1 teaspoon starch

Directions:

In a mixing bowl, beat the egg in a mixing bowl. Add the sour cream, ground black pepper, and starch and stir well. Sprinkle with the oatmeal flour. Take the cabbage and wash it. Grate the cabbage and combine the cabbage and egg mixture together. Use a hand mixer to combine everything. Add the olive oil and salt. Stir well and make cutlets from the mixture. Transfer the cutlets in the air fryer and close the lid. Cook for 10 minutes, then cool briefly and serve.

Creamy Buckwheat

Prep time: 10 minutes
Cooking time: 15 minutes
Servings: 3

Ingredients:

- 2 cups buckwheat
- 2 cups water
- 1 cup heavy cream
- 3 tablespoons brown sugar
- 1 tablespoon honey
- 1 vanilla pod
- 1 teaspoon nutmeg
- ⅓ cup cashews, chopped
- 1 tablespoon coconut

Directions:

Combine the buckwheat and water together in a mixing bowl. Add the cream and brown sugar and stir well. Transfer to the air fryer and add the vanilla pod and cream. Stir well. Sprinkle with the coconut and cashews and s and stir again. Close the lid and cook for 15 minutes. When the dish is cooked, remove it from the air fryer and cool briefly. Sprinkle it with the honey and stir well until the honey is dissolved. Sprinkle the dish with the nutmeg and serve.

Cheesy Bananas

Prep time: 15 minutes
Cooking time: 5 minutes
Servings: 3

Ingredients:

- 3 bananas
- 1 cup hard cheese
- 1 tablespoon condensed milk
- 1 teaspoon butter

Directions:

Peel the bananas. Combine the butter with the condensed milk in a mixing bowl and whisk until smooth. Make cuts lengthwise on every banana and fill the bananas with the condensed milk mixture. Slice the hard cheese and cover the bananas in cheese. Transfer the bananas to the air fryer and close the lid. Cook for 5 minutes or until the cheese browns. Remove the bananas from the air fryer and cool to room temperature. Transfer the bananas to the serving plate.

Cottage Cheese Casserole

Prep time: 10 minutes
Cooking time: 20 minutes
Servings: 4

Ingredients:

- 2 cups small curd cottage cheese
- 3 eggs
- 1 teaspoon vanilla sugar
- 2 bananas
- 1 teaspoon maple syrup
- ¼ cup sugar
- ¼ cup heavy cream
- 3 tablespoons milk
- ⅓ cup flour

Directions:

Add the cottage cheese to a mixing bowl and blend using a hand mixer until smooth. Beat the eggs into the cottage cheese for 1 minute. Sprinkle the mixture with the vanilla sugar, cream, and milk. Blend for 2 minutes, then add the flour and maple syrup. Peel the bananas and chop them roughly. Add the chopped bananas to the bowl and mix well. Transfer the casserole to the air fryer form and place the form in the air fryer. Cook for 20 minutes. Remove the casserole from the air fryer and cool for a few minutes. Cut the casserole into pieces and serve.

Bacon and Avocado Patties

Prep time: 5 minutes
Cooking time: 10 minutes
Servings: 3

Ingredients:

- 3 buns
- 2 cups yellow squash or zucchini1 bell pepper,, chopped
- 2 bacon slices
- 1 avocado, chopped
- 1 tablespoon hummus
- 1 cup cheese, shredded

Directions:

Add the squash, bell pepper and bacon to a bowl. Add the avocado and hummus and stir well. Add the cheese and stir again. Make small round patties and set the air fryer to 300°F. Place the patties on the grill and cook for 10 minutes. When done, place the patty on a bun and top with the favorite condiments.

Simple Egg Breakfast

Prep time: 4 minutes
Cooking time: 10 minutes
Servings: 2

Ingredients:

- 4 eggs
- 1 teaspoon yellow mustard
- ½ cup mayonnaise
- 2 green onions, chopped
- ½ teaspoon paprika
- Salt and ground black pepper to taste

Directions:

Mix the eggs, mustard and green onion in a bowl. Add the mayonnaise, salt, pepper, and paprika and mix well. Add the mixture to the baking tray. Place it in the air fryer and cook for 10 minutes. When cooked, remove the dish from the air fryer and serve.

Muffin Mix Breakfast

Prep time: 6 minutes
Cooking time: 12 minutes
Servings: 2

Ingredients:

- 1 tablespoon vegetable oil
- 1 el egg
- 1 whole wheat muffin
- Ground black pepper to taste
- 1 cup cheese, shredded
- 4 slices Canadian bacon

Directions:

Whisk the egg in a bowl. Add the black pepper and mix well. Grease the round baking tray with oil and pour the egg mixture. Add the cheese and bacon. Place the round baking tray in air fryer with the muffin. Let it cook for 12 minutes on 300°F. When cooked, remove the dish from the air fryer and serve.

Simple Bacon and Eggs

Prep time: 4 minutes
Cooking time: 10 minutes
Servings: 2

Ingredients:

- 3 eggs
- 3 egg whites
- ½ cup milk
- 3 mushrooms, diced
- 1 tablespoon bell pepper, diced
- 4 bread slices
- 2 slices bacon, chopped
- 3 slices cheese

Directions:

Whisk the eggs and egg whites in a bowl. Add the milk, mushrooms, green pepper, and bacon and mix well. Pour the mixture in the round baking tray and add the cheese to the top. Place the bread slices on the sides of the tray in the air fryer. Cook for 10 minutes on 300°F. Remove the dish when done and serve.

Air-fried Asparagus

Prep time: 6 minutes
Cooking time: 15 minutes
Servings: 2

Ingredients:
- 2 sliced of bread
- 1 avocado, sliced
- 3 slices deli ham
- 3 stalks asparagus
- ½ tomato, sliced
- 1 egg
- 1 tablespoon vegetable oil

Directions:

Whisk the egg in a bowl. Add the avocado, ham, and asparagus and mix well. Coat a round baking tray with the oil. Pour the mixture into the tray and top with the tomato slices. Place the tray into the air fryer. Place the bread pieces on the sides of the baking tray. Cook for 15 minutes on 300°F. Remove the dish when done and serve.

Beef with Mushrooms

Prep time: 5 minutes
Cooking time: 10 minutes
Servings: 3

Ingredients:
- 1 tablespoon mustard
- ½ tablespoon honey
- 1 garlic clove, minced
- ½ cup mayonnaise
- Salt and pepper to taste
- ½ pound beef, chopped
- 6 large mushrooms, chopped 1 onion, chopped
- 1 cup cheese, shredded
- Sandwich bread slices
- Oil – 1 tablespoon

Directions:

Put the beef into the bowl. Add the mustard, honey, garlic, mayonnaise, onion, cheese, and mushrooms and blend well. Coat the round baking tray with oil. Place the bread pieces at the bottom as a layer in the tray. Pour the mixture on top. Cook in the air fryer for 10 minutes. When cooked, remove the dish from the air fryer and serve.

Bacon and Ham Mix

Prep time: 5 minutes
Cooking time: 10 minutes
Servings: 2

Ingredients:
- 4 slices bacon
- 6 bread slices
- 1 cup ham, chopped
- 1 cup Cheddar cheese
- 3 eggs
- ½ cup milk
- Salt to taste

Directions:
Whisk the eggs in a bowl. Add the ham, cheese, milk, and salt. Blend well and add the bacon slices. Add the mixture to the round baking tray. Bake for 10 minutes in the air fryer on 300°F. When cooked, serve with the bread slices.

Chicken with Salsa

Prep time: 6 minutes
Cooking time: 18 minutes
Servings: 3

Ingredients:
- 2 cups salsa
- 1 tablespoon
- 1 tablespoon adobo sauce
- 1 pound chicken boneless and skinless breast, chopped
- Salt and ground black pepper to taste
- Cheddar cheese, shredded
- Cilantro, for garnish

Directions:
Put the chicken into the bowl. Add the salsa, tomato sauce, adobo sauce, and cheese. Mix well and add the salt and pepper. Make small patties out of the mixture and place them in the air fryer. Cook for 18 minutes on 300°F. When ready, garnish with the cilantro and serve.

Steak Strips

Prep time: 4 minutes
Cooking time: 15 minutes
Servings: 2

Ingredients:
- 1 small steak, cut into 5 strips
- Salt and ground black pepper to taste
- 6 slices ciabatta bread
- 2 tablespoons garlic, minced
- 1 tomato, chopped
- ½ cup fresh basil, minced
- ½ cup cheese, shredded

Directions:
Mix the cheese with basil in a bowl. Add the garlic, tomato, salt, and pepper and mix well. Pour the mixture into the round baking tray and add the steak strips. Bake in the air fryer for 15 minutes. When done, serve with bread.

Potato Mix Breakfast

Prep time: 5 minutes
Cooking time: 10 minutes
Servings: 2

Ingredients:

- 2 cups provolone
- 1 pound steak, sliced.
- 1 onion, chopped
- 1 potato, diced

- 1 tablespoon butter
- Salt and ground black pepper to taste
- 1 tablespoon vegetable oil
- 4 bread slices

Directions:

Add the cheese and potato in a bowl. Add the onion, butter, salt and pepper and blend well. Coat the round baking tray with oil and pour the mixture in the pan, placing the steak on top. Cook for 10 minutes on 300°F. When ready, serve it with the bread.

Potato Rissoles

Prep time: 15 minutes
Cooking time: 15 minutes
Servings: 5

Ingredients:

- 4 large potatoes
- 1 teaspoon butter
- ¼ cup flour
- 1 teaspoon salt
- 1 teaspoon starch
- ½ cup beef, minced
- 1 tablespoon barbecue sauce

Directions:

Peel the potatoes and then grate them. Transfer the grated potato in the mixing bowl and add flour and salt. Add the starch and stir well. Melt the butter and combine it with the minced beef, stirring well. Combine the minced meat mixture and the potato mixture. Make medium-sized rissoles from the mixture and transfer them to the air fryer. Close the lid and cook for 15 minutes. Remove the rissoles from the air fryer and let them rest briefly. Serve with the BBQ sauce.

Mushroom Boats

Prep time: 10 minutes
Cooking time: 20 minutes
Servings: 3

Ingredients:

- ⅓ cup mushrooms
- 1 teaspoon dill
- ¼ cup cheese
- 1 tablespoon butter
- 10 ounces puff pastry
- 1 egg
- 1 potato

Directions:

Take the puff pastry and roll it out using a rolling pin. Cut the puff pastry to match the size of the muffin form pan. Transfer the puff pastry to the muffin forms. Slice the mushrooms and chop the dill and combine in a mixing bowl. Add the butter and egg and stir well. Peel the potato and grate it. Add the potato to the mushroom mixture. Grate the cheese. Transfer the mushroom mixture to the puff pastry and sprinkle them with the grated cheese. Transfer the muffin pan to the air fryer and cook for 20 minutes. Remove the mushroom boards from the air fryer and serve hot.

Sweet Rice with Raisins and Prunes

Prep time: 10 minutes
Cooking time: 15 minutes
Servings: 4

Ingredients:

- 2 cups basmati rice
- 3 tablespoons brown sugar
- 1 teaspoon vanilla sugar
- 2 cups water
- 2 cups milk
- 1 teaspoon nutmeg
- ½ cup raisins
- ⅓ cup prunes
- ½ cup nuts

Directions:

Combine water and milk together and stir well. Take the rice and transfer it to the air fryer basket. Pour the milk mixture into it and stir well. Sprinkle the mixture with the vanilla sugar, brown sugar, and nutmeg and stir well. Cut the raisins in half and chop the prunes. Crush the nuts. Combine the fruit and nuts and mix well. Add the nut's mixture in the rice mass and stir well again. Close the air fryer lid and cook for 15 minutes or until the rice absorbs all the liquid. Remove the rice from the air fryer and transfer it to a serving bowl. , let them rest briefly before serving. Add honey, if desired.

Vegetarian Millet

Prep time: 10 minutes
Cooking time: 15 minutes
Servings: 2

Ingredients:

- 2 cups millet
- 1 teaspoon salt
- 4 cups vegetable stock
- 1 carrot
- 1 onion
- 1 tablespoon butter
- 1 teaspoon basil

Directions:

Take the millet and combine it with the vegetable stock. Sprinkle the mixture with salt and stir well. Sprinkle the mixture with the basil. Peel the onion and carrot and chop them into same-sized pieces. Add the vegetables to the millet mixture and stir well. Open the air fryer lid and add the millet mixture. Add the butter and close the lid. Cook for 25 minutes or until the vegetables are soft. Remove the millet from the air fryer and stir well. Transfer to serving bowls.

Chicken Boards with Pineapple

Prep time: 15 minutes
Cooking time: 20 minutes
Servings: 4

Ingredients:

- 10 ounces boneless and skinless chicken breast, boiled
- 1 cup pineapple
- ½ cup hard cheese
- 10 ounces puff pastry
- 1 teaspoon butter
- 1 teaspoon salt

Directions:

Roll the puff pastry out using a using a rolling pin. Take the muffin forms and cut the dough to fit in the muffin forms. Put puff pastry in every form. Chop the chicken or cut it into strips. Chop the pineapple into small pieces. Combine the chicken and pineapple in a mixing bowl. Add the butter and salt. Grate the hard cheese. Fill the muffin forms with the chicken mixture and sprinkle with the grated cheese. Take the small amount of the dough and cover every muffin form. Open the air fryer lid and add the muffin pan. Close the lid and cook for 20 minutes. When the dish is cooked, remove the pan from the air fryer and remove the muffin forms and serve .

Apple Casserole

Prep time: 15 minutes
Cooking time: 20 minutes
Servings: 4

Ingredients:

- 1 cup sour apples
- 1 teaspoon ground cinnamon
- 1 tablespoon brown sugar
- 1 cup rolled oats
- ½ cup heavy cream
- 1 teaspoon starch
- 1 tablespoon butter
- ⅓ cup flour

Directions:

In a mixing bowl, combine the oats and butter in a mixing bowl and add the starch and cream. Mix well. Add the flour and knead the dough. Chop the apples into medium-sized pieces and sprinkle them with the cinnamon and brown sugar. Stir well. Grate half of the dough into the casserole pan. Add half of the apple mixture. Grate the remaining part of the dough into the pan and top with the remaining apple mixture. Open the air fryer lid and transfer the casserole pan to the air fryer basket. Close the lid and cook for 20 minutes. When the casserole is cooked, let rest for 5 minutes before serving.

Breakfast Pizza

Prep time: 10 minutes
Cooking time: 7 minutes
Servings: 2

Ingredients:
- 1 cup sour cream
- 1 cup flour
- ¼ cup sweet corn
- ½ cup chicken breast, boiled
- 1 teaspoon paprika
- 1 teaspoon salt
- 1 teaspoon basil
- 1 bell pepper
- 1 cup Parmesan cheese
- ½ teaspoon baking soda

Directions:
In a mixing bowl, combine the sour cream, flour, and basil in a mixing bowl. Sprinkle with the salt and mix well using a hand mixer. Sprinkle it with the baking soda and stir the batter well. Pour the batter into the air fryer form. Remove the seeds from the pepper and chop it. Sprinkle the pizza dough with the pepper. After this, chop the chicken. Sprinkle the pizza dough with the chicken and corn. Grate the Parmesan cheese and sprinkle the pizza with the cheese. Transfer the pizza to the air fryer and close the lid. Cook for 7 minutes. Remove the pizza from the air fryer and serve.

Eggs in Sweet Potato

Prep time: 10 minutes
Cooking time: 10 minutes
Servings: 3

Ingredients:
- 3 sweet potatoes
- 3 eggs
- 1 tablespoon tomato paste
- 1 teaspoon basil
- 1 teaspoon ground black pepper
- 1 teaspoon paprika
- 8 ounces bacon
- 1 teaspoon olive oil
- 3 garlic cloves
- 1 tablespoon greens

Directions:
Wash the sweet potatoes and cut them in half lengthwise. Remove the flesh from the potatoes. Mince the sweet potato meat and combine it with the basil, pepper, paprika, and oil and stir well. Then peel the garlic cloves and mince it. Combine the minced garlic and bacon together and stir well. After this add tomato paste and stir well again. Chop the greens. Fill the sweet potato shells with the bacon mixture and add spiced potato flesh. Beat the egg in a small bowl and brush onto every potato shell. Open the air fryer lid and transfer the sweet potatoes. Cook for 10 minutes and remove it from the air fryer. Sprinkle with the chopped greens and serve.

Easy Quiche

Prep time: 10 minutes
Cooking time: 20 minutes
Servings: 4

Ingredients:

- ⅓ cup flour
- 2 eggs
- ½ cup heavy cream
- ½ cup broccoli
- 1 onion

- 2 tomatoes
- 1 cup Cheddar cheese
- 1 tablespoon butter
- 1 teaspoon ground black pepper

Directions:

In a mixing bowl, combine the flour and eggs in a mixing bowl and mix well. Add the cream slowly and mix until smooth. Sprinkle the dough with the pepper. Wash the broccoli and cut into small florets. Peel the onion and chop it. Slice the tomato. Combine all the vegetables in a mixing bowl and stir. Add the vegetable mixture to the batter and stir. Pour the batter into the baking dish. Transfer the mixture to the air fryer and cook for 20 minutes. Remove the quiche from the air fryer and let it rest before cutting into pieces and serving.

Simple Frittata

Preparation time: 10 minutes
Cooking time: 10 minutes
Servings: 3

Ingredients:

- ½ Italian sausage, sliced
- 3 eggs
- 4 cherry tomatoes, cut in halves
- ½ cup parsley, minced

- 1 tablespoon olive oil
- 1 tablespoon parmesan, grated
- Salt and ground black pepper, to taste

Directions:

Add the tomatoes and sausage to the baking dish and preheat the air fryer at 360°F. Bake for 5 minutes. Mix the eggs with salt, pepper, cheese, parsley and oil and whisk well. Remove the baking dish, add the eggs mixture and place the sausage and tomatoes on top. Spread evenly in the fryer and bake for 5 minutes. Cut into slices and serve.

Tofu Scramble

Preparation time: 10 minutes
Cooking time: 35 minutes
Servings: 4

Ingredients:

- 2 tablespoons soy sauce
- 1 block tofu, cubed
- 1 teaspoon turmeric
- 2 tablespoons olive oil
- ½ teaspoon onion powder
- ½ teaspoon garlic powder
- 2½ cup red potatoes, cubed
- ½ cup yellow onion, chopped
- 4 cups broccoli florets
- Salt and ground black pepper, to taste

Directions:

Mix the tofu with 1 tablespoon oil, salt, pepper, soy sauce, garlic, and onion powder, turmeric and onion. Toss to coat, and set aside. In another bowl, mix the potatoes with the remaining oil, Salt and pepper and toss to coat. Put the potatoes in the air fryer preheated to 350°F and bake for 15 minutes, shaking once after 8 minutes. Add the tofu and reserved marinade, spread in the air fryer and bake for 15 minutes. Mix the broccoli with reserved marinade, add it to the fryer, and cook for 5 minutes. Divide between plates and serve.

English Breakfast

Preparation time: 10 minutes
Cooking time: 20 minutes
Servings: 4

Ingredients:

- 8 sausages, sliced
- 8 slices bacon
- 10 ounces canned baked beans, drained
- 4 eggs
- 8 slices of toast

Directions:

Put sausage and bacon in the air fryer, preheat at 350°F, and cook for 10 minutes. Transfer to a plate and set aside. Put the beans in one ramekin and the eggs in another one. Put them in the air fryer and cook for 10 minutes at 370°F. Divide the sausage and bacon on plates, add the eggs on the side, and serve.

Breakfast Sandwich

Preparation time: 10 minutes
Cooking time: 6 minutes
Servings: 1

Ingredients:

- 1 slice English bacon
- 1 egg
- 1 English muffin cut in halves
- Salt and ground black pepper

Directions:

Put the egg in a ramekin and place in the air fryer. Season it with salt and pepper. Add bacon and muffin halves as well. Cook at 400°F for 6 minutes. Assemble the sandwich and serve.

Breakfast Burrito

Preparation time: 10 minutes
Cooking time: 10 minutes
Servings: 2

Ingredients:

- 4 slices cooked turkey breast
- ½ red bell pepper, sliced
- 2 eggs
- 1 small avocado, peeled, pitted and sliced
- 2 tablespoons salsa
- Salt and ground black pepper, to taste
- 1/8 cup mozzarella cheese, grated
- Tortillas for serving

Directions:

In a bowl, whisk the eggs with salt and pepper, pour them into a pan, and place it in the air fryer's basket. Cook at 400°F for 5 minutes, take the pan out of the fryer and transfer eggs to a plate. Arrange tortillas on a working surface. Divide the eggs onto them and the turkey, bell pepper, cheese, salsa, and avocado to each one. Roll the burritos and place them in the air fryer after you've lined it with aluminum foil. Heat the burritos at 300°F for 3 minutes, divide them between plates and serve.

Polenta Bites

Preparation time: 10 minutes
Cooking time: 15 minutes
Servings: 4

Ingredients:

- 1 cup cornmeal
- 3 cups water
- Salt
- 1 tablespoon butter
- ¼ cup potato starch
- Vegetable oil cooking spray
- 1 tablespoon coconut oil
- Maple syrup
- Powdered sugar

Directions:

Put the water for the polenta in a bowl and heat on medium heat. Add the cornmeal, stir well, and cook for 10 minutes. Add the butter, stir again, and cook for 2 minutes. Take off the heat and set aside to cool down. Take spoonfuls of polenta, shape them into balls, and place them on a lined baking sheet. Spray the air fryer basket with cooking oil, place the polenta balls on it, and spray them as well. Cook at 380°F for 8 minutes, flip balls, and cook them for 8 minutes. Divide polenta balls on plates, sprinkle powdered sugar on them, and serve with maple syrup.

Cinnamon Toast

Preparation time: 10 minutes
Cooking time: 5 minutes
Servings: 6

Ingredients:

- 1 stick butter, softened
- 12 bread slices
- ½ cup sugar
- Ground black pepper
- 1½ teaspoons vanilla extract
- 1½ teaspoons ground cinnamon

Directions:

In a bowl, mix the butter with cinnamon, sugar, vanilla, and Ground black pepper and stir well. Spread the mixture onto bread slices, put them in the air fryer, cook at 400°F for 5 minutes, divide them between plates, and serve.

Tasty Soufflé

Preparation time: 5 minutes
Cooking time: 8 minutes
Servings: 2

Ingredients:

- 2 eggs
- 2 tablespoons cream
- 1 red chile pepper, seeded and chopped
- 2 tablespoons parsley, minced
- Salt and ground black pepper, to taste

Directions:

In a bowl, mix the eggs with salt, pepper, cream, chile pepper, and parsley and whisk well. Pour into two ramekins, place them in the air fryer and cook for 390°F for 8 minutes and serve.

Greasy Breakfast Potatoes

Preparation time: 10 minutes
Cooking time: 35 minutes
Servings: 4

Ingredients:

- 3 potatoes, cubed and soaked in water for 30 minutes
- 2 tablespoons clarified butter or vegetable oil
- 1 yellow onion, peeled and chopped
- Salt and ground black pepper, to taste
- 1 red bell pepper, seeded and chopped
- 1 teaspoon onion powder
- 1 teaspoon garlic powder
- 1 teaspoon sweet paprika

Directions:

In a bowl, mix the onion powder, garlic powder, paprika, salt, and pepper and stir. Coat the air fryer with some of the butter. Drain the potatoes, pat them dry, and put them in a bowl. Add the rest of the butter, toss to coat, and transfer to the fryer. Add the onion, bell pepper, and spices. Toss to coat and cook at 370°F for 30 minutes and serve.

Onion and Cheese Omelet

Preparation time: 5 minutes
Cooking time: 15 minutes
Servings: 2

Ingredients:

- 2 eggs
- 1 yellow onion, sliced
- 1 teaspoon soy sauce
- Vegetable oil cooking spray
- Ground black pepper
- 1 tablespoon cheddar cheese, grated

Directions:

In a bowl, mix the eggs, soy sauce, and pepper and whisk well. Spray the air fryer with some cooking oil spray, preheat the air fryer at 350F, add the onion slices, and cook for 10 minutes. Add the whisked eggs and cheese and cook for 5 minutes. Divide between two plates and serve.

Breakfast Casserole

Preparation time: 10 minutes
Cooking time: 15 minutes
Servings: 2

Ingredients:

- 1 yellow onion, chopped
- 1 teaspoon garlic, minced
- 1 teaspoon olive oil
- 1 carrot, chopped
- 2 celery stalks, chopped
- ½ cup shiitake mushrooms, chopped
- ½ cup red bell pepper, chopped
- Salt and ground black pepper, to taste
- 1 teaspoon dried oregano
- ½ teaspoon red pepper flakes
- ½ teaspoon ground cumin
- ½ teaspoon dried dill
- 7 ounces firm tofu, cubed
- 2 tablespoons yogurt
- 1 tablespoon lemon juice
- 2 tablespoons water
- ½ cup quinoa, cooked
- 2 tablespoons active yeast

Directions:

Heat up a pan with the oil on medium-high heat. Add the garlic and onion, stir, and cook for 3 minutes. Add the bell pepper, celery and carrot, stir, and cook for 3 minutes. Add the salt, pepper, mushrooms, oregano, dill, cumin and pepper flakes, stir, and cook for 3 minutes. In a food processor, mix the tofu with yogurt, yeast, lemon juice, and water and puree until smooth. Add the quinoa and blend again. Add the sautéed veggies and stir. Pour everything into a baking dish and cook everything at 350°F for 15 minutes. Divide the between plates and serve.

Baked Eggs

Preparation time: 10 minutes
Cooking time: 20 minutes
Servings: 4

Ingredients:

- 7 ounces ham, chopped
- 4 eggs
- 1 pound baby spinach
- 4 tablespoons cream milk
- Salt and ground black pepper, to taste
- 1 tablespoon olive oil
- 1 tablespoon butter

Directions:

Coat 4 ramekins with the butter and place them on a working surface. Heat up a pan with the oil on medium heat. Add the spinach and cook for a few minutes. Divide the spinach and ham into ramekins. Crack an egg into each ramekin, add 1 tablespoon of milk on top, and season with salt and pepper. Place the ramekins in the air fryer and bake at 350°F for 20 minutes. Serve warm.

Eggs in Bread Bowls

Preparation time: 10 minutes
Cooking time: 20 minutes
Servings: 4

Ingredients:

- 4 dinner rolls, tops cut off and some of the bread inside removed
- 4 eggs
- 1 tablespoon fresh parsley, chopped
- 1 tablespoon fresh tarragon, chopped
- 2 tablespoons chives, chopped
- Salt and ground black pepper, to taste
- 2 tablespoons Parmesan cheese, grated
- 4 tablespoons heavy cream

Directions:

Place the bread bowls on a lined baking sheet and crack an egg into each. Divide the parsley, tarragon, chives, and heavy cream equally into them and season with salt and pepper. Divide the cheese on top of each bread bowl, place them into the air fryer and bake at 350°F for 20 minutes. Take the bread bowls out of the air fryer and set aside for 5 minutes before serving.

Special Egg Breakfast

Preparation time: 10 minutes
Cooking time: 20 minutes
Servings: 4

Ingredients:

- 8 cremini mushrooms, sliced
- 1 garlic clove, minced
- 8 cherry tomatoes, cut in halves
- 4 slices bacon, chopped
- 7 ounces spinach, torn
- 4 pork sausages
- 4 eggs
- Salt and ground black pepper, to taste
- Vegetable oil cooking spray

Directions:

Place the tomatoes, garlic and mushrooms in a pan that you've sprayed with cooking oil. Add the salt and pepper and stir. Put the sausages and bacon in the pan as well, toss to coat, and place in the air fryer's basket. Cook for 10 minutes at 390°F. Put the spinach in a bowl, add some water to cover, put into a microwave over for a few seconds, and drain well. Add the spinach to the pan, add the eggs and cook in the air fryer for 5 to 6 minutes at 370°F. Serve hot.

Egg Muffins

Preparation time: 5 minutes
Cooking time: 15 minutes
Servings: 4

Ingredients:

- 1 egg
- 2 tablespoons vegetable oil
- 3 ounces milk
- 1 tablespoon baking powder
- 3.5 ounces white flour
- Mustard powder
- Worcestershire sauce
- ¼ cup Parmesan cheese, grated

Directions:

In a bowl, mix the egg with milk and whisk well. Add the baking powder, flour, and a pinch of mustard powder and stir well. Add a few drops of Worcestershire sauce and the cheese and stir well again. Pour the mixture into a muffin pan, then place in the air fryer's basket, and bake at 390°F for 15 minutes. Arrange muffins on a platter and serve.

Tomato Quiche

Preparation time: 10 minutes
Cooking time: 30 minutes
Servings: 2

Ingredients:

- 2 eggs
- ½ cup Gouda cheese, shredded
- 2 tablespoons yellow onion, chopped
- Salt and ground black pepper, to taste
- ¼ cup milk
- ¼ cup tomatoes, chopped

Directions:

In a bowl, mix the eggs with milk, cheese, salt, onion, and tomatoes and stir well. Pour the mixture into a ramekin, place in the air fryer's basket and cook at 340°F for 30 minutes. Take the ramekin out of the fryer, divide the quiche between two plates and serve.

Scrambled Eggs

Preparation time: 10 minutes
Cooking time: 10 minutes
Servings: 4

Ingredients:

- 7 ounces milk
- 4 eggs
- 2 tablespoons cheddar cheese, grated
- Vegetable oil cooking spray
- Salt and ground black pepper, to taste
- 8 cherry tomatoes, cut in halves

Directions:

In a bowl, mix the eggs, milk, salt and pepper and whisk well. Spray the air fryer with cooking oil, pour eggs into it, and cook at 350°F for 6 minutes. Scramble the eggs a bit and mix with the tomatoes and cheese. Cook for 3 minutes, divide scrambled eggs between plates and serve hot.

Sausage and Cheese Wraps

Preparation time: 10 minutes
Cooking time: 10 minutes
Servings: 4

Ingredients:

- 8 crescent roll dough pieces
- 8 small sausages
- 8 cheddar cheese slices
- Ketchup
- Barbecue sauce

Directions:

Separate the rolls, place them on a working surface, and unroll them. Divide the sausages and cheese on each roll, wrap, roll, and seal edges. Place 4 of the wraps in the air fryer, cook at 380°F for 3 minutes, and transfer to a plate. Repeat with the rest of the sausage rolls, arrange them on a plate and serve with ketchup and barbecue sauce on the side.

Breakfast Stromboli

Preparation time: 10 minutes
Cooking time: 15 minutes
Servings: 4

Ingredients:

- 12 ounces pizza crust
- 3 ounces red bell peppers, roasted and chopped roughly
- 3 cups Cheddar cheese, shredded
- Salt and ground black pepper, to taste
- 1 cup Mozzarella cheese, shredded
- ½ pound ham, cooked and chopped
- 1 tablespoon milk
- 1 egg yolk

Directions:

Roll out the pizza dough and place on a work surface. Place the cheddar cheese, mozzarella cheese, ham, roasted peppers, salt, and pepper on one side, fold with the other side of the pizza dough, and seal the edges closed. In a bowl, whisk the egg yolk with milk and brush the stromboli with the egg wash. Place the stromboli in the air fryer's basket and cook for 15 minutes at 360°F, flipping it every 5 minutes. Cut and serve.

Breakfast Pies

Preparation time: 10 minutes
Cooking time: 6 minutes
Servings: 4

Ingredients:

- 16 ounces canned candied yams, drained
- ½ teaspoon cinnamon, ground
- ¼ teaspoon allspice
- Salt
- 1 crescent dough sheet
- ½ cup confectioners' sugar
- 1 egg, whisked
- 2 tablespoons marshmallow cream
- ½ cup maple syrup

Directions:

In a bowl, mix the yams, salt, cinnamon, and allspice mash with a fork, and stir well. Place dough sheet on a work surface and cut into quarters. Spread the yam mixture on 2 pieces, top with marshmallow cream, and cover them with the remaining dough pieces. Seal the edges, brush the pies with the egg, place them in the air fryer, and cook at 400°F for 6 minutes. In a bowl, mix the maple syrup with confectioners' sugar and whisk well. Take the pies out of the fryer, divide between plates, and serve with the maple syrup glaze on top.

Lunch

Stuffed Eggplants

Prep time: 15 minutes
Cooking time: 20 minutes
Servings: 4

Ingredients:
- 2 large eggplants
- 1 onion
- 1 cup pork, minced
- 1 egg
- 1 teaspoon ground white pepper
- 1 teaspoon salt
- 1 tablespoon tomato paste
- 1 teaspoon mayonnaise
- ½ cup rice
- ½ cup chicken stock
- 2 tomatoes

Directions:

Wash the eggplants and cut them lengthwise into halves. Rub the eggplants with the salt and leave them for at least 5 minutes. In a mixing bowl, beat the egg in a mixing bowl. Whisk well and add the pork. Sprinkle the mixture with the white pepper, add the rice and stir well. Take the eggplant halves and remove the flesh from them. Chop the removed flesh, combine with the meat mixture, and stir well. Fill the eggplants with the meat mixture. Slice the tomatoes and cover the eggplant halves with it. Combine the tomato paste and mayonnaise. Stir the mixture and cover the eggplants with it. Transfer the eggplants to the air fryer and close the lid. Cook for 20 minutes. When the eggplants are cooked, remove them from the air fryer and serve hot.

Kale Rolls

Prep time: 20 minutes
Cooking time: 25 minutes
Servings: 7

Ingredients:
- 15 ounces kale
- 1 cup rice, cooked
- 2 cups chicken stock
- 1 cup minced chicken
- 1 egg
- 1 carrot
- 2 medium yellow onions
- 1 teaspoon salt
- 1 teaspoon black pepper
- 1 cup tomato juice
- 2 teaspoons sour cream

Directions:

Wash the kale leaves and dry them. In a mixing bowl, combine the rice, chicken, and egg. Sprinkle the mixture with the black pepper and salt and stir. Peel the carrot and grate it. Add the carrot to the rice mixture. Peel the onions and chop them. Add the onion to the mixing bowl and stir again. Take the kale leaves and fill them with the rice mixture. Make the rolls and transfer them to the air fryer basket. In a mixing bowl, combine the sour cream, tomato juice, and chicken stock in a bowl and stir well. Pour the liquid into the air fryer basket and close the lid. Cook the kale rolls for 25 minutes. When the kale rolls are cooked, let them cool briefly. Remove them from the air fryer and serve the dish warm.

Thai-style Rice

Prep time: 15 minutes
Cooking time: 20 minutes
Servings: 3

Ingredients:
- 2 cups rice
- 4 cup beef broth
- 1 tablespoon soy sauce
- 1 teaspoon sriracha
- 1 teaspoon brown sugar
- 2 garlic cloves
- 1 teaspoon fresh ginger
- 1 carrot
- 1 teaspoon salt
- 1 tablespoon lemon juice
- ⅓ cup pineapple

Directions:
In a mixing bowl, combine the rice and pineapple in a bowl and stir well. In a separate bowl, combine the sriracha, soy sauce, brown sugar, and salt. Stir well and pour it in with the rice. Stir it again and set it aside. Peel the garlic and carrot. Mince the garlic and grate the carrot. Add the vegetables to the rice and stir well. Transfer the rice in the air fryer and pour the in beef broth, mixing well. Close the lid and cook for 20 minutes. When the dish is cooked, remove it from the air fryer and serve.

Zucchini Loaf

Prep time: 15 minutes
Cooking time: 25 minutes
Servings: 6

Ingredients:
- 2 large zucchini
- 1 egg
- 1 cup wheat flour
- 2 egg whites
- 2 carrots
- 1 white onion
- ½ cup rolled oats
- 1 teaspoon salt
- 1 teaspoon ground black pepper
- ½ cup walnuts

Directions:
Wash the zucchini and grate them. Transfer the grated zucchini to a bowl and season with salt and ground black pepper. Add the eggs and stir. Peel the onion and the carrots and dice them. Add the vegetables to the mixing bowl with the grated zucchini. Add the wheat flour and whisk well. Take the loaf form for the air fryer and transfer the zucchini mixture to the form. Crush the walnuts and sprinkle the loaf with them. Transfer the zucchini loaf in the air fryer and close the lid. Cook for 25 minutes. When the loaf is done, remove it from the air fryer and let it rest before cutting and serving.

Tuna with Cheese Topping

Prep time: 20 minutes
Cooking time: 30 minutes
Servings: 4

Ingredients:

- 1 large tuna
- 1 cup Parmesan cheese
- 1 onion
- ½ lemon
- 1 tablespoon fresh ginger
- 1 teaspoon nutmeg
- 2 teaspoons salt
- ⅓ cup garlic

Directions:

Remove the skin from the tuna and separate it into two fillets. Rub the fillets with the salt and sprinkle with nutmeg. Peel the garlic and mince it. Sprinkle the tuna fillets with the garlic. Peel the onion and chop it. Slice the ginger and chop the lemon and combine them and stir well. Transfer the tuna fillets to the air fryer and sprinkle it with the chopped onion. Add the ginger mixture. Grate the Parmesan cheese and layer the cheese on the tuna and transfer the fish to the air fryer and close the lid. Cook the fish for 30 minutes. When the tuna is cooked, remove it from the air fryer and serve.

Warm Shrimp Salad

Prep time: 20 minutes
Cooking time: 20 minutes
Servings: 6

Ingredients:

- 13 ounces shrimp
- ½ cup bread crumbs
- 1 avocado
- 1 cup heavy cream
- 1 cup grated cheese
- 1 teaspoon paprika
- ½ cup tomato
- 1 tablespoon lemon juice
- 1 teaspoon salt
- 1 tablespoon brown sugar
- 2 sweet potatoes

Directions:

Peel and devein the shrimp and cut each of them in half. Sprinkle the shrimp with lemon juice and stir. Peel the potatoes and slice them. Sprinkle the potato slices with salt on both sides. Peel the avocado and chop it. Take the air fryer form and put the layer of potatoes into the form. Add the avocado and sprinkle the avocado layer with the paprika and add the bread crumbs. Slice the tomatoes and add them to the form. Add half of the grated cheese. Add the shrimp and the remaining cheese. In a mixing bowl, combine the brown sugar and cream in a mixing bowl and mix until smooth. Pour the sugar mixture onto the shrimp and transfer to the air fryer. Cook for 20 minutes. Remove the salad from the air fryer and let it cool briefly before serving.

Light Couscous Salad

Prep time: 15 minutes
Cooking time: 20 minutes
Servings: 2

Ingredients:
- 1 cup couscous
- 2 red bell peppers
- 1 red onion
- 2 teaspoons olive oil
- 2 cups chicken stock
- 1 teaspoon chile flakes
- 2 tomatoes
- ⅓ cup raisins
- 1 zucchini

Directions:
In a mixing bowl, combine the couscous and olive oil in a mixing bowl. Add the chicken stock and set aside. Peel the onion and remove the seeds from the bell pepper. Chop the vegetables, sprinkle them with the chile flakes and stir well. Chop the tomatoes and zucchini. Combine all the vegetables and stir well. Add the raisins and transfer the couscous mixture to the air fryer and the vegetables. Stir well and close the lid. Cook for 20 minutes or until the couscous absorbs all the water. Remove the dish from the air fryer and serve.

Broad Beans with Meat Sauce

Prep time: 20 minutes
Cooking time: 30 minutes
Servings: 4

Ingredients:
- 2 cups broad beans
- 1 red onion
- 1 cup tomato juice
- ½ cup beef stock
- 10 ounces minced beef
- 1 teaspoon salt
- 2 teaspoons sugar

Directions:
Combine the beans and beef stock in a mixing bowl. Add tomato juice and minced beef and stir well. Sprinkle it with salt and sugar and stir again. Peel the onion and dice it. Add the onion in the bean mixture and stir again. Transfer to the air fryer, close the lid, and cook for 30 minutes. When the dish is cooked, remove it from the air fryer, stir again, and serve warm.

Mushroom Wraps

Prep time: 15 minutes
Cooking time: 25 minutes
Servings: 8

Ingredients:

- 10 ounces puff pastry
- ½ cup mushrooms
- 2 yellow onion
- ½ teaspoon salt
- 1 teaspoon sugar
- 1 carrot
- 1 teaspoon butter
- 1 teaspoon olive oil

Directions:

Take the puff pastry and roll it using a rolling out. Cut small squares from the dough and spread them with butter. Peel the carrot and onions and chop them. Chop the mushrooms and combine the vegetables together. Stir well and sprinkle with salt. Transfer the mixture into the puff pastry squares and form the wraps from every square. Spread every wrap with the oil. Open the air fryer lid and transfer the mushroom wraps. Close the lid and cook for 25 minutes. Open the lid and leave the wraps in the air fryer for 3 minutes. Remove the wraps from the air fryer. Sprinkle the dish with butter, if desired, and serve.

Pork Roll with Chickpeas

Prep time: 20 minutes
Cooking time: 35 minutes
Servings: 4

Ingredients:

- 15 ounces pork
- ½ cup chickpeas, cooked
- 1 teaspoon butter
- ⅓ cup parsley
- 1 tablespoon olive oil
- 2 tablespoons tomato paste
- 1 onion

Directions:

Tenderize the pork and rub it with oil. Mince the parsley, combine it with the chickpeas and stir well. Peel the onion and chop it. Add the onion to the parsley mixture and stir. Transfer the parsley mixture to the meat and roll it. Spread the meat roll with tomato paste. Open the air fryer lid and transfer the pork roll to the fryer. Close the lid and cook for 35 minutes. When the pork roll is cooked, open the air fryer lid and remove the dish. Let the pork roll cool briefly before cutting into slices and serving into medium-sized pieces.

Vegetable Turnovers

Prep time: 15 minutes
Cooking time: 25 minutes
Servings: 6

Ingredients:

- 17 ounces puff pastry
- 2 bell peppers
- 1 cup cabbage
- 2 eggs, boiled
- 1 tablespoon tomato paste
- 1 garlic clove
- 1 teaspoon salt
- 1 teaspoon sugar
- 1 teaspoon olive oil

Directions:

Roll the puff pastry out using a rolling pin. Cut small squares from the dough and set it aside. Peel the eggs and chop them. Peel the garlic clove and mince it. Dice the cabbage. Combine the vegetables with the eggs and stir well. Sprinkle with the salt and sugar. Remove the seeds from the peppers and chop them. Add the peppers to the vegetable mixture. Add the tomato paste and stir well. Make turnovers from the puff pastry and vegetable mixture and coat them with the oil. Open the air fryer lid and add the turnovers. Close the lid and cook for 25 minutes. When the dish is cooked, remove the turnovers from the air fryer and let them cool briefly before serving.

Stuffed Dates

Prep time: 10 minutes
Cooking time: 5 minutes
Servings: 2

Ingredients:

- 10 dates
- 1 cup ricotta cheese
- ⅓ cup walnuts
- ¼ cup chicken breast, cooked and minced
- 1 tablespoon butter
- 1 tablespoon lemon juice

Directions:

Remove the pits from the dates and cut them in half lengthwise. In a mixing bowl, add the cheese to a mixing bowl with the chicken and stir well. Crush the nuts and add them to the cheese mixture. Add the lemon juice and butter until smooth. Fill the dates with the cheese mixture and transfer the dates in the air fryer. Close the lid and cook for 5 minutes. When the dish is cooked, remove the dates from the air fryer and serve.

Pasta Casserole

Prep time: 20 minutes
Cooking time: 20 minutes
Servings: 6

Ingredients:

- 1 cup pasta
- 1 cup broccoli
- 3 cups heavy cream
- 1 tablespoon fresh basil
- ½ cup hard cheese
- 1 teaspoon ground black pepper
- 1 teaspoon paprika
- 3 tablespoons butter

Directions:

Wash the broccoli and cut into florets. Chop the florets and combine them with basil, pepper, and paprika and stir well. Grate the cheese and combine it with the pasta and stir well. Transfer the broccoli to the air fryer and add the pasta. Add the cream and stir again. Add butter to the top of the dish and close the air fryer lid. Cook for 20 minutes. When the dish is cooked, remove it from the air fryer and let it cool for at least 5 minutes before serving.

Warm Creamy Chicken Salad

Prep time: 15 minutes
Cooking time: 30 minutes
Servings: 4

Ingredients:

- 1 eggplant
- 15 ounces boneless and skinless chicken breast
- 1 red onion
- 2 tablespoons barbecue sauce
- ½ teaspoon fresh dill
- 1 teaspoon heavy cream
- ½ cup chicken stock
- 3 tablespoons mayonnaise
- 1 teaspoon sour cream
- ½ cup black olives

Directions:

Cut the chicken into the strips and sprinkle it with the dill and stir well. Peel the eggplant and chop it. Combine the eggplant with the chicken strips. Peel the onion and chop it. In a separate bowl, combine the chicken stock, mayonnaise, sour cream, and barbecue sauce and stir well. Open the air fryer and transfer the chicken mixture. Add the black olives and mayonnaise mass and stir until smooth. Close the lid and cook for 30 minutes. When the salad is cooked, remove it from the air fryer and stir again before serving.

Tomato Beef Soup

Prep time: 20 minutes
Cooking time: 30 minutes
Servings: 6

Ingredients:
- 1 cup tomato juice
- 3 cups beef stock
- 4 medium potatoes
- 1 yellow onion
- ⅓ cup green peas
- 1 teaspoon ground black pepper
- 1 teaspoon salt
- 2 teaspoons heavy cream
- 10 ounces beef

Directions:

In a mixing bowl, combine the tomato juice and beef stock and stir well. Peel the onion and the potatoes and dice them. Chop the beef roughly. In a mixing bowl, In a mixing bowl, combine the vegetables and stir well. Sprinkle the mixture with the peas, pepper, and salt and stir well. Open the air fryer lid and add the vegetable mixture. Pour the cream on top and add the beef. Add the tomato juice and stir well. Close the lid and cook for 30 minutes. When the soup is done, all the ingredients should be soft. Remove the soup from the air fryer and ladle it into the serving bowls.

Fingerling Potatoes

Prep time: 15 minutes
Cooking time: 25 minutes
Servings: 4

Ingredients:
- 2 cups fingerling potatoes
- 1 white onion
- 1 bay leaf
- 1 cup fresh dill
- ⅓ cup heavy cream
- 1 cup chicken stock
- 1 teaspoon salt
- 1 teaspoon fresh cilantro
- 1 teaspoon fresh rosemary
- 1 tablespoon olive oil

Directions:

Wash the potatoes. Add the potatoes to a mixing bowl and sprinkle the, with the salt, cilantro, and rosemary and set aside. Chop the dill and combine it with the olive oil and stir well. Peel the onion and chop it. Open the air fryer lid and transfer the potatoes to the air fryer basket. Add the dill and bay leaf, then add the chopped onion and add the chicken stock. Add the cream and stir well. The liquid should cover the surface of the dish. Close the lid and cook for 25 minutes. Let the dish rest for 3 minutes and remove it from the air fryer. Serve hot.

Honey Ribs

Prep time: 15 minutes
Cooking time: 35 minutes
Servings: 4

Ingredients:

- 17 ounces pork ribs, deboned
- 1 tablespoon honey
- 3 tablespoons soy sauce
- 1 onion
- 1 teaspoon brown sugar
- 2 tablespoons lemon juice
- 5 tablespoons barbecue sauce

Directions:

In a mixing bowl, combine honey, soy sauce, and barbecue sauce until smooth and stir until smooth. Sprinkle the mixture with the brown sugar and stir until everything is dissolved. Chop the pork rib meat and top with the honey mixture and stir well. Set aside for 5 minutes. Peel the onion, sprinkle it with the lemon juice and stir well. Remove the pork ribs from the honey and combine the meat with the onion and stir well. Open the air fryer lid and transfer the ribs to the air fryer. Pour the honey onto the ribs and close the lid. Cook for 35 minutes. Open the air fryer lid and remove the dish from the air fryer and serve.

Sweet Carrot Mixture

Prep time: 10 minutes
Cooking time: 20 minutes
Servings: 4

Ingredients:

- 5 medium carrots
- 2 tablespoons sugar
- 2 cup cottage cheese
- 1 egg
- 1 teaspoon vanilla sugar
- 1 teaspoon cinnamon
- 3 tablespoons maple syrup

Directions:

Wash the carrots and peel them. Grate the carrots and mix with the vanilla sugar and cinnamon. Add the cottage cheese to a mixing bowl. Blend until smooth. Sprinkle the cottage cheese with the sugar and maple syrup. Stir well and add the egg. Blend for 2 minutes, then add the carrots and stir again. Open the air fryer lid and transfer the cottage cheese inside and close the lid. Cook for 20 minutes or until brown on top. Remove the dish from the air fryer and let it cool briefly before serving.

Potato Casserole

Prep time: 15 minutes
Cooking time: 30 minutes
Servings: 4

Ingredients:
- 4 potatoes
- 1 cup hard cheese
- 3 tomatoes
- 2 yellow onions
- 1 zucchini
- 1 teaspoon salt
- ¼ cup fresh parsley
- 1 teaspoon ground white pepper
- 1 teaspoon cilantro
- 1 cup chicken stock
- 8 ounces ham, diced

Directions:
Peel the potato and slice it. Transfer the potato to a mixing bowl and sprinkle it with the salt and cilantro and stir well. Dice the ham and chop the parsley. Wash the zucchini and chop it. Peel the onions and chop them. Transfer the chopped vegetables to the potato mixture and sprinkle it with the chopped parsley and ham. Wash the tomatoes and slice them. Grate the cheese. Open the air fryer lid and transfer the vegetable mixture to the air fryer basket. Sprinkle it with salt and white pepper. Add the sliced tomatoes. Add a layer of the grated cheese and close the lid. Cook for 30 minutes. When the dish is cooked, remove it from the air fryer and serve it.

Zucchini Crumble

Prep time: 15 minutes
Cooking time: 25 minutes
Servings: 4

Ingredients:
- 2 cups bread crumbs
- 3 zucchini
- 2 eggs
- ½ cup heavy cream
- ¼ cup flour
- 1 teaspoon ground white pepper
- 1 teaspoon cilantro
- 1 teaspoon sour cream
- 1 teaspoon chili pepper
- 8 ounces Cheddar cheese
- 3 tomatoes
- 1 carrot

Directions:
Wash the zucchini and slice them. Transfer the zucchini to a mixing bowl and sprinkle them with the white pepper and cilantro, stirring well. In another bowl, beat the egg, then add the sour cream, cream, and flour and mix well. Grate the Cheddar cheese. Peel the carrot and slice the carrot and tomatoes. Open the air fryer and sprinkle the air fryer basket with the ⅓ of the bread crumbs. Make a layer from the zucchini, carrots, and tomatoes. Pour the ⅓ of the batter and sprinkle the mixture with the bread crumbs again. Repeat these steps 5 times. Sprinkle the last layer with the grated cheese and close the lid. Cook for 25 minutes. Remove from the air fryer and let it cool briefly before serving.

Salmon with Potatoes, Fennel, and Dill

Preparation time: 10 minutes
Cooking time: 22 minutes
Servings: 2

Ingredients:

- 3 potatoes, thinly sliced
- 4 tablespoons butter, softened
- ½ fennel bulb, thinly sliced
- ½ cup fresh dill, chopped
- 8 cherry tomatoes, cut in halves
- 2 salmon fillets
- Salt and ground black pepper, to taste
- ¼ cup vermouth, dry

Directions:

Put some water in a pan, add some salt, and bring to a boil on medium-high heat. Add the potatoes and blanch them for 2 minutes. Drain the potatoes and pat them dry. Transfer the potatoes to a bowl and mix them with, salt, pepper, half of the butter and fennel and toss to coat. Divide the vegetable mix into 2 parchment paper pieces, add 1 salmon fillet on each, season with salt and pepper, add tomatoes on top of salmon, also divide the rest of the butter, and the vermouth, fold packets and place once of them in the preheated air fryer. Cook for 400°F for 10 minutes, take out of the fryer and place on a plate. Repeat with the other packet, open them and serve with chopped dill on top.

Cod with Grapes

Preparation time: 10 minutes
Cooking time: 15 minutes
Servings: 2

Ingredients:

- 2 black cod fillets
- Salt and ground black pepper, to taste
- 1 fennel bulb, thinly sliced
- 1 cup grapes, cut in halves
- 3 cups kale leaves, shredded
- ½ cup pecans
- 2 teaspoons balsamic vinegar
- Olive oil

Directions:

Place the fish in the air fryer's basket, season with the salt and pepper. Drizzle some olive oil on top and cook at 400°F for 10 minutes. Take the fish out of the fryer and place on a plate. In a bowl, mix the pecans with grapes, fennel, ½ tablespoon oil, salt, and pepper and toss to coat. Transfer this mixture to the fryer's basket and cook at 400°F for 5 minutes. Divide fish on plates, add the grapes on the side and serve with the kale mixed with ½ tablespoon oil, salt, pepper, and balsamic vinegar.

Glazed Turkey Breast

Preparation time: 10 minutes
Cooking time: 1 hour
Servings: 6

Ingredients:
- 1 large turkey breast
- 2 teaspoons olive oil
- ½ teaspoon smoked paprika
- 1 teaspoon thyme, dried
- ½ teaspoon sage, dried
- Salt and ground black pepper, to taste
- 2 tablespoons Dijon mustard
- ¼ cup maple syrup
- 1 tablespoon butter, soft

Directions:
Brush the turkey breast with the olive oil, season with salt, pepper, thyme, paprika, and sage and toss to coat. Put the turkey breast in the air fryer's basket and cook at 350°F for 25 minutes. Flip the breast onto the other side and cook for 12 minutes. Flip the turkey breast again and cook for another 12 minutes. Heat up a pan with the maple syrup on medium heat, add the butter and mustard, stir well, and cook for 2 minutes. Drizzle this over the turkey breast, and cook at 350°F for 5 minutes. Leave the turkey breast rest for a few minutes before serving.

Air-fried Potato Pancakes

Prep time: 10 minutes
Cooking time: 15 minutes
Servings: 6

Ingredients:
- 2 eggs
- 2 tablespoons olive oil
- 3 cups potatoes, peeled and grated
- 2 onions, peeled and grated
- 3 tablespoons sour cream
- 1 teaspoon sea salt
- Ground black pepper

Directions:
Preheat the air fryer to 340°F. Spread the oil on the pan. Beat 2 eggs into the potatoes, and then add the onions. Season with salt and pepper and mix until combined. Pour the mixture on the pan and cook at 350°F for 15 minutes. Serve with sour cream.

Eggplant Panini

Preparation time: 30 minutes
Cooking time: 30 minutes
Servings: 2

Ingredients:

- 1 eggplant, peeled and sliced
- 2 teaspoons parsley, dried
- Salt and ground black pepper, to taste
- ½ cup bread crumbs
- ½ teaspoon Italian seasoning
- ½ teaspoon garlic powder
- ½ teaspoon onion powder
- 2 tablespoons milk
- 4 bread slices
- Cooking spray
- ½ cup mayonnaise
- ¾ cup tomato sauce
- 2 tablespoons parmesan, grated
- 2 cups mozzarella cheese, grated
- ½ cup fresh basil, chopped

Directions:

Season the eggplant slices with salt and pepper and aside for 30 minutes. Pat them dry. In a bowl, mix the parsley with bread crumbs, Italian seasoning, onion powder, garlic powder, salt, and pepper and stir. In another bowl, mix the milk with mayonnaise and stir well. Brush the eggplant slices with mayonnaise, dip them in bread crumbs, and place them on a lined baking sheet. Spray the eggplant with cooking oil, place the baking sheet in the air fryer's basket and cook them at 400°F for 15 minutes, flipping them after 8 minutes. Brush each bread slice with olive oil and arrange 2 of them on a working surface. Add Mozzarella and Parmesan on each, add baked eggplant slices, spread tomato sauce and basil and top with the other bread slices, greased side down. Grill sandwiches on preheated grill for 10 minutes, place them on serving plates, cut each in half, and serve right away.

Cheesy Pork Belly Casserole

Prep time: 10 minutes
Cooking time: 55 minutes
Servings: 6

Ingredients:

- ½ pound sliced pork belly
- 1 onion
- 2 cups grated raw potatoes,
- 4 eggs,
- 1 cups ricotta cheese
- ½ cup curd
- 1 cup mascarpone cheese
- 2 tablespoons of olive oil
- Sea salt
- Ground black pepper
- 3 tablespoons heavy cream

Directions:

Preheat the air fryer to 340°F. Lightly oil a baking dish. Chop the pork belly into cubes and then dice the onion. Cook the meat with onion in the air fryer for about 10 minutes until browned. Shift the meat with onion into a separate bowl. Add the potatoes, eggs, curd, mascarpone cheese, and ricotta cheese. Season with the sea salt and pepper. Transfer the mixture into a prepared baking dish. Cook at 280°F for 45 minutes until the cheese is melted. Serve with cream.

Baked Potatoes with Bacon

Prep time: 10 minutes
Cooking time: 35 minutes
Servings: 3

Ingredients:

- 200 ounces of bacon
- 3 Potatoes of average size, washed
- 3 tablespoons olive oil
- 1 tablespoon salt
- 1 tablespoon sour cream
- 1 tablespoon garlic
- 1 teaspoon fresh dill

Directions:

Preheat the air fryer to 340°F. Cut the potatoes in half but not all the way. Rub the garlic evenly onto the potatoes. Place the slices of bacon in the middle of the potatoes. Sprinkle with the olive oil, salt, and dill. Place into the basket of the air fryer. Cook at 350°F for 35 minutes. Serve with sour cream.

Baked Potatoes with Sour Cream

Prep time: 10 minutes
Cooking time: 20 minutes
Servings: 4

Ingredients:

- 8 potatoes
- 3 tablespoons sour cream
- 30 ounces cheddar cheese
- 2 teaspoons garlic, minced
- 1 tablespoon shallots,
- 1 teaspoon of basil,
- 1 teaspoon celery
- 1 teaspoon fresh parsley
- Allspice
- Sea salt
- Ground black pepper

Directions:

Boil the potatoes in their skins until half cooked. Cool slightly and cut halfway through. Fill the middle of the potatoes with a mixture of sour cream, garlic, shallots, celery, basil, and parsley. Preheat the air fryer to 390°F. Place the potatoes to the air fryer and cook at 350°F for 20 minutes.

Sweet Potato Fries

Prep time: 10 minutes
Cooking time: 1 hour
Servings: 2

Ingredients:

- 2 large potatoes
- 2-3 tablespoons sunflower oil
- ¼ teaspoon curry powder
- ¼ teaspoon coriander
- Sea salt
- ¼ teaspoon ground ginger
- ¼ teaspoon ground cumin
- ¼ teaspoon cinnamon

Directions:

Preheat the air fryer to 400°F. Cut the potatoes in thin sticks. Place the potatoes on the baking pan and sprinkle with oil. Season with spices and toss in the pan to spread spices evenly. Cook for an hour, stirring every 15 minutes. Serve with ketchup

Cheesy Crab Sticks

Prep time: 5 minutes
Cooking time: 5 minutes
Servings: 3

Ingredients:
- 1 pack crab sticks
- 2 tablespoons cheddar cheese
- 1 egg
- Sea salt
- 1 cup panko bread crumbs
- 1 tablespoon olive oil

Directions:

Whisk an egg with the salt. Dip the crab sticks into the egg, and then coat them with the bread crumbs. Store in the refrigerator for 20-30 minutes to set the dish. Preheat the air fryer to 350°F . Sprinkle crab sticks with oil. Place into the basket of the air fryer. Cook the crab sticks and cook for 5 minutes, turning them every minute. While hot, sprinkle with grated cheese and serve.

Salmon Patty Cakes

Prep time: 10 minutes
Cooking time: 5 minutes
Servings: 4

Ingredients:
- 1 can salmon in sauce
- 4 mushrooms
- 1 egg
- Sea salt
- Allspice

Directions:

Preheat the air fryer to 350°F. Pour the sauce from canned salmon. Slice the mushrooms. Place the ingredients in a bowl and combine them. Mold the mixture into small patties. Cook them in the air fryer for 5 minutes at 350°F.

Air-fried Rolls

Prep time: 20 minutes
Cooking time: 25 minutes
Servings: 4

Ingredients:

- 50 ounces macaroni
- 1 tablespoon olive oil
- 200 ounces forcemeat
- 1 onion, peeled and sliced
- 3 teaspoons garlic, ground
- 1 packet puff pastry
- 1 tps sea salt
- a pinch of allspice

Directions:

Boil the macaroni until al dente. Drain and chop the macaroni into small pieces. Combine the forcemeat with onion and garlic in a frying pan. Add oil and cook until forcemeat is half cooked. Mix the meat with the macaroni. Take one sheet of puff pastry and cut it in half. Fill the pastry with the mincemeat and twist into rolls. Cook the rolls in the air fryer for 8 minutes at 350°F .

Cheesy Mushrooms

Prep time: 5 minutes
Cooking time: 15 minutes
Servings: 3

Ingredients:

- 9 large button mushrooms
- 2 tablespoons Cheddar cheese
- 1 egg
- 1 cup panko bread crumbs
- 1 tablespoon olive oil
- Sea salt
- Ground black pepper

Directions:

Whisk an egg with some salt. Combine bread crumbs with cheese and pepper. Plunge every champignon into egg, and then powder them with the bread crumbs mixture. Preheat the air fryer to 320°F. Place champignon into the basket of the Air Fryer. After that sprinkle with oil. Cook for 15 minutes at 320°F, until golden brown.

Eggs with Sour Cream

Prep time: 5 minutes
Cooking time: 15 minutes
Servings: 2

Ingredients:

- 2 tablespoons sour cream
- 2 ounces of bacon, sliced
- 4 eggs
- 1 tablespoon olive oil
- 2 tablespoons cheddar cheese
- 1 tablespoon of shallots,chopped
- Ground black pepper
- Sea salt

Directions:

Sprinkle oil on the baking pan and place bacon slices on it. Beat the eggs in a mixing bowl. Add the sour cream, salt, and spices and whisk them with the eggs. Pour the egg mixture on the top of bacon and sprinkle with the cheese. Cook for 13 minutes at 310°F in the air fryer. Serve with the chopped shallots and toasted bread.

Eggs with Shrimp

Prep time: 15 minutes
Cooking time: 15 minutes
Servings: 4

Ingredients:

- 1 teaspoon butter
- 2 tablespoons olive oil
- 2 average onions chopped
- 2 tablespoons bell peppers
- 4 tablespoon of shallots
- 9 eggs
- 1 cup shrimps
- ¼ cup of panko bread crumbs
- 30 ounces cheddar cheese

- 2 teaspoons garlic, minced
- 1 teaspoon fresh basil,
- 1 teaspoon celery
- 1 teaspoon fresh parsley
- Ground black pepper
- Paprika
- Sea salt
- Allspice

Directions:

Use 4 cocottes or ramekins and coat them with olive oil. Dice the bell peppers. Place the chopped onion, peppers and shrimp in the frying pan and sauté with oil for 2 minutes at 420°F. minutes Add the shallots, garlic and parsley, and cook for 1 minute. minutes Place the mixture into a mixing bowl and let it cool. In another bowl, whisk 1 of egg with the panko bread crumbs and cheese and mix thoroughly. Put the half of the mixture over the bottom of each cocotte. Beat two eggs into each cocotte. Sprinkle with the salt, pepper, and paprika. Cook at 400°F for 10 minutes. Top with the basil and celery and serve.

Quince Pie

Prep time: 20 minutes
Cooking time: 40 minutes
Servings: 6

Ingredients:

- 4 eggs
- 1 cup milk
- 1 cup wheat flour
- Vanilla extract
- 3 tablespoons butter
- 2 quinces

- Powdered sugar
- ½ cup sugar
- Salt
- 1 teaspoon honey
- ½ teaspoon ground cardamom
- 1/8 teaspoon ground cinnamon

Directions:

Peel and cut quinces in thin pieces. Beat the eggs in a bowl. Add the flour, and a few drops of the vanilla extract and blend. Set the dough aside for 15 minutes. Preheat the air fryer to 420°F. Coat the frying pan with melted butter. Place quinces on the pan, and then add the cardamom, cinnamon, and salt and cook for 7 minutes. Add the sugar and cook for another 3 minutes. Add the butter on the top to melt. Pour the batter on the quinces and cook for 20 minutes. Sprinkle with powder sugar or honey, if desired.

Scrambled Cauliflower

Prep time: 5 minutes
Cooking time: 15 minutes
Servings: 4

Ingredients:

- 1 large cauliflower, cut into florets
- 1 tablespoon olive oil
- 1 teaspoon turmeric
- 1 tablespoon of cheddar cheese
- 4 tablespoons wheat flour
- 1 egg
- Sea salt
- Ground black pepper

Directions:

Whisk an egg with some salt, pepper, and turmeric. Boil the cauliflower in the water with some salt, drain and let cool. Coat the florets with the egg, and then dip them in the flour. Preheat the air fryer to 320°F. Place the cauliflower into the basket of the air fryer and sprinkle with oil. Cook for 15 minutes, until golden brown. Serve with the shredded cheese sprinkled on top.

Marinated Cauliflower with Potatoes

Prep time: 5 minutes
Cooking time: 15 minutes
Servings: 4

Ingredients:

- 1 large cauliflower
- 1 tablespoon olive oil
- 1 teaspoon turmeric
- Sea salt
- Ground black pepper
- 1 glove garlic, minced
- Onion powder
- 1 onion, chopped
- 5 potatoes, peeled and chopped
- 1 cup panko bread crumbs

Directions:

For marinade, combine the bread crumbs with oil, turmeric, and onion in a bowl. Add the garlic powder and onion powder, and toss. Preheat the air fryer to 400°F. Sprinkle some oil on the frying pan and add the potatoes. Cook the potatoes for 20 minutes, shaking the pan every 5 minutes. Add the cauliflower and marinade and cook for 20 minutes. Sprinkle with salt and pepper and serve warm.

Sausage Patties

Prep time: 20 minutes
Cooking time: 25 minutes
Servings: 4

Ingredients:

- 8 ounces wheat flour
- 4 ounces butter
- 1 tablespoon sunflower oil
- 11 ounces sausage links
- 1 egg
- Sea salt
- Allspice

Directions:

Preheat the air fryer to 320°F. Combine flour, egg, and butter in a bowl. Add the oil and some water and knead the dough until smooth. Roll out the dough into a square shape. Cut into smaller squares. Put the sausage in the center of each square and roll up. Make cuts on the top of every roll so that dough can expand. Mold the mixture into small patties. Air fry for 5 minutes at 320°F.

Hot Dogs

Prep time: 5 minutes
Cooking time: 15 minutes
Servings: 4

Ingredients:

- 4 buns
- 4 hot dogs
- 1 teaspoon condiments

Directions:

Preheat the air fryer to 320°F. Place the hot dogs inside of each bun. Air fry for 5 minutes at 320°F. Serve with mustard, ketchup, relish, or other condiments.

Ground Meat Burger Pockets

Prep time: 20 minutes
Cooking time: 25 minutes
Servings: 4

Ingredients:

- 8 ounces wheat flour
- 4 ounces butter
- 4 ounces force meat
- 1 egg
- 1 onion, peeled and grated
- 1 potato, peeled and grated
- 1 tablespoon sunflower oil
- 1 teaspoon Italian herbs
- 1 teaspoon sesame seeds
- Sea salt
- Allspice

Directions:

Combine the flour, egg and butter in a bowl. Add the oil and some water and knead the dough until smooth. Roll out the dough into a square shape. Combine the forcemeat, spices, potato, and onion with some oil and mix thoroughly. Put the meat mixture on a pan and cook until brown. Put the cooked meat in the center of the square and roll up on all sides. Coat the burgers with egg and place them to the air fryer. Cook for 25 minutes at 390°F. Sprinkle with sesame seeds and serve.

Pear-Squash Porridge

Prep Time: 10 minutes
Cooking Time: 15 minutes
Servings: 3

Ingredients:

- 1 squash, washed
- 3 pears
- ½ cup stock or water
- 2 tablespoons honey
- ½ teaspoon cinnamon
- 1/8 teaspoon cloves
- 1/8 teaspoon ginger
- Salt

Directions:

Preheat the air fryer to 320°F. Cut the unpeeled pears from the cores. Place a whole, uncut squash into a bowl and add the pears, stock, and spices. Air fry for 8 minutes at 350°F. Add the honey and salt. Use a blender and puree for 30 seconds or until smooth. Serve with cinnamon.

Millet

Prep Time: 10 minutes
Cooking Time: 10 minutes
Servings: 6

Ingredients:

- 1 cups millet, rinsed well
- 2 cups water
- 2 tablespoons honey
- ½ teaspoon vanilla extract
- 1/4 teaspoon ground cinnamon
- Sea salt
- milk
- Fresh berries
- Sliced almonds

Directions:

Place the millet, water, honey, vanilla extract, cinnamon, and salt in the air fryer pan and stir well. Air fry for 8 minutes at 350°F. Remove the millet and serve sprinkled with cinnamon. Add milk, berries, and sliced almonds, if desired..

Sweetened Air-fried Squash

Prep Time: 10 minutes
Cooking Time: 20 minutes
Servings: 6

Ingredients:
- 1 squash
- 2 tablespoons sugar

Directions:
Preheat the air fryer to 350°F. Washed and peel the squash and cut it into squares. Place to the air fryer pan. Sprinkle the sugar and toss well. Air fry for 8 minutes at 350°F. Serve sprinkled with cinnamon.

Peach Cake

Prep time: 10 minutes
Cooking time: 40 minutes
Servings: 4

Ingredients:
- 8 ounces wheat flour
- 3 ounces butter
- 4 ounces sugar
- 7 ounces canned peaches, chopped
- 2 ounces cocoa butter, melted
- 1 egg
- 2 tablespoons milk

Directions:
Preheat the air fryer to 390°F Combine the flour and butter in a bowl. Add the sugar, peaches with syrup and cocoa butter. Whisk an egg with milk in a separate bowl. Combine the egg mixture with the flour mixture. Stir in the cake dough on the frying pan. Cook at 390°F or 35 minutes. Garnish with fresh mint, if desired.

Muffin Pizza

Prep time: 10 minutes
Cooking time: 30 minutes
Servings: 4

Ingredients:
- 13 ounces wheat flour
- 4 slices ham
- 1 egg
- 1 onion, peeled and diced
- 4 ounces cheese, grated
- 2 tablespoons sunflower oil
- 1 cup milk
- 1 teaspoon fresh dill

Directions:
Preheat the air fryer to 320°F. Sprinkle the ham with oil and fry in a frying pan. Add onions and sauté for 5 minutes. In a separate bowl, mix the dill, flour, and cheese. Knead the dough and add the milk, oil, and egg. Mix well and combine the dough with the ham and onions. Cook in the muffin cases for 20 minutes at 320°F.

Mini Croissants with Cheese

Prep time: 5 minutes
Cooking time: 20 minutes
Servings: 6

Ingredients:

- 6 ounces self-rising flour
- 1 ounce butter
- 1 egg
- 4 ounces cheese

- 2 tablespoons milk
- 1 teaspoon parsley
- Salt
- Ground black pepper

Directions:

Preheat the air fryer to 320°F. In a bowl, combine the flour, salt, pepper, butter, milk, egg, and parsley. If the dough is sticky, add a small amount of the oil. Roll the dough into 3 smooth squares and cut in half diagonally. Put the cheese inside on each piece of dough and roll up like a croissant. Place these mini croissants in the frying basket. Cook for 20 minutes at 320°F.

Bacon-wrapped Hot Dogs

Prep time: 5 minutes
Cooking time: 13 minutes
Servings: 6

Ingredients:

- 6 bacon slices
- 6 hot dogs

- 2 tablespoons mustard
- 3 leaves lettuce

Directions:

Preheat the air fryer to 320°F. Wrap each hot dog in the slice of bacon. Place them in the frying basket. Cook for 13 minutes at 320°F and serve with mustard.

Bagel with Cheese and Tuna

Prep time: 5 minutes
Cooking time: 5 minutes
Servings: 2

Ingredients:

- 2 savory brioche
- 4 ounces cheddar cheese, shredded

- 1 can canned tuna
- 4 slices cucumber

Directions:

Preheat the air fryer to 320°F. Cut the bagels in half, put the cheese inside and place them in the frying basket. Cook for 3 minutes at 320°F until the cheese melted and bread is crispy. Remove from the air fryer. Drain the liquid from tuna and mash it. Put the tuna on top of the cheese, add the cucumber slices, and serve with mustard.

Bagel with Tuna and Tomatoes

Prep time: 5 minutes
Cooking time: 10 minutes
Servings: 4

Ingredients:
- 4 bagels with seeds
- 1 can canned tuna
- 1 tablespoon mayonnaise
- 1 green onion
- 1 tomato, sliced
- 125 ounces Cheddar cheese
- 1 lemon, juiced
- Salt

Directions:
Preheat the air fryer to 480°F. Cut the bagels in half, place them in the frying basket. Fry until bread is crispy and remove from the air fryer. Drain the liquid from tuna, mash it, and add to a bowl. Chop the onion and mix it with the tuna. Add the mayonnaise and lemon juice and mix well. Add salt to taste. Put ¼ of the tuna on each bagel half and garnish with a slice of tomato on top. Sprinkle with the grated cheese. Place them in the frying basket. Cook for 2 minutes at 320°F until tuna becomes warm. Repeat the process with the other halves of bagel and serve.

Hearty Omelet

Cooking time: 10 minutes
Servings: 4

Ingredients:
- 9 ounces cooked sausage
- 8 ounces Parmesan cheese
- 5 eggs
- ¾ cup milk
- ¼ cup mineral water
- 1 tomatoes
- Fresh dill
- Green onion
- Salt
- 1 tablespoon sunflower oil

Directions:
Cut the sausage and tomato into small cubes. Slice the cheese thinly. Mince the dill and onion. In a bowl, beat the eggs, add the milk water, and salt and whisk thoroughly. Preheat the air fryer to 320°F. Place the sausage to the air fryer pan and fry for 3 minutes. Add the cheese, stirring until it lightly melted. Add the oil and pour the egg mixture. Cook for 7 minutes at 320°F and serve with tomatoes.

Bun with Ham and Pineapple

Prep time: 5 minutes
Cooking time: 5 minutes
Servings: 2

Ingredients:

- 2 whole wheat buns
- 2 slices unsmoked ham
- 2 pineapple rings
- 2 teaspoons cheddar cheese, shredded
- 2 tablespoons ketchup

Directions:

Preheat the air fryer to 320°F. Cut the buns in half; place them in the frying basket. Fry until bread is crispy and remove them from the air fryer. Put the ham, a ring of pineapple and cheese on each half of a bun. Place them in the frying basket. Cook for 3 minutes at 320°F until the cheese is lightly melted. Serve with ketchup.

Bacon and Pear Sandwich

Prep time: 5 minutes
Cooking time: 5 minutes
Servings: 2

Ingredients:

- 3 tablespoons honey
- 1 tablespoon mustard
- 2 teaspoons sugar
- 4 slices rye bread
- 1 pear
- 4 slices smoked ham
- ½ cup watercress

Directions:

Preheat the air fryer to 320°F. Put the bread into the air fryer. Air fry for 2 minutes at 320°F and fry until the bread is crispy and remove from the air fryer. Cool briefly and set aside. Mix the honey, mustard, and sugar. Spread the mixture on the slices of bread. Cut the pear in half, without removing from the skin. Remove the core. Cut in thick slices. Put a couple of pear slices on each slice of bread. Top with bacon. Add watercress and serve.

Puff Pastry-wrapped Sausages

Prep time: 5 minutes
Cooking time: 25 minutes
Servings: 12

Ingredients:

- 9 ounces puff pastry
- 14 ounces Polish sausage
- 6 tablespoon ketchup
- 6 cherry tomatoes, diced
- 2 teaspoons balsamic vinegar
- 2 teaspoons water

Directions:

Preheat the air fryer to 430°F. Roll out the dough layer 8 inches by 12 inches and ¼-inch thick, cut into strips about ½-inch wide. Cut the sausages in half, and wrap each sausage into one strip of dough. Place them on a baking sheet so that the ends of the dough strips are on the bottom. Air fry for 20 minutes at 320°F until the dough is crispy. Mix ketchup, vinegar, water, and tomatoes to make a sauce to serve with the sausages.

Pasta Salad

Preparation time: 10 minutes
Cooking time: 15 minutes
Servings: 6

Ingredients:

- 1 green bell pepper, seeded and chopped
- 1 orange bell pepper, seeded and chopped
- 1 zucchini, sliced
- 1 red bell pepper, seeded and chopped
- Salt and ground black pepper, to taste
- 1 yellow squash, chopped
- 1 red onion, peeled and diced
- 4 ounces cremini mushrooms, cut in half
- 1 teaspoon Italian seasoning
- 1 pound penne rigate, cooked and drained
- 1 cups cherry tomatoes, cut in half
- ½ cup Kalamata olives, pitted and halved
- 3 tablespoons balsamic vinegar
- 2 tablespoons basil, chopped
- ¼ cup olive oil

Directions:

In a bowl, mix the bell peppers with the squash, zucchini, mushrooms, onion, half of the olive oil, salt, pepper, and Italian seasoning. Toss to coat and transfer to the air fryer. Cook at 380°F for 15 minutes, shaking halfway through. In a bowl, mix the pasta with cooked vegetables, olives, tomatoes, salt, pepper, vinegar, and the rest of the oil. Toss to coat and chill in the refrigerator. Sprinkle basil on top, divide on plates, and serve.

Cheeseburgers

Preparation time: 10 minutes
Cooking time: 20 minutes
Servings: 2

Ingredients:

- 2 hamburger buns
- 12 ounces beef, ground
- 2 teaspoons mustard
- Salt and ground black pepper, to taste
- 3 tablespoons onion, chopped
- 4 teaspoons ketchup
- 4 cheddar cheese slices
- 8 dill pickle chips

Directions:

In a bowl, mix ground beef with salt, pepper, ketchup, onion, and mustard and stir well. Divide this mixture into 4 pieces and shape into patties. Place half of the cheese on 2 meat patties and 4 pickle chips, top with the other 2 patties and press well. Place burgers in the air fryer's basket and cook at 370°F for 20 minutes, flipping them after 10 minutes. Divide cheeseburgers on 2 buns, top with the rest of the pickle chips and cheese. Serve with the favorite condiments.

Macaroni and Cheese

Preparation time: 10 minutes
Cooking time: 25 minutes
Servings: 4

Ingredients:

- 2 cups macaroni, cooked and drained
- 1 teaspoon cornstarch
- 2 cups cheddar cheese, shredded
- 2 cups heavy cream
- Salt and ground black pepper, to taste

Directions:

In a bowl, mix 1½ cup of the cheese with the cornstarch and stir. Add the macaroni, salt, pepper, and cream and stir. Pour this into the air fryer's basket, cover with aluminum foil and cook at 310°F for 15 minutes. Sprinkle the rest of the cheese on top and cook for 10 minutes. Let macaroni and cheese cool for a few minutes before dividing between plates and serve.

Chicken Pie

Preparation time: 10 minutes
Cooking time: 25 minutes
Servings: 4

Ingredients:
- 1½ cups canned cream of celery soup
- 6 chicken tenders
- Salt and ground black pepper, to taste
- 2 potatoes, peeled chopped
- 1 bay leaf
- 1 thyme sprig
- 1 tablespoon milk
- 1 egg yolk
- 5 buttermilk biscuit dough pieces
- ½ cup heavy cream

Directions:

In a pot, mix chicken with the soup, potatoes, cream, bay leaf, thyme, salt, and pepper, stir well, and bring to a boil over medium-high heat. Pour this into the air fryer's basket, cover and cook at 320°F for 15 minutes. Add the biscuits into the air fryer's basket, brush with egg yolk mixed with milk, and cook at 300°F for 10 minutes. Divide between plates and serve.

Air-fried Sirloin Steak

Preparation time: 10 minutes
Cooking time: 15 minutes
Servings: 1

Ingredients:
- 6 ounces sirloin steak
- 1 cup flour
- 1 cup panko bread crumbs
- 3 eggs, whisked
- Salt and ground black pepper, to taste
- 1 teaspoon onion powder
- 1 teaspoon garlic powder
- 6 ounces ground pork sausage
- 2 cups milk
- 2 tablespoons flour

Directions:

In a bowl, mix the bread crumbs salt, pepper, onion powder, and garlic powder and stir. Put 1 cup flour in a bowl. Put the eggs in another bowl. Dredge the steak in the flour, then the egg, and finally in the bread crumbs and place it in the fryer's basket. Cook at 370°F for 12 minutes, take out of the fryer and place on a serving plate. Heat up a pan over medium heat, add the sausage meat. Brown for a few minutes, stirring frequently, and drain the grease, reserving 2 tablespoons in the pan. Add flour to the sausage, stir and cook for 1 minute. Add the milk, salt and pepper, cover and cook gravy for 3 minutes. Drizzle this over steak and serve.

Pork Loin and Potatoes

Preparation time: 10 minutes
Cooking time: 25 minutes
Servings: 2

Ingredients:

- 2 pounds pork loin
- Salt and ground black pepper, to taste
- 2 red potatoes, roughly chopped
- ½ teaspoon garlic powder
- ½ teaspoon red pepper flakes
- 1 teaspoon parsley
- Balsamic glaze

Directions:

Put pork loin and potatoes in the basket of the air fryer and add the salt, pepper, pepper flakes, garlic powder and parsley. Toss to coat, cover, and cook at 390°F for 25 minutes. Transfer the pork loin to a cutting board and let rest for 5 minutes. Slice and put on a platter. Add potatoes on the side, drizzle balsamic glaze on top, and serve.

Turkey-stuffed Bread

Preparation time: 10 minutes
Cooking time: 30 minutes
Servings: 2

Ingredients:

- 1 tablespoon turkey meat, cooked and shredded
- ½ cup spinach, chopped
- 3.5 ounces cheddar cheese, shredded
- 3.5 ounces soft cheese
- 8 ounces flour
- 5 ounces milk
- 1 teaspoon yeast
- 1 tablespoon butter
- Salt and ground black pepper, to taste

Directions:

Mix the butter with the flour and rub until you obtain bread crumbs. Add the turkey, yeast, milk, salt and pepper and knead until a dough forms. Roll the dough on a working surface. In a bowl, mix a handful of spinach with cheeses, stir and spread onto dough. Roll the dough into a loaf shape and place it in the baking pan of the air fryer. Cook at 400°F for 20 minutes and at 350°F for 6 minutes. Slice the stuffed bread and serve warm with a dip of the choice.

Turkey Patties

Preparation time: 10 minutes
Cooking time: 10 minutes
Servings: 4

Ingredients:

- 6 mushrooms, cleaned and trimmed
- 1 teaspoon garlic powder
- 1 teaspoon onion powder
- Salt and ground black pepper, to taste
- 1 ¼ pounds turkey meat, ground
- Vegetable oil cooking spray

Directions:

Put the mushrooms in the blender and puree them. Add the salt and pepper and pulse a few times. In a bowl, mix the turkey with the mushrooms, salt, pepper, onion powder, and garlic powder and stir well. Shape patties from this mixture and spray them with cooking oil. Place the patties in the air fryer's basket and cook at 320°F for 10 minutes. Divide them between plates and serve with French fries on the side.

Air-fried Cheese Ravioli

Preparation time: 10 minutes
Cooking time: 5 minutes
Servings: 6

Ingredients:

- 1 box cheese ravioli
- 10 ounces marinara sauce
- Olive oil
- 1 cup buttermilk
- 2 cups bread crumbs
- ¼ cup Parmesan cheese, grated

Directions:

Pour the buttermilk in a bowl and the bread crumbs in another bowl. Dip each ravioli piece in the buttermilk and then in bread crumbs. Place them in the air fryer on a baking pan. Drizzle some olive oil over them, cook at 400°F for 5 minutes, and arrange them on a plate. Sprinkle Parmesan cheese on top and serve.

Fish Tacos

Preparation time: 10 minutes
Cooking time: 12 minutes
Servings: 4

Ingredients:

- 4 tortillas
- 1 yellow onion, chopped
- 2 grilled ears of corn, corn cut from the cob
- 4 fish fillets
- ½ cup mango salsa
- 1 red bell pepper, seeded and chopped
- Mixed greens like spinach, radicchio, and lettuce
- 4 tablespoons cheddar, grated
- Tortilla chips

Directions:

Heat a pan on medium high heat, add the onion and bell pepper, stir well, and cook for 4 minutes. Add the corn, stir, and cook for 2 minutes and take off the heat. Put the fish fillets in the air fryer and cook at 400°F for 6 minutes. Transfer fish to a cutting board and chop it. Place the tortillas on a working surface, add onion mix in the middle of each, and divide the fish pieces and mango salsa between them. Add some tortilla chips to each tortilla, divide the mixed greens evenly, and top with grated cheese. Wrap the tacos, place them in the lined air fryer and cook at 350°F for 6 minutes. Divide tacos between plates and serve.

Shrimp Pasta

Preparation time: 10 minutes
Cooking time: 25 minutes
Servings: 3

Ingredients:

- 5 ounces spaghetti
- 8 ounces shrimp, peeled and deveined
- Salt and ground black pepper, to taste
- 5 garlic cloves, minced
- 1 teaspoon chile flakes
- ½ teaspoon chicken bullion
- 1 tablespoon butter
- 2 tablespoons olive oil
- Salt and ground black pepper to taste

Directions:

Put some water in a pot, add some salt, bring to a boil on medium-high heat, add spaghetti, cook for 8 minutes, drain and set aside. Put 1 tablespoon oil, the butter and shrimp in the air fryer and cook at 350°F for 10 minutes. Add the pasta, salt, pepper, chicken bouillon, chile flakes, garlic, and remaining oil, toss to coat, and cook for 5 minutes more. Divide between plates and serve.

Beef Stew

Preparation time: 10 minutes
Cooking time: 25 minutes
Servings: 4

Ingredients:

- 2 pounds beef, cut into medium chunks
- 2 carrots, peeled and chopped
- 4 potatoes, peeled and chopped
- Salt and ground black pepper, to taste
- 1 quart beef stock
- ½ teaspoon smoked paprika
- ½ cup fresh thyme, chopped
- 4 tablespoons Worcestershire sauce

Directions:

Put the beef in the air fryer. Add the carrots, potatoes, stock, salt, pepper, paprika, Worcestershire sauce, and a pinch of thyme and stir. Cook at 380°F for 25 minutes. Divide into bowls and serve.

Mediterranean Vegetables

Preparation time: 10 minutes
Cooking time: 20 minutes
Servings: 4

Ingredients:

- ½ cup cherry tomatoes, cut in halves
- Salt and ground black pepper, to taste
- 1 parsnip, peeled and diced
- 1 zucchini, diced
- 1 green bell pepper, cut into strips
- 1 carrot, peeled and sliced
- 1 teaspoon mixed herbs
- 2 tablespoons honey
- 2 teaspoons garlic, minced
- 6 tablespoons olive oil
- 1 teaspoon mustard

Directions:

Put zucchini into the air fryer. Add the bell pepper, parsnip, carrot, and a few tomatoes. Add half of the oil, salt and pepper and mix well. Cook at 360°F for 15 minutes. In a bowl, mix the rest of the oil with some salt and pepper, plus the honey, mustard, mixed herbs, and garlic and stir well. Pour this over the vegetables, toss to coat, and cook for 5 minutes at 370°F. Divide between plates and serve.

Five-cheese Bread

Preparation time: 10 minutes
Cooking time: 5 minutes
Servings: 2

Ingredients:

- 1 bread loaf
- 2 teaspoons garlic, minced
- 4 ounces butter
- 2 tablespoons cheddar cheese grated
- 2 tablespoons mozzarella cheese, grated
- 2 tablespoons goat cheese, shredded
- 2 tablespoons soft cheese
- 2 tablespoons edam cheese, shredded
- Salt and ground black pepper, to taste
- 2 teaspoons chives, chopped

Directions:

Heat up a pan with the butter on medium heat, add the chives, garlic, salt, and pepper. Stir and cook for 2 minutes. Make slits into the bread and drizzle the garlic and butter mix into them. Divide the cheese evenly between the slits, place the bread in the air fryer, and cook at 370°F for 5 minutes. Serve hot.

Sloppy Joes

Preparation time: 10 minutes
Cooking time: 30 minutes
Servings: 2

Ingredients:

- 7 ounces beef, ground
- 5 potatoes, cut into wedges
- 1 onion, chopped
- 7 ounces canned tomatoes, diced
- 2 tablespoons cheddar, grated
- 1 tablespoon tomato puree
- 1 tablespoon garlic, minced
- 2 tablespoons olive oil
- Salt and ground black pepper, to taste
- 1 tablespoon oregano, chopped
- 1 tablespoon thyme, chopped
- 1 tablespoon Italian seasoning
- 1 teaspoon basil, chopped

Directions:

Place the potato wedges and 1 tablespoon oil in the preheated air fryer and cook at 360°F for 20 minutes, shaking them every 6 minutes. Heat up a pan with the rest of the oil on medium heat, add the onions, stir, and cook for 3 minutes. Add the garlic, beef, tomato puree, canned tomatoes, Italian seasoning, oregano, thyme, basil, salt, and pepper, stir and cook for 10 minutes. Pour this onto the potato wedges in the air fryer, cook for 5 minutes at 360F, divide between plates, and serve with grated cheese on top.

Meatball Sandwich

Preparation time: 10 minutes
Cooking time: 27 minutes
Servings: 4

Ingredients:

- 3 baguettes
- 14 ounces beef, ground
- 7 ounces tomato sauce
- 1 small onion, chopped
- 1 egg, whisked
- 1 tablespoon bread crumbs
- 2 tablespoons cheddar cheese, grated
- 1 tablespoon fresh oregano, chopped
- 1 tablespoon olive oil
- Salt and ground black pepper, to taste
- 1 teaspoon fresh thyme
- 1 teaspoon fresh basil, chopped

Directions:

In a bowl, mix the beef with the salt, pepper, onion, bread crumbs, egg, cheese, oregano, thyme, and basil, and stir well. Shape into meatballs and place them on a working surface. Put the oil in the air fryer heat up at 370°F and add the meatballs. Cook for 12 minutes, flipping them half way. Add half of the tomato sauce and cook for 10 minutes more. Slice baguettes more than half way through, divide meatballs and sauce on them and serve with the rest of the tomato sauce on the side.

Snacks and Appetizers

Pea and Carrots Bread Rolls

Prep time: 20 minutes
Cooking time: 15 minutes
Servings: 4

Ingredients:

- 1 cup of peas
- 1 carrot
- 6 bread slices
- 4 shallots, minced
- ½ teaspoon basil, minced
- 1 onions, diced
- ½ teaspoon fresh marjoram
- ½ teaspoon fresh oregano
- 2 lettuce leaves
- 2 tablespoons olive oil
- Salt
- Ground black pepper

Directions:

Boil the peas with some salt and puree until smooth. In a pan, fry the carrot, onion, shallots, and basil for a few minutes until translucent. Add the marjoram and oregano and stir. Add the mixture to the peas. Mix well and set aside. Form 8 balls from the [pea mixture. Brush one side of each bread slice with water. Wring the water from the bread. Mix the bread with the peas. Preheat the air fryer to 350°F. Sprinkle the rolls and the air fryer pan with oil. Put the rolls in the air fryer. Cook for 12-13 minutes until bread rolls are crispy. Serve with ketchup on lettuce leaves.

Potato Chips with Paprika

Prep time: 5 minutes
Cooking time: 15 minutes
Servings: 2

Ingredients:

- 4 sweet potatoes
- 2 cups of water
- Salt
- ½ teaspoon paprika
- ½ teaspoon turmeric
- 1 tablespoon olive oil

Directions:

Peel the potatoes and cut them into thin slices. In a bowl add the water with teaspoon salt and the turmeric. Dip the potatoes in the brine and soak for 3 minutes. Drain the potatoes and coat them with olive oil. Preheat the air fryer at 350°F. Cook the potatoes in the air fryer for 10-12 minutes. Sprinkle the chips with paprika and serve.

Cabbage Rolls

Prep time: 15 minutes
Cooking time: 20 minutes
Servings: 5

Ingredients:

- 1 small white cabbage
- 1 egg
- 1 carrot
- ½ teaspoon black pepper
- Sugar
- 1 teaspoon balsamic vinegar
- 1 teaspoon salt
- 2 tablespoons vegetable oil
- 2 teaspoons parsley
- 10 spring roll sheets
- 2 tablespoons wheat flour
- 1 cup of water

Directions:

Take the spring roll sheets from the freezer and thaw for the 1 hour. Chop the cabbage into thin strips. Peel and grate the carrot and add the carrots and cabbage to a bowl. Add the parsley, balsamic vinegar, salt, and a pinch of sugar and mix well. Cook this carrot and cabbage mixture on the air fryer pan with a little oil for 10 minutes. Beat an egg in another bowl and add some pepper. Add it to the filling and stir. Let it cool briefly. In a separate bowl, mix the water with flour. Take a spring roll sheet and cut in half. Take a tablespoon of the filling and put on the sheet. Roll the sheet and dip it in the flour paste. Do the same with the rest of the filling. Preheat the air fryer to 350°F. Cook the cabbage rolls for 10-12 minutes and serve.

Pita Chips

Prep time: 5 minutes
Cooking time: 15 minutes
Servings: 4

Ingredients:

- 1 pita bread
- 1 tablespoon olive oil
- 1 teaspoon poultry seasoning

Directions:

Preheat the air fryer to 350°F. Cut pita bread into strips. Sprinkle the strips with olive oil. Put the strips into the air fryer for 3 minutes. Repeat with the rest of the strips. Sprinkle with poultry seasoning and serve with soup or chicken broth.

Imitation Crab Crisps

Prep time: 15 minutes
Cooking time: 15 minutes
Servings: 4

Ingredients:

- 2 ounces imitation crab
- 2 tablespoons vegetable oil
- Salt
- 1 teaspoon cheese powder

Directions:

Preheat the air fryer to 350°F. Cut the imitation crab into thin slices. Sprinkle with oil and cheese seasoning. Mix well and add to a baking pan. Cook in the air fryer for 12 minutes until crispy.

Air-fried Pickled Summer Squash

Prep time: 10 minutes
Cooking time: 5 minutes
Servings: 4

Ingredients:

- 2 slices pickled summer squash
- 1 egg
- 5 tablespoons milk
- 2 tablespoons wheat flour
- ½ teaspoon garlic minced
- ½ teaspoon mustard
- 2 tablespoons olive oil

Directions:

Drain the pickled squash on a paper towel. In a bowl, mix the milk with the egg. Add the garlic and mustard and mix well. Cut the squash into thin slices. Dip the slices in flour, then in the egg mixture, then flour again. Preheat the air fryer to 350°F. Sprinkle with oil in the air frying basket. Cook in the air fryer for 3-5 minutes until crispy.

Air-fried Cauliflower

Prep time: 5 minutes
Cooking time: 20 minutes
Servings: 6

Ingredients:

- 1 cauliflower head, broken into florets
- 1 tablespoon olive oil
- 1 egg
- 5 tablespoons milk
- 2 tablespoons wheat flour
- Salt
- Ground black pepper
- 1 tablespoon butter (or any vegetable oil)

Directions:

Boil the cauliflower florets in salted water for 10 minutes. Mix the milk and egg in a bowl with salt and pepper. Dip the florets in the flour, then into the egg mixture, and then into the flour again. Preheat the air fryer to 350°F. Sprinkle with oil in the air frying basket. Cook in the air fryer for 3-5 minutes until crispy. Serve with garlic sauce.

Seasoned Chickpeas

Prep time: 15 minutes
Cooking time: 15 minutes
Servings: 4

Ingredients:
- 14 ounce canned chickpeas
- 1 tablespoon olive oil
- 1 teaspoon any seasoning

Directions:
Preheat the air fryer to 350°F. Drain chickpeas and season them and mix with olive oil. Add them to the air fryer and cook for 10-12 minutes.

Couscous

Prep time: 15 minutes
Cooking time: 15 minutes
Servings: 4

Ingredients:
- 2 cups couscous, cooked
- 1 tablespoon olive oil
- 1 tablespoon garlic, minced
- 1 cup cauliflower floret
- 1 carrot, peeled
- 6 slices smoked sausage
- 2 tablespoons cheddar cheese

Directions:
Preheat the air fryer to 350°F. Dice the cauliflower carrot. Add some water and garlic and cook in the air fryer for 3-5 minutes. Add the smoked sausage slices and cook for 5 minutes. Combine with the couscous and mix well. Cook in the air fryer for 3-4 minutes, then drizzle with cheese and serve.

Air-fried Green Beans

Prep time: 5 minutes
Cooking time: 15 minutes
Servings: 4

Ingredients:

- 1 pound green beans, washed and trimmed
- 1 lemon
- Salt to taste
- Ground black pepper to taste
- ¼ teaspoon vegetable oil

Directions:

Preheat the air fryer to 350°F. Put the green beans in the air fryer and squeeze the lemon juice on them. Add a pinch of salt and pepper and drizzle the oil over top. Cook in air fryer at 400°F for 10-12 minutes and serve.

Chicken Balls

Prep time: 10 minutes
Cooking time: 15 minutes
Servings: 4

Ingredients:

- 14 ounces skinless and boneless chicken breast
- 1 cup bread crumbs
- 2 egg yolks
- 1 teaspoon turmeric
- 1 teaspoon salt
- 1 teaspoon ginger
- 2 tablespoons heavy cream
- 1 teaspoon olive oil

Directions:

Pour the olive oil in the air fryer basket. Take the chicken and chop it roughly. In a mixing bowl, combine the egg yolks and salt together. Whisk until smooth. Add the ginger and cream and stir again. Add the turmeric and stir again. Take the chicken pieces and dip them into the egg mixture. Coat the chicken pieces with the bread crumbs and transfer the chicken to the air fryer. Close the lid and cook for 15 minutes. Remove the dish from the air fryer and let it cool briefly before serving.

Spicy Potato Logs

Prep time: 10 minutes
Cooking time: 10 minutes
Servings: 4

Ingredients:

- 3 cups mashed potatoes
- ⅓ cup cheddar cheese
- 1 teaspoon paprika
- 1 egg
- 1 teaspoon nutmeg
- 1 teaspoon salt
- 3 tablespoons flour
- 1 teaspoon starch

Directions:

In a mixing bowl, combine the mashed potatoes and egg. Use a hand mixer and mix until smooth. Sprinkle the mixture with the nutmeg, salt, paprika, and starch. Stir well again. Grate the Cheddar cheese. Make the small logs from the mashed potato mixture and dip the logs in the flour. Sprinkle the logs with the grated cheese. Transfer the potato logs to the air fryer and close the lid. Cook for 10 minutes, let it cool briefly and serve.

Minced Meat Pockets

Prep time: 15 minutes
Cooking time: 20 minutes
Servings: 6

Ingredients:

- 10 ounces puff pastry
- 1 cup minced pork
- 1 white onion
- 1 teaspoon sour cream
- 1 teaspoon black pepper
- 1 teaspoon salt
- 1 teaspoon butter

Directions:

Take the puff pastry and roll it out using a rolling pin. Make the small squares from the dough. Peel the onion and dice it. In a mixing bowl, combine the chopped onion and minced pork. Sprinkle the mixture with the salt, pepper, and sour cream and stir well. Add the butter and stir again until smooth. Put 1 teaspoon of the meat mixture on the every dough square and make the pockets from them. Transfer the pockets to the air fryer and close the lid. Cook for 20 minutes. When the dish is cooked, remove it from the air fryer, let it rest briefly and serve.

Tomato Circles with Basil

Prep time: 10 minutes
Cooking time: 10 minutes
Servings: 4

Ingredients:

- 4 tomatoes
- 1 cup Parmesan cheese
- 4 tablespoons dried basil
- 1 teaspoon salt
- 1 teaspoon paprika
- 1 teaspoon turmeric
- 6 ounces boneless and skinless chicken breast

Directions:

Wash the tomatoes and cut into the thick slices. Dice the chicken and combine it with the paprika, salt, and turmeric. Stir well. Transfer the tomato slices to the air fryer basket. Add the chopped chicken. Grate the cheese and sprinkle the tomatoes with the grated cheese. Sprinkle the dish with the basil. Close the lid and cook for 10 minutes. When the dish is cooked, let them rest briefly before serving cooked, let it rest briefly and serve.

Salmon Bites

Prep time: 15 minutes
Cooking time: 25 minutes
Servings: 4

Ingredients:

- 1 cup butter
- 1 cup flour
- 1 teaspoon salt
- 10 ounces salmon fillet
- ½ cup sour cream
- 1 tablespoon tomato sauce
- 1 teaspoon black pepper
- ¼ cup chives
- 1 cup cheddar cheese, grated

Directions:

Chop the butter and transfer it to the mixing bowl. Sift the flour and add salt. Stir the mixture and knead the dough. Take the air fryer forms and make small boards. Chop the salmon fillet and chives. Combine the chopped salmon and black pepper and mix well. Sprinkle it with the sour cream and stir well. Mince the chives, combine them with the grated cheese and stir well. Transfer the salmon mixture to the boards and sprinkle them with the grated cheese mixture. Add the tomato sauce. Transfer the salmon to the air fryer and close the lid. Cook for 25 minutes. When the dish is cooked, remove it cooked, let it rest briefly and serve.

Sausage Spirals

Prep time: 15 minutes
Cooking time: 25 minutes
Servings: 4

Ingredients:

- 10 ounces yeast dough
- 8 ounces sausages
- 1 teaspoon cayenne pepper
- 1 teaspoon chile flakes
- 3 tablespoons tomato sauce
- 1 cup hard cheese
- 1 teaspoon salt
- 1 teaspoon olive oil

Directions:

In a mixing bowl, combine the cayenne pepper, chile flakes, salt, and olive oil and stir well. Roll the dough using a rolling pin. Chop the sausages and grate the cheese. In a mixing bowl, combine the grated cheese and chopped sausages together. Sprinkle it with the spice mixture and stir well. Add the tomato sauce and stir again. Spread the yeast dough with the sausage mixture and roll it. Cut the sausage rolls into thick circles and transfer them in the air fryer. Close the lid and cook for 25 minutes. When the dish is cooked, remove it from the air fryer, let it cool briefly, and serve.

Stuffed Bell Peppers

Prep time: 15 minutes
Cooking time: 30 minutes
Servings: 5

Ingredients:
- 5 bell peppers
- ½ cup minced chicken
- ½ cup minced beef
- 1 egg
- 1 yellow onion
- 1 teaspoon salt
- ½ cup Parmesan cheese

Directions:
Wash the bell peppers and cut them across into halves. Remove the seeds from the peppers. In a mixing bowl, combine the meats together. Sprinkle the mixture with the salt and add the egg. Stir well. Peel the onion and dice it. Add the onion to the meat mixture and stir well. Grate the Parmesan cheese. Transfer the meat mixture to the peppers and sprinkle them with the grated Parmesan cheese. Transfer the peppers in the air fryer and close the lid. Cook for 30 minutes, let it rest briefly, and serve.

Puff Pastry Sausages

Prep time: 20 minutes
Cooking time: 30 minutes
Servings: 4

Ingredients:
- 2 garlic cloves
- 4 sausages
- 1 tablespoon sesame seeds
- 1 teaspoon ground black pepper
- 2 tablespoons olive oil
- 8 ounces puff pastry
- 1 egg yolk

Directions:
Roll the puff pastry using a rolling pin and make squares from the dough. Peel the garlic clove and mince it. Sprinkle the dough squares with the minced garlic and pepper. Spray them with the olive oil. Put a sausage in every square and roll them. Whisk the egg and spread the sausage rolls with the egg mixture. Sprinkle them with the sesame seeds. Transfer the dish to the air fryer and close the lid. Cook the sausage rolls for 30 minutes. When the dish is cooked, remove it cooked, remove it from the air fryer, let it rest briefly and serve.

Date Rolls

Prep time: 10 minutes
Cooking time: 15 minutes
Servings: 4

Ingredients:
- 4 bacon strips
- 4 dates
- ⅓ cup cheddar cheese
- 1 teaspoon paprika

Directions:

Remove the pits from the dates. Grate the Cheddar cheese and combine it with the paprika and stir well. Fill the dates with the cheese mixture. Take the bacon strips and wrap the dates in the bacon. Transfer the dish in the air fryer and cook for 15 minutes. Remove the dish from the air fryer and let it cool briefly before serving.

Stuffed Mushroom Caps

Prep time: 15 minutes
Cooking time: 25 minutes
Servings: 6

Ingredients:
- 6 mushroom caps
- 1 carrot
- 1 yellow onion
- 1 tablespoon olive oil
- 1 teaspoon basil
- 1 teaspoon black pepper
- 2 tablespoons pumpkin, chopped

Directions:

Wash the mushroom caps and then peel the onion and carrot. Dice the onion and grate the carrot. Combine the carrot and onion in a mixing bowl. Add the olive oil, basil, and pepper and stir well. Add the pumpkin and stir again. Fill the mushroom caps with the carrot mixture. Open the air fryer lid and transfer the stuffed mushroom caps to the basket. Close the lid and cook for 25 minutes. When the dish is cooked, remove it cooked, remove it from the air fryer, let it rest briefly and serve.

Sausage Buns

Prep time: 10 minutes
Cooking time: 7 minutes
Servings: 4

Ingredients:

- 14 ounces puff pastry
- 2 eggs
- 4 sausages
- 1 teaspoon fresh basil
- 1 teaspoon fresh cilantro
- 1 teaspoon paprika
- 6 ounces Cheddar cheese
- 1 tablespoon tomato sauce

Directions:

Separate the egg yolks and egg whites and put them into separate bowls. Then whisk the egg parts gently. Sprinkle the egg yolk mixture with the paprika and cilantro and stir well. Take the puff pastry and roll it out using a rolling pin. Make medium-sized squares from the puff pastry. Spread the puff pastry squares with the egg yolk mixture. Put the Cheddar cheese in every square and add the sausage and tomato sauce. Roll the puff pastry and spread it with the whisked egg white. Sprinkle the dish with the basil. Open the air fryer lid and put the sausage buns inside. Close the lid and cook for 7 minutes until the top is crunchy. Remove the dish from the air fryer and let it cool briefly before serving.

Onion Circles

Prep time: 10 minutes
Cooking time: 8 minutes
Servings: 3

Ingredients:

- 3 large white onions
- 2 eggs
- 1 cup bread crumbs
- ½ cup wheat flour
- 1 teaspoon salt
- 1 teaspoon ground black pepper
- 1 teaspoon oregano
- ½ teaspoon chile pepper
- 2 tablespoons heavy cream

Directions:

Peel the onions and cut them into thick slices. Separate the onion slices. In a mixing bowl, beat the eggs in a mixing bowl. Whisk until smooth. Add cream and sprinkle the liquid with the salt and ground black pepper and stir well. Put the flour in a separate mixing bowl and sprinkle it with the oregano and chile pepper and stir well. Take the onion pieces and dip them in the egg mixture, then dip them into the flour mixture. Then, dip the onions in the egg mixture again. Finally, dip the onions in the bread crumbs. Open the air fryer lid and add the onions. Close the lid and cook for 8 minutes. When the dish is cooked, remove it cooked, remove it from the air fryer, let it rest briefly and serve.

Lush Eggs

Prep time: 15 minutes
Cooking time: 10 minutes
Servings: 6

Ingredients:

- 1 teaspoon butter
- 1 cup crackers
- 1 teaspoon paprika
- ¼ cup dill
- 4 ounces sausage
- ½ teaspoon baking soda
- 1 teaspoon lemon juice
- 1 teaspoon ground black pepper
- 4 eggs
- 3 tablespoons heavy cream

Directions:

In a mixing bowl, beat the eggs in a mixing bowl. Whisk the mixture and add the baking soda and lemon juice and stir well. Add cream and paprika. Stir the mixture again. Chop the sausage into the tiny pieces. Chop the dill. Combine the chopped sausages and dill and transfer the mixture in the egg mixture and stir. Sprinkle the mixture with the pepper and stir well. Spread butter on the crackers. Place the into the air fryer muffin form. Pour the egg mixture in every muffin form. Transfer the muffin form to the air fryer and close the lid. Cook for 10 minutes. When it is cooked, cool briefly and remove the dish from the muffin forms and serve.

Parmesan Chips

Prep time: 10 minutes
Cooking time: 8 minutes
Servings: 5

Ingredients:

- 1 cup Parmesan cheese
- 1 teaspoon ground thyme
- 1 teaspoon salt
- 1 teaspoon ground black pepper
- ½ teaspoon basil

Directions:

Grate the Parmesan cheese and sprinkle it with the ground thyme, salt, pepper, and basil and stir well. Take the air fryer form and make the circles from the Parmesan mixture. Transfer the form to the air fryer and close the lid. Cook for 8 minutes. When the dish is cooked, remove it from the air fryer and let it cool completely before serving.

Sweet Chicken Bites

Prep time: 15 minutes
Cooking time: 15 minutes
Servings: 4

Ingredients:

- 15 ounces boneless and skinless chicken breast
- 1 tablespoon barbecue sauce
- 1 tablespoon sesame seeds
- 1 teaspoon salt
- 1 tablespoon lemon juice
- 1 teaspoon honey
- 1 teaspoon soy sauce
- 1 tablespoon lime zest
- 4 tablespoons chicken stock

Directions:

Chop the chicken fillet into medium-sized pieces. In a mixing bowl, combine the lemon juice, barbecue sauce, salt, honey, and soy sauce. Stir the mixture until smooth. Add lime zest and stir again. Combine the chopped chicken and liquid mixture together in the mixing bowl and stir well. Set aside for Set aside for at least 5 minutes. Add the chicken stock and stir it again. Sprinkle the chicken with the sesame seeds. Open the air fryer lid and transfer the chicken to the basket. Close the lid and cook for 15 minutes. When the dish is cooked, remove it from the air fryer and let it rest briefly before serving.

Beef Puffs

Prep time: 20 minutes
Cooking time: 25 minutes
Servings: 5

Ingredients:

- 1 egg
- 1 cup fresh dill
- 2 cups minced beef
- 1 white onion
- 1 egg yolk
- 1 teaspoon salt
- 1 teaspoon paprika
- 1 teaspoon butter
- 1 teaspoon nutmeg
- 1 teaspoon turmeric
- 1 tablespoon lemon juice
- 15 ounces puff pastry

Directions:

In a mixing bowl, beat the egg in a mixing bowl and add the salt, paprika, nutmeg, turmeric, and lemon juice and stir well. Add the minced beef and mix well using your hands. Peel the onion and chop it. Mince the fresh dill and add the dill and onion to the minced meat mixture and mix well. Whisk the egg yolk in a separate bowl. Take the puff pastry and roll it using a rolling pin. Make medium-sized puff squares from the dough. Transfer the minced beef mixture to the dough squares and make the puffs. Sprinkle the meat puffs with the whisked egg yolk and transfer to the air fryer. Cook for 25 minutes. When it is done, remove the puffs from the air fryer and let them cool before serving.

Herbed Parsley Balls

Prep time: 10 minutes
Cooking time: 20 minutes
Servings: 4

Ingredients:

- 13 ounces minced chicken
- 1 cup fresh parsley
- 1 tablespoon dried thyme
- 1 teaspoon salt
- 1 egg
- 1 teaspoon corn starch
- 1 teaspoon paprika
- ¼ cup fresh cilantro
- ⅓ cup flour
- ¼ cup chives

Directions:

Wash the parsley and mince it. Mince the cilantro and chives. Combine the herbs in a mixing bowl. Add the egg and dried thyme and stir well. Sprinkle the mixture with paprika and add minced chicken and corn starch. Stir again. Add salt and stir again. Make medium-sized balls from the mixture and flatten them slightly. Transfer the balls to the air fryer. Cook for 20 minutes. When it is done, remove them from the air fryer and serve.

Potato Cups

Prep time: 20 minutes
Cooking time: 15 minutes
Servings: 6

Ingredients:

- 1 teaspoon dry yeast
- 1 cup skim milk
- 2 cups flour
- 1 cup mashed potatoes
- 1 onion
- 1 carrot
- ½ cup chopped chicken fillet
- 1 teaspoon sugar
- ½ teaspoon salt

Directions:

In a mixing bowl, combine the dry yeast and skim milk together. Stir until smooth. Add the salt and sugar and stir again. Sift the flour into the yeast mixture. Knead the dough and let it rest. Peel the onion and dice it. Combine the chopped onion and mashed potatoes together. Stir until smooth. Peel the carrot and grate it. In a mixing bowl, combine the grated carrot and the chicken and mix well. Take the air fryer form and make dough cups. Add the meat mixture and the mashed potato mixture. Transfer the dough cups to the air fryer and cook for 15 minutes. When the dish is cooked, remove it cooked, remove it from the air fryer, let it rest briefly and serve.

Creamy Parmesan Potatoes

Prep time: 10 minutes
Cooking time: 15 minutes
Servings: 3

Ingredients:

- 3 large potatoes
- ½ cup heavy cream
- 1 cup Parmesan cheese
- ⅓ cup chives
- 1 teaspoon paprika
- 1 teaspoon salt
- 1 teaspoon ground black pepper
- 1 teaspoon oregano
- 1 tablespoon butter
- 1 onion

Directions:

Peel the onion and chop it. Wash the potatoes and cut them into halves. Grate the Parmesan cheese and combine it with the cream in a mixing bowl. Remove the flesh from the potatoes. Combine the potato flesh and the cheese together. Chop the chives and add it to the cheese. Sprinkle the cheese with the paprika, salt, pepper, and oregano and stir well. Fill the potatoes shells with the cheese. Add the butter on top of every potato. Transfer the stuffed potatoes to the air fryer and close the lid. Cook for 15 minutes and serve.

Eggplant Spicy Toast

Prep time: 15 minutes
Cooking time: 15 minutes
Servings: 4

Ingredients:

- 4 white bread slices
- 1 eggplant
- 1 teaspoon olive oil
- 2 tomatoes
- 2 garlic cloves
- 1 teaspoon fresh basil
- 1 tablespoon Parmesan cheese, grated
- 1 teaspoon salt
- 1 teaspoon cilantro

Directions:

Peel the garlic cloves and mince them. Combine the garlic and olive oil. Sprinkle the mixture with the basil and cilantro and stir well. Slice the eggplant into thin pieces and rub them with salt. Set the eggplant aside for 5 minutes. Wash the tomatoes and slice them. Rub the white bread slices with the garlic mixture. Place the sliced tomatoes on the bread. Add the sliced eggplant and sprinkle the toasts with grated Parmesan cheese. Transfer the toasts in the air fryer and close the lid. Cook for 15 minutes. When the dish is cooked, let it cool briefly and serve.

Side Dishes

Avocados with Jalapeños

Prep time: 3 minutes
Cooking time: 15 minutes
Servings: 2

Ingredients:

- 4 avocados, pitted and peeled
- 2 tablespoons lime juice
- 2 tablespoons lemon juice28 ounces canned tomatoes, diced½ cup red onion, diced

- 1 jalapeño pepper, seeded and minced3 garlic cloves, peeled and minced Salt and pepper to taste

Directions:

Mash the avocados into the bowl. Mix the lime juice, lemon juice, tomatoes, red onions, jalapeño pepper, and garlic with the salt and pepper. Pour the mixture into the air fryer and cook for 15 minutes. Remove the dish when done and serve.

Chicken Broth Rice

Prep time: 4 minutes
Cooking time: 20 minutes
Servings: 3

Ingredients:

- 1 tablespoon olive oil
- 2 red onions, peeled and chopped
- 2 garlic cloves, peeled and minced
- 2 cups white rice
- 2 cups chicken broth

- 1 cup fresh parsley, minced
- Salt and pepper to taste
- 1 cup dried cherries
- Hazelnuts, for garnishing

Directions:

Add the olive oil and garlic to the air fryer. In a bowl, add the onion, chicken broth, rice, salt, and pepper, dried cherries, and parsley. Cook for 20 minutes on 300ºF in the air fryer. When ready, garnish with hazelnuts and serve.

Sweet Potato Mix

Prep time: 4 minutes
Cooking time: 10 minutes
Servings: 3

Ingredients:

- 2 pounds sweet potatoes, cooked and mashed
- 2 garlic cloves, peeled and minced
- Salt and pepper to taste
- 1 tablespoon dried parsley
- 1 tablespoon dried sage

- 1 tablespoon dried rosemary
- 1 tablespoon dried thyme
- 1 cup milk
- 2 tablespoons butter
- 1 cup Parmesan cheese, grated

Directions:

Add the butter and garlic into the air fryer. Mix the sweet potatoes, salt and pepper, parsley, sage, rosemary, thyme, milk, and Parmesan cheese. Cook for 10 minutes on 300ºF. Remove the dish when done and serve.

Pink Rice

Prep time: 2 minutes
Cooking time: 15 minutes
Servings: 2

Ingredients:
- 2 cups pink rice4 cups water
- 1 tablespoon salt

Directions:

Add the rice, water and salt to the air fryer. Cook in the air fryer for 15 minutes on 300°F, let it cool briefly and serve.

Saffron Rice

Prep time: 2 minutes
Cooking time: 15 minutes
Servings: 2

Ingredients:
- 1 tablespoon saffron threads, crushed
- 2 tablespoons hot milk.
- 1 onion, peeled and chopped
- 2 cups rice
- 2 cups vegetable broth
- Salt and pepper to taste
- 1 tablespoon ground cinnamon
- 1 tablespoon honey
- 1 cup almonds, crushed
- 1 cup dried currants

Directions:

Add the milk and rice to a bowl. Add the onion, broth, salt, pepper, cinnamon, honey, and currants and mix well. Cook in the air fryer for 15 minutes on 300°F. When ready, garnish with the saffron threads and almonds and serve.

Dried Cherries Mix

Prep time: 3 minutes
Cooking time: 15 minutes
Servings: 3

Ingredients:
- 1 cup whole grain farro
- 1 cup apple cider vinegar
- 1 tablespoon lemon juice
- 1 tablespoon olive oil
- Salt to taste
- 1 cup dried cherries, chopped
- 2 green onions, minced
- 1 cup mint leaves, minced
- 2 cups fresh cherries, pitted and cut in half

Directions:

Add the oil and farro to a bowl. Add the vinegar, lemon juice, salt, dried cherries, green onions, and mint leaves and mix well. Cook in the air fryer for 15 minutes on 300°F. When ready, garnish with fresh cherries and serve.

Simple Corn Muffins

Prep time: 3 minutes
Cooking time: 15 minutes
Servings: 3

Ingredients:
- 17 ounces packaged corn muffin mix
- 1 cup milk
- 2 eggs
- 1 tablespoon vegetable oil

Directions:

Add the muffin mix and milk to a bowl. Whisk in the eggs and stir well. Coat the muffin baking tray with oil. Pour the mixture into the tray's cups. Bake in the air fryer for 15 minutes on 300°F. When cooked, remove the dish from the air fryer and serve.

Baked Avocados

Prep time: 4 minutes
Cooking time: 10 minutes
Servings: 3

Ingredients:
- 2 avocados, mashed
- 1 small onion, peeled and chopped
- 1 garlic clove, peeled and minced
- 1 tomato, diced
- 1 tablespoon lime juice
- Salt and pepper to taste
- 1 tablespoon cayenne pepper

Directions:

Add the avocados and onion to a bowl. Mix the garlic, tomato, lime juice, cayenne pepper, salt, and pepper. Pour the mixture into the round baking tray. Cook in the air fryer for 10 minutes on 300°F. When cooked, remove the dish from the air fryer and serve.

White Rice with Herbs

Prep time: 2 minutes
Cooking time: 15 minutes
Servings: 2

Ingredients:
- 2 tablespoons olive oil
- 1 onion, peeled and chopped
- 2 garlic cloves, peeled and minced
- 2 cups vegetable broth
- 2 cups sun-dried tomatoes, chopped
- Salt to taste
- 1 bay leaf
- 2 tablespoons fresh oregano, minced
- 2 tablespoons fresh rosemary
- 2 tablespoons fresh basil, minced
- 1 cup fresh parsley, minced
- 2 cups white rice

Directions:

Add the olive oil and onion to a bowl. Add the garlic, broth, tomatoes, bay leaf, oregano, rosemary, basil, parsley and rice and stir well. Cook in the air fryer for 15 minutes on 300°F. When ready, sprinkle with salt and serve.

Chicken Broth with Harvest Grains

Prep time: 4 minutes
Cooking time: 10 minutes
Servings: 3

Ingredients:

- 2 tablespoons butter
- 2 cups chicken broth
- 2 cups harvest grains blend
- Salt and pepper to taste

Directions:

Add the butter and harvest grains blend to a bowl. Add the salt, pepper, and chicken broth and mix well. Pour the mixture into the air fryer. Cook for 10 minutes on 300°F. When cooked, remove the dish from the air fryer and serve.

Sweet Potatoes with Cream

Prep time: 4 minutes
Cooking time: 15 minutes
Servings: 2

Ingredients:

- 2 pounds sweet potatoes, peeled and cubed
- 1 cup brown sugar
- 2 tablespoons butter
- 1 tablespoon vanilla extract
- 1 teaspoon ground cinnamon
- 1 teaspoon ground nutmeg
- 1 egg
- 2 tablespoons heavy cream

Directions:

Add the sweet potatoes and brown sugar into a bowl. Mix the butter, vanilla extract, cinnamon, powder, and cream. Whisk the egg in a separate bowl and add it to the mixture. Pour the mixture into the round baking tray. Cook in the air fryer for 15 minutes on 300°F. When cooked, remove the dish from the air fryer and serve.

Spicy Rice with Vegetable Broth

Prep time: 3 minutes
Cooking time: 10 minutes
Servings: 3

Ingredients:

- 1 cup vegetable broth
- 1 cup rice
- 1 avocado, chopped
- 1 cup fresh cilantro, chopped
- 1 cup hot sauce
- Salt and pepper to taste

Directions:

Add the vegetable broth to a bowl with the rice, avocado, cilantro, hot sauce, salt, and pepper and mix well. Cook in the air fryer for 10 minutes on 300°F. When cooked, remove the dish from the air fryer and serve.

Corn Fritters with Cheese

Prep time: 5 minutes
Cooking time: 10 minutes
Servings: 12

Ingredients:

- 6 ounces self-rising flour
- 1 teaspoon baking powder
- 2 eggs
- 1 cup milk
- 7 ounces canned corn, drained
- 3 ounces cheese, shredded
- 2 tablespoons fresh parsley, minced
- 2 teaspoons olive oil

Directions:

Preheat the air fryer to 320°F. Whisk the flour, baking powder, eggs and milk in a bowl until smooth. Add the cheese, corn and parsley and mix well. Sprinkle oil on the air fryer pan. Put 6 portions of dough with a spoon dipped in water and fry on both sides. Repeat with the remaining dough. Serve with ketchup.

Green Peas and Ham Pie

Prep time: 5 minutes
Cooking time: 50 minutes
Servings: 6

Ingredients:

- 9 ounces premade pie dough
- 9 ounces green peas
- 4 eggs
- 2 cups sour cream
- 3 ounces cheese, grated
- 3 ounces ham, diced
- Salt
- Ground black pepper

Directions:

Preheat the air fryer to 390°F. Roll out the dough on a floured surface and place on the air fryer pan. Cook for 15 minutes at 390°F. Mix the peas, eggs, and sour cream with salt and pepper in a bowl. Add the cheese and ham and mix well. Pour the mixture onto the dough. Cook for 35 minutes at 350°F until the filling covered with a crispy crust. Cool and serve.

Pasta Envelopes with Ricotta Cheese

Prep time: 5 minutes
Cooking time: 25 minutes
Servings: 4

Ingredients:

- 9 ounces lasagna
- 1 tablespoon olive oil
- 9 ounces ricotta cheese
- 2 ounces arugula
- 25 ounces tomato sauce
- 2 ounces Parmesan cheese, shredded
- Salt

Directions:

Lasagna sheets, place in a large bowl, and pour boiling water so that the water covers them completely. Let stand for 5 minutes. Preheat the air fryer to 390°F. Sprinkle oil on the baking pan. Drain the lasagna. In the center of every sheet, place 1 tablespoon of ricotta cheese. Sprinkle the arugula with salt, fold the sheet in half to form rectangle. Put them on the air frying pan. Coat the lasagna envelopes with sauce, sprinkle with Parmesan cheese and cook for 10-12 minutes until the cheese is melted and lasagna is hot.

Double Sandwich

Prep time: 5 minutes
Cooking time: 20 minutes
Servings: 3

Ingredients:

- 6 slices bacon
- 9 slices whole wheat bread
- 9 ounces low-fat soft cheese
- 1 carrot, peeled and grated
- 6 lettuce leaves
- 12 cucumber slices
- 2 tomatoes slices

Directions:

Preheat the air fryer to 390°F. Fry the bacon on both sides for 5 minutes. Cut the crust from the bread and fry the bread in the air fryer. Mix the cheese with the carrot. Spread this mixture on the bread slices. On 3 slices of bread, place 2 lettuce leaves, cucumber, and tomato and cover with a piece of bread. Put 2 slices of bacon on these sandwiches and cover with bread with cheese mixture so that the cheese is on the bottom. Cut the sandwiches into triangles and serve

Ham and Sweet Bell Pepper Rolls

Prep time: 5 minutes
Cooking time: 10 minutes
Servings: 4

Ingredients:

- 4 whole wheat pita breads
- 4 slices unsmoked ham
- 2 red bell peppers
- 2 tablespoons cheddar cheese
- Ground black pepper

Directions:

Preheat the air fryer to 320°F. Open up the pita bread and put the slice of ham on top. Sprinkle with pepper and cheese and wrap roll as tightly as possible, starting with the opposite edge. Place rolls on the air fryer pan. Cook for 15 minutes at 320°F until the cheese melts. Serve with mustard

Spicy Falafel Balls

Prep time: 5 minutes
Cooking time: 15 minutes
Servings: 6

Ingredients:

- 14 ounces canned chickpeas, drained and rinsed
- 1 teaspoon cumin ground
- 1 teaspoon coriander ground
- 2 tablespoons parsley chopped
- 1 teaspoon fresh herbs (basil, marjoram, oregano, rosemary, sage, or thyme)
- 1 egg
- 6 lettuce leaves
- 6 pita breads
- 2 tablespoons sunflower oil
- 1 onion, peeled and minced
- 1 clove garlic, peeled and crushed

Directions:

Preheat the air fryer to 320°F. Sprinkle oil on the pan and fry the onion and garlic. Put the onion, garlic, and spices in with the chickpeas and mash the mixture. Add the parsley, spice mixture, egg, and salt. Mix with your hands and roll into 6 balls. Cook the falafel balls for 3 minutes from each side in the air fryer. Serve hot or cold falafel wrapped in pita bread with lettuce and vegetables.

Crispy Sausages

Prep time: 5 minutes
Cooking time: 13 minutes
Servings: 6

Ingredients:
- 6 pork sausage links
- 6 tortillas
- 2 tablespoons tomato sauce
- 1 onion, peeled and sliced
- 1 teaspoon mustard seeds
- 2 tablespoons olive oil
- Salt

Directions:
Preheat the air fryer to 320°F. Sprinkle oil onto the air fryer pan. Place the sausages on it and cook for 10 minutes. Move the sausages to the edge of the pan. Add the onion, sprinkle with mustard seeds and salt and cook for 10-15 minutes until the onion is golden brown and sausages is ready. Warm the tortillas in the pan so that they soften and fold easily. Place a sausage with some onion in the center of each tortilla, pour the sauce on top, and serve.

Bacon and Egg Sandwich

Prep time: 5 minutes
Cooking time: 10 minutes
Servings: 1

Ingredients:
- 2 thick bread slices
- 1 ham slice
- 1 egg
- 2 tablespoons milk
- 1 teaspoons sunflower oil
- 3 tablespoons butter
- 2 teaspoons salsa sauce
- Salt

Directions:
Spread the bread with a thin layer of butter, put on one piece of ham and cover with the second piece of bread. Cut diagonally in half. Whisk the egg with the milk and salt. Preheat the air fryer to 320°F. Sprinkle oil on the frying basket. Dip the sandwiches in the egg mixture on both sides. Cook for 2 minutes at 320°F on each side. Serve with salsa.

Chicken Sandwich

Prep time: 5 minutes
Cooking time: 15 minutes
Servings: 8

Ingredients:

- 4 ounces boiled chicken
- 1 carrot
- ½ red bell pepper
- 2 tablespoons sweet canned corn
- 4 slices whole wheat bread

- 1 tablespoon mayonnaise
- 1 teaspoon lemon juice
- 1 teaspoon butter
- Salt

Directions:

Preheat the air fryer to 320°F. Dice the chicken and mix with the pepper. Peel and grate carrot. Mix everything with the corn in a bowl. Add the mayonnaise, lemon juice, and salt. Mix well and spread the slices of bread with a little butter. Place them in the frying basket. Cook in the air fryer for 3 minutes at 320°F. Cool briefly add the stuffing and make 2 sandwiches. Serve with mustard.

Cheese Buns

Prep time: 10 minutes
Cooking time: 25 minutes
Servings: 8

Ingredients:

- 5 ounces self-rising flour
- 5 ounces whole-wheat flour
- 1 teaspoon baking powder
- 2 ounces butter
- 3 ounces cheese, shredded

- 1 egg
- 1 tablespoon active dry yeast
- 2 tablespoons yogurt
- 4 tablespoons milk

Directions:

Preheat the air fryer to 370°F. Sift the flour and baking powder together in a bowl. Add the butter and mash until fine crumbs form. Add half of the cheese, stir, and make a hole in the middle of the bread crumb mixture. Whisk the eggs, yeast, yogurt, and milk in a separate bowl. Pour this mixture into the hole in the flour and stir to get soft but not sticky dough. Put the dough on a floured surface and roll out to ¼-inch thick. Use the cookie form to make circles. Gather the remains of the dough roll and make another 4 circles. Put the buns on the pan and sprinkle with milk and cheese. Cook in the air fryer for 13 minutes at 370°F. When cooked, remove the dish from the air fryer and serve.

Mexican Pizza

Prep time: 5 minutes
Cooking time: 15 minutes
Servings: 8

Ingredients:

- 2 whole wheat pita breads or tortillas
- 3 ounces cheddar cheese
- 4 ounces boiled chicken, diced
- 1 tomato, sliced

- 2 teaspoons olive oil
- Salt
- Ground black pepper

Directions:

Preheat the air fryer to 320°F. Sprinkle the oil on the air fryer pan. Add the cheese on half of the tortillas. Add the chicken on top and top with some tomato slices. Season with salt and pepper. Cook in the air fryer until the cheese melts, then fold in half and fry until crisp. Put the pizza on a plate and cut into triangles. Repeat again with the other tortilla.

Tortillas with Beans

Prep time: 5 minutes
Cooking time: 10 minutes
Servings: 2

Ingredients:

- 14 ounces canned beans in chili sauce
- 3-4 cherry tomatoes, coarsely chopped
- 4 whole wheat pita breads or tortillas
- 3 ounces cheddar cheese

- 1 tomato
- 1 avocado
- 1 teaspoon lemon juice
- a half of onion
- 1 tablespoon chopped cilantro
- 2 teaspoons olive oil

Directions:

Preheat the air fryer to 320°F. Sprinkle the oil on the air fryer pan. Add cheese to half of the tortillas. Add the chicken on top and top with tomato slices. Season with salt and pepper. Cook in the air fryer until the cheese melts, then fold in half and fry until crisp. Put the tortillas on a plate and cut into triangles. Repeat again with another tortilla.

Pita Bread with Beans

Prep time: 5 minutes
Cooking time: 10 minutes
Servings: 4

Ingredients:

- 14 ounces canned white beans
- 1 clove garlic, peeled
- 2 tablespoons olive oil
- 1 teaspoon juice of lemon
- 4 whole wheat pita breads
- ½ cucumber, chopped
- 4 tomatoes
- Salt
- Ground black pepper

Directions:

Drain the liquid from beans and rinse with water. Add the beans with the garlic, oil, and lemon juice to a blender. Puree in a blender until smooth. Season with salt and pepper. Preheat the air fryer to 320°F. Put the pitas into the air fryer, add some water and warm them. Cut the pitas from one side and open to make pocket. Put the beans, cucumbers and tomatoes into the pocket of the bread. Repeat with the other pitas.

Pizza with Vegetables

Prep time: 20 minutes
Cooking time: 40 minutes
Servings: 4

Ingredients:

- 7 ounces wheat flour
- 1 teaspoon salt
- 1 teaspoon dry yeast
- 1 cup warm water
- 2 tablespoons olive oil
- Salt
- Ground black pepper
- 2 red bell peppers
- 1 onion, peeled and diced
- 1 teaspoon olive oil
- 1 tablespoon tomato paste
- 5 ounces fresh Mozzarella cheese
- 12 cherry tomatoes
- 3 tablespoons frozen peas, thawed
- 2 tablespoons Parmesan cheese

Directions:

Preheat Air fryer to 440°F. Mix the flour, salt, and yeast in a bowl. Pour the warm water in the bowl and stir until a soft dough forms. Roll the dough into a 12-inch diameter pizza shell. Sprinkle the pan with oil and then add the bell pepper and onion. Cook for 10 minutes. Spread tomato paste onto pizza shell and then add the toppings. Cut the Mozzarella cheese into thin slices and top the pizza. Add the tomatoes and peas. Sprinkle with the Parmesan cheese. Cook in the air fryer for 15-20 minutes, let it rest for a few minutes and serve.

Stuffed Sweet Potatoes

Prep time: 5 minutes
Cooking time: 15 minutes
Servings: 8

Ingredients:

- 24 small sweet potatoes
- 8 slices bacon
- 7 ounces sweet canned corn
- 3 tablespoons honey
- 1 teaspoon mustard
- 2 teaspoons olive oil
- 1 bunch green onions, minced
- Salt
- Ground black pepper

Directions:

Rinse and dry the potatoes in advance. Puncture the skin with a fork and cook in the microwave oven for 10-12 minutes, turning after 5 minutes. Cut the potatoes in half lengthwise, remove a third of the potato flesh, and add to a bowl. Preheat the air fryer to 320°F. Sprinkle the oil on the air fryer pan. Cut the bacon into large pieces, add to the potatoes and mix with the con, honey, mustard, and onions. Add salt and pepper to taste and mix thoroughly. Fill the potatoes and cook in the air fryer for 10 minutes at 430°F.

Garlic Eyes with Cream Sauce

Prep time: 5 minutes
Cooking time: 30 minutes
Servings: 12

Ingredients:

- 5 ounces pizza dough mix
- 1 teaspoon olive oil
- 1 garlic clove, peeled and minced
- 2 tablespoons parsley, minced
- 12 green olives, pitted
- 1 egg
- 1 cup sour cream
- 1 teaspoon lemon juice
- 2 tablespoons chives, chopped
- Salt
- Ground black pepper

Directions:

Put the pizza dough mix in a bowl. Add the water and olive oil according to the instructions on the package. The dough must be sticky. Put the dough in a warm place until it doubles in volume for 20-30 minutes. Preheat the air fryer to 320°F. In a bowl, mix the sour cream, lemon juice and chives. Sprinkle the oil on the air fryer pan. Smooth the dough on a flat floured surface and sprinkle it with garlic and parsley. Stir to allow garlic and parsley mix with the dough. Divide the dough into 12 small pieces and roll the balls. Coat the balls with the egg and bake in the air fryer until golden brown. Decorate each ball with an olive. Serve with the sauce.

Snail Pizza

Prep time: 5 minutes
Cooking time: 25 minutes
Servings: 12

Ingredients:

- 14 ounces thawed puff pastry
- 6 tablespoon pasta sauce
- 4 ounces ham, sliced thin
- 4 ounces cheddar cheese, grated
- 1 egg
- 1 teaspoon oregano seasoning
- Salt
- Ground black pepper

Directions:

Preheat the air fryer to 320°F. Sprinkle oil on the air fryer pan. Roll out the dough to make a rectangle measuring 16 inches by 13 inches. Cover the dough with the sauce, leaving ¼-inch uncovered at the edges. Place the ham on it and sprinkle with cheese. Roll the dough up into a roll as tightly as possible. Put it in the refrigerator for 10 minutes. Cut the roll into 12 equal parts and lay it flat surface. Sprinkle with beaten egg and seasoning. Cook for 10-15 minutes and serve.

Sweet Potato Patties

Prep time: 5 minutes
Cooking time: 40 minutes
Servings: 4

Ingredients:

- 4 sweet potatoes
- 4 eggs
- 1 cup cheddar cheese, grated
- 2¾ tablespoons flour
- 3 tablespoons parsley, finely chopped
- Sea salt
- Cayenne pepper
- 1 teaspoon coriander
- 3 tablespoons olive oil
- ¾ cup bread crumbs

Directions:

Peel and cut potatoes into small cubes. Put the potatoes in hot salted water and cook for 15 minutes. Mash the potatoes and set aside. Combine two of the eggs, cheese, flour, parsley, salt, pepper, and coriander and mix well. Divide the potato mixture into pieces in the size of a walnut, roll the balls and set aside. Preheat the air fryer to 360°F. Combine the oil and bread crumbs. Dredge the patties into the flour, then the eggs and finally the bread crumbs. Cook in the air fryer for 7-8 minutes or until crispy.

Potato with Swiss Cheese

Prep time: 10 minutes
Cooking time: 35 minutes
Servings: 6

Ingredients:

- 6 sweet potatoes
- 2 eggs
- ½ cup sour cream
- Ground black pepper
- Salt
- Coriander
- ½ cup Swiss cheese, grated

Directions:

Preheat the air fryer to 320°F. Peel and cut the potatoes in thin slices. Combine the eggs and sour cream in a pan. Sprinkle with a pinch of salt, pepper, and coriander. Place the potato slices into the cooking basket. Cover them with the egg and cream mixture by pouring it from the pan on top of the potatoes. Cook for 25 minutes. Remove the potatoes to a serving dish and top with the cheese.

Air-fried Vegetables

Prep time: 5 minutes
Cooking time: 25 minutes
Servings: 6

Ingredients:

- 13 ounces thawed puff pastry
- 1 cup radish
- Parsley
- 2 white onions
- 1 small squash
- 1 tablespoon celery seeds
- 1 tablespoon vegetable oil
- Ground black pepper
- Salt

Directions:

Preheat the air fryer to 320°F. Peel and chop the radish and squash into ½-inch cubes and slice the onions into rings. Combine all the vegetables with the celery seeds and vegetable oil. Sprinkle with salt and pepper. Put all vegetables into the cooking basket. Cook for 25 minutes, stirring occasionally.

Peppery Cauliflower

Prep time: 15 minutes
Cooking time: 20 minutes
Servings: 4

Ingredients:

- 15 ounces cauliflower
- 1 teaspoon salt
- 2 egg yolks
- 1 cup heavy cream
- 1 teaspoon ground white pepper
- 1 teaspoon ground black pepper
- 4 tablespoons flour
- 1 teaspoon cilantro
- 1 teaspoon chile pepper
- 2 tablespoons butter

Directions:

Wash the cauliflower and cut into florets. Transfer the cauliflower to the mixing bowl and sprinkle it with salt and stir well. In a separate mixing bowl, add the egg yolk and stir. Add the cream and continue to whisk it until smooth. Sprinkle the liquid with the cilantro, chile pepper, butter, white pepper, and black pepper and stir well. Add the flour and mix well until smooth. Dip the florets in the yolk mixture and place in the air fryer and close the lid. Cook for 20 minutes and serve immediately.

Garlic Red Apples

Prep time: 10 minutes
Cooking time: 15 minutes
Servings: 4

Ingredients:

- 6 red apples
- ½ cup garlic clove
- 1 teaspoon salt
- 3 tablespoons honey
- 1 teaspoon ground ginger
- 1 teaspoon brown sugar
- 1 tablespoon lemon juice
- 1 teaspoon olive oil
- ⅓ teaspoon cinnamon
- 1 tablespoon fresh parsley

Directions:

Wash the red apples very and slice them. Sprinkle the apples with the lemon juice. Chop the parsley and combine it with the cinnamon, olive oil, brown sugar, salt, and ginger and stir again. Transfer the sweet mixture to the sliced apples and stir it. Add honey and stir it again. Peel the onion and mince it. Sprinkle the apple mixture with the minced onion and stir again. Set aside. Open the air fryer lid and transfer the apple mixture in the basket. Close the lid and cook for 15 minutes. When the dish is cooked, let it cool briefly and serve.

Sweet and Crispy Carrot Sticks

Prep time: 10 minutes
Cooking time: 20 minutes
Servings: 4

Ingredients:
- 4 carrots
- 1 egg yolk
- ½ cup heavy cream
- 1 teaspoon water
- 2 tablespoons whole wheat flour
- 1 teaspoon salt
- 1 tablespoon oregano
- 1 teaspoon butter
- 1 teaspoon stevia

Directions:

Wash the carrots and peel them. Make medium-sized sticks from the carrots and sprinkle them with salt and stir well. In another bowl, and combine the whole wheat flour, oregano, butter, and stevia. Add the egg yolk and cream and stir the mixture well, and then add water. Use a hand mixer and mix until smooth. Dip the carrot sticks in the flour mixture. Transfer the carrot sticks to the air fryer basket and close the lid. Cook for 20 minutes or until a crunchy crust forms. Open the air fryer lid and remove the dish from the basket. Let the carrot sticks cool briefly and then serve.

Potato Pancakes

Prep time: 20 minutes
Cooking time: 15 minutes
Servings: 4

Ingredients:
- 4 large potatoes
- 3 garlic cloves
- 1 yellow onion
- 1 egg
- 2 tablespoons flour
- 1 teaspoon starch
- 1 teaspoon ground white pepper
- ⅓ cup fresh cilantro
- 1 teaspoon dried dill
- ½ teaspoon salt
- 1 teaspoon flax seed

Directions:

Peel the potatoes and grate them. Transfer the potatoes to a mixing bowl and sprinkle it with the starch and cilantro. Add the dill and flex seeds and stir well. Peel the onion and the garlic cloves and dice them. Combine the vegetables, then chop the cilantro and combine it with the onion mixture. Add this to the potato mixture and stir well. Add the flour and egg and stir well. Take the air fryer tray and make the pancakes from the potato dough. Transfer the air fryer tray with the potato pancakes to the air fryer and close the lid. Cook for 15 minutes, then remove the pancakes from the air fryer and serve.

Roasted Asparagus

Prep time: 15 minutes
Cooking time: 25 minutes
Servings: 4

Ingredients:

- 2 cups asparagus
- ½ cup cashews
- ⅓ cup raisins
- 1 cup water
- 1 teaspoon honey
- 1 teaspoon soy sauce
- 1 tablespoon cilantro
- 1 teaspoon cayenne pepper
- ½ teaspoon salt

Directions:

Wash the asparagus and cut it into halves. Transfer the asparagus to a mixing bowl, sprinkle it with the cilantro and salt and stir well. Combine the cashews and raisins in a mixing bowl. Add the honey and soy sauce and stir well. Sprinkle it with the cayenne pepper and stir again. Combine the asparagus and soy sauce mixture together and stir well. Open the air fryer lid and add the asparagus mixture. Pour the water into the dish and close the lid. Cook for 25 minutes. Open the instant bowl lid, and remove the asparagus and serve.

Spicy Brussels Sprouts

Prep time: 15 minutes
Cooking time: 25 minutes
Servings: 6

Ingredients:

- 15 ounces Brussels sprouts
- 1 teaspoon cardamom
- 1 teaspoon cayenne pepper
- 1 teaspoon black pepper
- 1 cup Parmesan cheese
- 1 teaspoon coriander
- ½ teaspoon thyme
- 1 teaspoon salt
- 2 tablespoons butter
- 1 cup chicken stock
- 1 teaspoon sriracha
- 1 white onion

Directions:

Wash the Brussels sprouts and cut them into halves. Transfer the Brussels sprouts to a mixing bowl and sprinkle it with the cardamom, cayenne pepper, black pepper, coriander, and thyme. Add the salt and stir well. Peel the onion and dice it. Combine the onion with the sriracha and chicken stock and stir well. Grate the Parmesan cheese. Combine the Brussels sprouts and onion mixtures and stir well. Open the air fryer lid and transfer the onion mixture to the air fryer basket. Sprinkle the dish with the cheese and stir well. Close the lid and cook for 25 minutes. When the dish is done, remove it from the air fryer and serve.

Mushrooms with Sour Cream

Prep time: 15 minutes
Cooking time: 30 minutes
Servings: 4

Ingredients:

- 3 cups mushrooms
- ½ cup milk
- 2 tablespoons butter
- 1 onion
- ⅓ cup walnuts
- ½ cup beef broth
- 1 teaspoon ginger
- 1 teaspoon turmeric
- 1 tablespoon cilantro
- 3 apricots
- 1 teaspoon sugar
- ½ teaspoon kosher salt

Directions:

Slice the mushrooms and sprinkle them with the ginger and cilantro in a mixing bowl and stir well. Chop the apricots roughly. Peel the onion and chop it. Combine the onion with the apricots in another bowl and stir well. Crush the nuts. Transfer the sliced mushrooms and onion mixture to the air fryer basket. Sprinkle the mixture with the crushed nuts, turmeric, sugar, and kosher salt. Stir the mixture well. Add the butter. Combine the beef broth and milk together in a mixing bowl and stir well. Pour the liquid into the air fryer basket and close the lid. Cook for 30 minutes. When the dish is cooked, remove it from the air fryer. Let it cool and serve.

Honey Butternut Squash

Prep time: 15 minutes
Cooking time: 20 minutes
Servings: 4

Ingredients:

- 3 cups butternut squash
- 1 teaspoon brown sugar
- 1 teaspoon stevia extract
- 1 tablespoon coriander
- ½ teaspoon turmeric
- 1 teaspoon cardamom
- 1 teaspoon sesame seeds
- 1 tablespoon flax seeds
- ½ cup water
- 1 carrot

Directions:

Peel the butternut squash and chop it into medium-sized pieces. Sprinkle it with the cardamom and stir. In a mixing bowl, combine the sugar, stevia extract, coriander, turmeric, sesame seeds, and flax seeds and stir well. Peel the carrot and chop it into the same size pieces as the squash was chopped. Combine the carrot and squash and stir well. Sprinkle it with the spice mixture and stir well. Transfer the mixture to the air fryer and add the water. Close the lid and cook for 20 minutes. When the dish is cooked, open the air fryer lid and stir well before serving.

Sweet Corn

Prep time: 10 minutes
Cooking time: 20 minutes
Servings: 4

Ingredients:
- 4 cups sweet corn
- ½ cup yogurt
- 1 cup milk
- 1 teaspoon cilantro
- ½ cup hard cheese
- 1 onion
- 1 cup shrimp
- 1 teaspoon salt
- ½ teaspoon ground white pepper

Directions:
Put the sweet corn in a mixing bowl, sprinkle it with the cilantro and stir well. Grate the hard cheese and combine the cheese with the yogurt and milk and stir well. Add salt and stir until the salt is dissolved. Peel and devein the shrimp and sprinkle them with the pepper. Peel the onion and chop it. Add the chopped onion to the shrimp. Combine all the ingredients in a mixing bowl until smooth. Transfer the mixture to the air fryer basket and close the lid. Cook for 20 minutes. Remove the corn from the air fryer and stir again. Transfer the dish to the serving plates.

Zucchini Sticks

Prep time: 15 minutes
Cooking time: 15 minutes
Servings: 4

Ingredients:
- 2 zucchinis
- 1 tablespoon soy sauce
- 1 teaspoon cardamom
- 1 teaspoon salt
- ½ teaspoon ground black pepper
- 1 tablespoon sunflower oil
- 1 teaspoon thyme
- 1 teaspoon cardamom
- 1 teaspoon lemon juice
- 3 tablespoons water
- 1 teaspoon red wine

Directions:
Take the zucchinis and wash them. Cut each one in half, then make medium-sized strips from the zucchini and add them in the mixing bowl. In a mixing bowl, combine the salt, pepper, thyme, and cardamom. Stir the spice mixture and add red wine. Stir again until the salt is dissolved. Add lemon juice and stir again. Pour the mixtures onto the zucchini sticks and stir. Add the water and lemon juice and stir. and stir well. Open the air fryer lid and transfer the zucchini to the air fryer basket. Coat the mixture with the sunflower oil and close the lid. Cook for 15 minutes. When the zucchini is cooked, remove them from the air fryer and serve.

Air-fried Parsnips

Prep time: 15 minutes
Cooking time: 15 minutes
Servings: 4

Ingredients:

- 2 parsnips
- 1 tablespoon chile flakes
- 1 teaspoon sugar
- 1 teaspoon honey
- ½ cup water

- 1 egg
- 1 teaspoon ground black pepper
- 1 teaspoon cilantro
- ½ tablespoon olive oil

Directions:

Wash the parsnips and peel them, then cut them into strips. Transfer the parsnip strips to a mixing bowl and add honey and stir well. In a mixing bowl, beat the egg and sprinkle it with the sugar, pepper, and cilantro and stir well. Add the chile flakes and water stir until smooth. Open the air fryer lid and add olive oil to the air fryer basket. Transfer the parsnip to the air fryer and add the egg mixture. Stir well and close the lid. Cook for 15 minutes. Remove the dish from the water and serve.

Sweet Peaches and Ham

Prep time: 15 minutes
Cooking time: 20 minutes
Servings: 4

Ingredients:

- 4 peaches
- 2 cups ham
- 1 cup Cheddar cheese
- 1 teaspoon oregano

- 1 tablespoon fresh dill, chopped
- ⅓ cup heavy cream
- 1 onion
- 2 sweet potatoes

Directions:

Wash the peaches, remove the pits, and chop into bite-sized pieces. Slice the ham and combine it with the peaches. Grate the cheese. In a mixing bowl, combine the dill and oregano and stir well. Add the cream and stir again. Peel the sweet potatoes and onion. Chop the vegetables and combine them. Sprinkle the vegetables with the spice mixture. Add the peach mixture and mix well. Sprinkle the mixture with the grated cheese and stir again. Transfer the mixture to the air fryer and close the lid. Cook for 20 minutes. When the dish cooked, remove it from the air fryer, let it cool briefly, and serve.

Sweet Chickpeas

Prep time: 15 minutes
Cooking time: 30 minutes
Servings: 6

Ingredients:

- 5 cups canned chickpeas
- 1 cup bread crumbs
- 1 teaspoon ground black pepper
- 7 cups chicken stock
- 1 teaspoon chile flakes
- 1 tablespoon sugar
- ½ teaspoon salt
- 1 tablespoon olive oil

Directions:

Drain and rinse the chickpeas. In a mixing bowl, combine the olive oil and salt. Add the chile flakes and stir. Sprinkle the chickpeas with the olive oil mixture and stir well. Add the sugar and pepper and stir again. Open the air fryer lid and transfer the chickpea mixture to the air fryer. Pour the chicken stock into the air fryer and close the lid. Cook for 30 minutes. When the dish is cooked, remove it from the air fryer and drain the liquid from the chickpeas. Transfer the dish to a serving plate and sprinkle it with the bread crumbs.

Pumpkin Stew

Prep time: 20 minutes
Cooking time: 15 minutes
Servings: 4

Ingredients:

- 3 cups sweet pumpkin
- 2 zucchinis
- 1 cup fresh parsley
- 2 cups chicken stock
- 1 sweet potato
- 2 red onions
- 1 teaspoon basil
- 1 teaspoon ground black pepper
- 1 teaspoon ground white pepper
- 1 teaspoon cilantro
- 1 tablespoon tomato paste

Directions:

Peel the pumpkin and chop it into medium-sized pieces. Sprinkle the chopped pumpkin with cilantro and white pepper and stir well. Peel the onion and sweet potato. Chop the vegetables into the same size as the pumpkin. Add the vegetables to the pumpkin mixture, sprinkle it with the basil and pepper and stir again. Wash the zucchini, chop it, and add it to the pumpkin. Add the tomato paste and mix again. Chop the parsley and it to the mixing bowl. Open the air fryer lid and transfer the pumpkin mixture. Pour the chicken stock on top and stir well. Close the lid and cook for 15 minutes. When the dish is cooked, remove it from the air fryer and let it cool briefly before serving.

Honey Red Onion Petals

Prep time: 15 minutes
Cooking time: 10 minutes
Servings: 4

Ingredients:

- 8 large red onions
- ½ cup parsley
- 1 tablespoon brown sugar
- ½ tablespoon salt
- 1 tablespoon olive oil
- 2 tablespoons water
- 1 teaspoon apple cider vinegar
- 1 teaspoon lemon juice

Directions:

Peel the red onions, make the petals from them, and transfer them to a mixing bowl. Sprinkle the mixture with the brown sugar and salt and stir well. Add the olive oil and lemon juice. Add the apple cider vinegar and stir well. Set aside for at least 5 minutes. Chop the parsley, add it to the mixture and stir. Open the air fryer lid and add the onion petals and water and stir well. Close the lid and cook for 10 minutes. Remove the onion petals from the air fryer and serve.

Lentil and Chicken Salad

Prep time: 15 minutes
Cooking time: 30 minutes
Servings: 4

Ingredients:

- 3 cups lentils
- 1 boneless and skinless chicken breast
- 6 cups chicken stock
- ½ cup fresh cilantro
- ½ cup fresh parsley
- ½ cup bacon
- 1 teaspoon sugar
- 1 teaspoon salt
- 1 tablespoon butter
- 1 teaspoon black pepper
- 3 tablespoons heavy cream

Directions:

Cut the chicken into strips and transfer to a mixing bowl. Sprinkle the meat with the salt and pepper. Add the cream and stir well. Set aside for at least 5 minutes. Chop the cilantro and dill. Open the air fryer lid and transfer the lentils to the air fryer basket. Add the greens and stir. Add the chicken stock and sugar. Chop the bacon and add it to the lentils. Stir again. Add chicken strips and stir well. . Close the lid and cook for 30 minutes. When it is done, remove the dish from the air fryer and serve.

Lentils with Rice Noodles

Prep time: 10 minutes
Cooking time: 10 minutes
Servings: 7

Ingredients:

- 2 cups rice noodles
- 4 cups lentils
- 1 cup parsnip
- 6 cups water
- 1 teaspoon soy sauce
- 1 teaspoon pineapple juice
- 1 teaspoon salt
- 2 tablespoons olive oil
- 1 teaspoon sriracha
- 1 tablespoon fish sauce
- 1 yellow onion

Directions:

Peel the parsnip and chop into tiny pieces. In a mixing bowl, combine the chopped parsnip and lentils and stir well. Combine the soy sauce and the fish sauce together in the mixing bowl. Stir the liquid and add the sriracha and salt. Add the pineapple juice and olive oil and stir again. Peel the onion, dice it, and add to the mixing bowl. Pour the water into the mixture and stir well. Transfer the mixture to the air fryer and add the rice noodles. Cook for 10 minutes, then open the air fryer lid and stir again. Remove the dish from the air fryer and transfer to serving plates.

Crusty Potatoes

Prep time: 15 minutes
Cooking time: 30 minutes
Servings: 4

Ingredients:

- 1 cup granola
- 1 teaspoon butter
- 2 teaspoons olive oil
- 1 teaspoon salt
- 6 potatoes
- 1 cup minced beef
- 1 cup fresh basil, chopped
- 3 yellow onions
- 1 cup heavy cream

Directions:

Peel the potatoes and slice them. Sprinkle the potatoes with the salt and olive oil and stir well. Peel the onions and chop them. Take the air fryer form and transfer the sliced potato onto it. Add the minced beef and onion to the potatoes and sprinkle with the basil. Pour the cream onto the mixture and sprinkle it with the granola. Transfer the form to the air fryer and close the lid. Cook for 30 minutes. When the dish is cooked, remove it from the air fryer and let it cool briefly before serving.

Rice with Cottage Cheese and Pumpkin

Prep time: 15 minutes
Cooking time: 20 minutes
Servings: 4

Ingredients:

- 2 onions
- 1 teaspoon salt
- 2 teaspoons brown sugar
- 1 cup rice, cooked
- ½ cup spinach
- ⅓ cup cottage cheese
- 1 butternut squash
- ¼ cup sweet corn
- 1 teaspoon paprika

Directions:

Peel the onions and dice them. Transfer the onions to the mixing bowl and sprinkle them with the brown sugar. Add the salt and stir well. Wash the butternut squash and remove the seeds. Cut the squash into quarters. Add the cooked rice to the mixing bowl with the onion. Add the cottage cheese and stir well. Sprinkle it with the sweet corn and paprika and stir again. Chop the spinach and add it to the mixture. Fill the squash quarters with the rice mixture and transfer to the air fryer. Close the lid and cook for 20 minutes. When the dish is cooked, let it rest briefly and serve.

Couscous with Pumpkin Seeds

Prep time: 15 minutes
Cooking time: 25 minutes
Servings: 4

Ingredients:

- 3 cups couscous
- 6 cups chicken stock
- 1 teaspoon salt
- 3 tablespoons butter
- ¼ cup heavy cream
- 1 cup pumpkin seeds
- 1 cup pumpkin
- 3 bell peppers
- 1 cup fresh basil

Directions:

Transfer the couscous to the air fryer and add the chicken stock. Sprinkle the mixture with the salt and add the butter and stir well. Remove the seeds from the bell peppers and chop them. Peel the pumpkin and chop it. Combine the vegetables in a mixing bowl and add the pumpkin seeds. Mince the basil and add it to the vegetable mixture. Transfer the vegetable mixture to the air fryer and stir well. Close the lid and cook for 25 minutes. When the dish is cooked, the couscous will have absorbed all the liquid. Stir the cooked dish and serve.

Bacon and Corn Pudding

Preparation time: 10 minutes
Cooking time: 90 minutes
Servings: 6

Ingredients:

- 4 bacon strips, chopped
- 1 tablespoon butter
- 2 cups corn kernels
- 1 yellow onion, chopped
- ¼ cup celery, chopped
- ½ cup red bell pepper, chopped
- 1 teaspoon thyme, chopped
- 2 teaspoons garlic, minced

- Salt and ground black pepper, to taste
- ½ cup heavy cream
- 1½ cups whole milk
- 3 eggs
- Cayenne pepper
- 3 cups bread, cubed
- 1 cup Monterey jack cheese, grated
- 3 tablespoons Parmesan cheese, grated

Directions:

Heat a pan on medium heat, add the bacon, cook until it browns, transfer to a bowl, and set aside. Heat up the pan again, add the corn, stir and cook for 10 minutes. Add the celery, onion and bell pepper, stir, and cook for 5 minutes. Add the salt, black pepper, garlic and thyme, stir, and cook for 1 minute, take off heat and transfer to a bowl. Add the bacon, milk, cream, eggs, salt, pepper, bread cubes, cayenne pepper, and Monterey jack cheese and stir everything. Pour this into a greased casserole that fits the air fryer, cook at 320°F for 30 minutes, sprinkle with Parmesan cheese, and cook for 30 minutes. Let the pudding cool down before serving.

Potato Wedges

Preparation time: 10 minutes
Cooking time: 25 minutes
Servings: 4

Ingredients:

- 2 potatoes, cut into medium-sized wedges
- Salt and ground black pepper, to taste
- 1 tablespoon vegetable oil

- Sour cream
- Sweet chili sauce, to taste

Directions:

Put potatoes in a bowl, add oil, and toss to coat them. Transfer wedges to the preheated air fryer, cook at 360°F for 15 minutes. Flip them and cook for 10 minutes. Serve them as a side dish with sour cream and chives.

Seasoned Stuff Mushrooms

Preparation time: 10 minutes
Cooking time: 15 minutes
Servings: 3

Ingredients:
- 10 large mushrooms, stems removed
- 1 tablespoon dried mixed herbs
- 1 tablespoon Cheddar cheese, grated
- 1 tablespoon Mozzarella cheese, grated
- Olive oil
- 2 teaspoons dried dill
- Salt and ground black pepper, to taste

Directions:
Season mushrooms with the salt, pepper, and mixed herbs and drizzle some oil on them. Place them in the air fryer and cook at 360°F for 6 minutes. Add the Cheddar and Mozzarella cheeses and dill and cook for 8 minutes. Divide between plates and serve.

Corn with Feta and Lime

Preparation time: 10 minutes
Cooking time: 15 minutes
Servings: 2

Ingredients:
- 2 corns on the cob
- Salt and ground black pepper, to taste
- Olive oil
- Juice from 2 limes
- 2 teaspoons paprika
- ½ cup feta cheese, crumbled

Directions:
Rub the corn on the cob with salt, pepper, paprika and oil and place them in the air fryer. Cook at 400°F for 15 minutes. Divide on plates, drizzle lime juice on the cobs and sprinkle feta crumbles on them. Serve hot.

Roasted Brussels Sprouts

Preparation time: 10 minutes
Cooking time: 2 hours
Servings: 8

Ingredients:

- 3 pounds Brussels sprouts, cut in halves
- Olive oil
- 1 pound bacon, chopped
- 4 tablespoons butter
- 4 shallots, chopped
- 4 tablespoons flour
- Salt and ground black pepper, to taste
- 1 cup milk
- 4 tablespoons prepared horseradish
- 2 cups heavy cream
- ¼ teaspoon ground nutmeg
- 1 tablespoon fresh thyme

Directions:

In a bowl, mix sprouts with a drizzle of oil, salt and pepper, toss to coat, put in the air fryer, and cook at 400°F for 30 minutes. Transfer them to a plate and set aside. Put the bacon in the air fryer and cook for 10 minutes. Add the shallots, salt and pepper, cook for 10 minutes, transfer to paper towels, and drain the grease. Heat up a pan with the butter on medium heat, add the flour and stir well. Add the milk and heavy cream, stir and cook for 5 minutes. Add the salt, pepper, nutmeg, thyme, and horseradish, stir well and take off the heat. Spread the Brussels sprouts in a baking dish that fits the air fryer, add the horseradish cream, bacon and shallot mix, and cook in the air fryer for 30 minutes at 350°F. Divide between plates and serve.

Air-fried Eggplant

Preparation time: 10 minutes
Cooking time: 25 minutes
Servings: 6

Ingredients:

- 3 eggplants, cut into medium cubes
- 1 tablespoon duck fat, hot
- 1 teaspoon onion powder
- 1 teaspoon garlic powder
- 1 teaspoon lemon zest
- 2 bay leaves
- Salt and ground black pepper, to taste
- 3 teaspoons Italian seasoning
- 1 teaspoon olive oil
- Juice of ½ lemon

Directions:

Put the duck fat in the air fryer. Add the eggplant, onion powder, garlic powder, salt, pepper, lemon zest, Italian seasoning, and bay leaves and cook at 320°F for 25 minutes. Transfer eggplant to a bowl, add the lemon juice and olive oil, toss to coat, divide between plates and serve.

Onion Rings

Preparation time: 10 minutes
Cooking time: 10 minutes
Servings: 3

Ingredients:

- 1 medium onion, cut into slices and rings separated
- 1 ¼ cups white flour
- Salt, to taste

- 1 egg
- 1 cup milk
- 1 teaspoon baking powder
- ¾ cup bread crumbs

Directions:

In a bowl, mix the flour with salt and baking powder and stir. Dip the onion rings in flour and place them on a plate. Add the milk and egg to flour mix and whisk well. Dip the onion rings in the flour mix, dredge them in bread crumbs and put them in the air fryer. Cook at 360°F for 10 minutes. Divide between plates and serve.

Roasted Carrots

Preparation time: 10 minutes
Cooking time: 12 minutes
Servings: 4

Ingredients:

- 3 cups baby carrots
- Salt and ground black pepper, to taste

- 1 tablespoon honey
- 1 tablespoon olive oil

Directions:

In a bowl, mix the carrots with salt, pepper, oil, and honey and toss to coat. Transfer carrots to the air fryer and cook at 400°F for 12 minutes. Divide between plates and serve.

Garlic and Parsley Potatoes

Preparation time: 10 minutes
Cooking time: 40 minutes
Servings: 3

Ingredients:

- 3 large potatoes
- Salt and ground black pepper, to taste
- 2 tablespoons extra virgin olive oil
- 1 tablespoon garlic, minced
- Sour cream for serving
- 1 teaspoon fresh parsley, chopped

Directions:

Prick the potatoes with a fork and place them in the air fryer's basket. Add the salt, pepper, garlic, parsley, and oil, toss to coat and cook at 390°F for 40 minutes. Divide them between plates and serve with sour cream on top.

Zucchini Fries

Preparation time: 10 minutes
Cooking time: 20 minutes
Servings: 3

Ingredients:

- 2 egg whites
- 3 zucchinis, cut in medium-sized sticks
- 2 tablespoons Parmesan cheese, grated
- ½ cup bread crumbs
- Salt and ground black pepper, to taste
- Vegetable oil cooking spray
- ¼ teaspoon garlic powder

Directions:

In a bowl, mix the egg whites with salt and pepper and whisk well. In another bowl, mix the bread crumbs with the cheese and garlic powder and stir. Dip the zucchini sticks in the egg mix and then dredge in bread crumbs. Place them in the air fryer's basket, spray some cooking oil over them, and cook at 420°F for 20 minutes. Divide them between plates and serve.

Baked Rice

Preparation time: 10 minutes
Cooking time: 20 minutes
Servings: 4

Ingredients:

- 2 cups cooked rice
- 1 tablespoon butter
- Salt and ground black pepper, to taste
- 4 garlic cloves, minced
- 1 veal sausage, chopped
- 2 tablespoons carrot, chopped
- 3 tablespoons broccoli, diced
- 3 tablespoons Cheddar cheese, grated
- 2 tablespoons Mozzarella cheese, shredded
- 10 tablespoon creamy butter sauce

Directions:

Put the butter in the air fryer and heat for 2 minutes. Add the garlic and heat for 2 minutes. Add the broccoli, carrots, salt, pepper, sausage, rice, and sauce, stir and cook at 350°F for 10 minutes. Sprinkle the rice with the cheeses and cook for 10 minutes more. Divide between plates and serve.

Calamari Rings

Preparation time: 10 minutes
Cooking time: 8 minutes
Servings: 2

Ingredients:
- 2 ounces calamari, sliced into thin rings
- 1 egg, whisked
- Salt and ground black pepper, to taste
- 1 tablespoon paprika
- Juice of 1 lemon
- Peel from 1 lemon, grated
- 1 tablespoon fresh parsley, chopped
- 1 cup rolled oats

Directions:
Put the oats in a food processor, blend well, transfer to a bowl and add the salt, pepper, lemon zest, parsley, and paprika and stir. Put whisked egg in another bowl. Put calamari rings in a bowl, add salt, pepper and lemon juice, toss to coat, and set aside for a few minutes. Dip calamari rings in oat mixture, then in flour, and again in oats and place them in the air fryer pan lined with aluminum foil. Cook at 350°F for 8 minutes, divide between plates and serve.

Cauliflower Rice

Preparation time: 10 minutes
Cooking time: 20 minutes
Servings: 4

Ingredients:
- 4 tablespoons soy sauce
- ½ block firm tofu, cubed
- 1 cup carrots, peeled and chopped
- ½ cup yellow onions, peeled and chopped
- 1 teaspoon turmeric
- 3 cups cauliflower, minced
- 1½ teaspoons sesame oil
- 1 tablespoon rice vinegar
- ½ cup broccoli, chopped
- 1 tablespoon ginger, minced
- 2 garlic cloves, peeled and minced
- ½ cup frozen peas, thawed

Directions:
In a bowl, mix the tofu with 2 tablespoons soy sauce and the onions, turmeric and carrots, toss to coat, transfer into the air fryer and cook at 370°F for 10 minutes, shaking halfway through. In a bowl, mix the cauliflower with the remaining soy sauce and the sesame oil, garlic, vinegar, ginger, broccoli, and peas and stir. Add to the tofu mix in the air fryer, toss to coat and cook at 370°F for 10 minutes. Divide between plates and serve.

French Fries

Preparation time: 10 minutes
Cooking time: 30 minutes
Servings: 4

Ingredients:

- 6 potatoes peeled, cut into strips, soaked in water for 30 minutes, drained and patted dry
- Salt and ground black pepper, to taste
- 2 tablespoons extra virgin olive oil

Directions:

Put the potatoes in a bowl, add the salt, pepper and oil and toss to coat. Place the potatoes in the cooking basket of the air fryer and cook at 360°F for 30 minutes. Divide between plates and serve.

Potato Croquettes

Preparation time: 10 minutes
Cooking time: 25 minutes
Servings: 4

Ingredients:

- 4 potatoes, cubed
- 1 cup Parmesan cheese, grated
- Salt and ground black pepper, to taste
- Nutmeg
- 2 egg yolks
- 2 tablespoons white flour plus ¼ cup white flour
- 3 tablespoons chives, chopped
- 3 tablespoons vegetable oil
- 2 eggs, whisked
- ¼ cup bread crumbs

Directions:

Put some water in a pot, add the salt and potatoes, bring them to a boil on medium-high heat, cook for 15 minutes, drain, transfer to a bowl, and mash them with a potato masher. Add the egg yolks, salt, pepper, nutmeg, cheese, chives and 2 tablespoons flour and stir well. In a bowl, mix vegetable oil with bread crumbs and stir. Put the eggs in a bowl and ¼ cup flour in another one. Shape balls from the potato dough, dip them in flour, then eggs, and finally in bread crumbs at the end and place them in the cooking basket of the air fryer. Cook at 390°F for 8 minutes, divide between plates and serve.

Potato Chips

Preparation time: 10 minutes
Cooking time: 30 minutes
Servings: 4

Ingredients:

- 4 potatoes, scrubbed, peeled into thin chips, soaked in water for 30 minutes, drained and patted dry
- Salt to taste
- 1 tablespoon extra virgin olive oil
- 2 teaspoons fresh rosemary, chopped

Directions:

In a bowl, mix the potatoes with the salt and oil toss to coat and place them in the cooking basket of the air fryer. Cook at 330°F for 30 minutes, transfer them to plates and serve with rosemary sprinkled on top.

Avocado Chips

Preparation time: 10 minutes
Cooking time: 10 minutes
Servings: 3

Ingredients:
- 1 avocado, pitted, peeled and sliced
- Salt and ground black pepper, to taste
- ½ cup panko bread crumbs
- Liquid from 15 ounces canned white beans

Directions:

In a bowl, mix the bread crumbs with salt and pepper and stir. In another bowl, put liquid from beans. Dip avocado pieces in liquid and then in the bread crumbs. Place the avocado chips in the air fryer's basket and cook at 390°F for 10 minutes, shaking halfway through. Divide between plates and serve.

Vegetable Fries

Preparation time: 10 minutes
Cooking time: 30 minutes
Servings: 4

Ingredients:
- 4 parsnips, cut into thin sticks
- 2 sweet potatoes, cut into sticks
- 4 carrots, cut in sticks
- Salt and ground black pepper, to taste
- 2 tablespoons fresh rosemary, chopped
- 2 tablespoons olive oil
- Garlic powder
- Cornmeal

Directions:

Put the vegetables in a bowl, add the oil, garlic powder, salt, pepper, cornmeal and rosemary and toss to coat. Put the sweet potatoes in the preheated air fryer, cook them for 10 minutes at 350°F and transfer them to a platter. Add the parsnips to the air fryer, cook for 5 minutes and transfer to the sweet potato fries. Add the carrots, cook for 15 minutes and transfer to the platter with the other vegetable fries. Keep warm until it is time to serve.

Polenta Rounds

Preparation time: 10 minutes
Cooking time: 35 minutes
Servings: 4

Ingredients:
- 18 ounces pre-cooked polenta roll
- 1 tablespoon olive oil
- Vegetable oil cooking spray

Directions:

Cut the polenta roll in medium-sized slices and brush them with the olive oil. Coat the air fryer basket with vegetable oil spray and place the polenta rounds in the air fryer basket. Cook at 400°F for 25 minutes, flipping them after 10 minutes. Serve by themselves or with fish.

Roasted Cabbage

Preparation time: 10 minutes
Cooking time: 20 minute
Servings: 2

Ingredients:
- ½ cabbage head, cored and chopped
- 1 yellow onion, peeled chopped
- Salt and ground black pepper, to taste
- 4 bacon slices, chopped
- 1 cup whipping cream
- Tabasco sauce
- 2 tablespoons cornstarch

Directions:
Put the cabbage and onion on aluminum foil. In a bowl, mix the cornstarch with cream, salt, pepper, and a dash of Tabasco sauce and stir well. Pour onto the cabbage and onion mixture. Add the bacon, seal the edges of the foil, place in air fryer and cook at 400°F for 20 minutes. Divide between plates and serve.

Snacks and Appetizers

Fried Beef Croquettes

Prep time: 5 minutes
Cooking time: 20 minutes
Servings: 4

Ingredients:
- 1 red onion
- 1 pound beef forcemeat
- 1 tablespoon fresh dill, chopped
- 1 clove garlic, peeled and minced
- 1 egg
- ½ teaspoon sea salt
- Cayenne pepper
- ¾ cup bread crumbs

Directions:
Preheat the air fryer to 360°F. Peel and dice the onion. Put the beef, onion, garlic and dill into a bowl and combine. Add egg, salt and pepper. Divide the forcemeat into pieces in the size of a walnut and roll into balls. Cover the croquettes with bread crumbs. Transfer the croquettes to the basket of the air fryer. Cook for 15 minutes and serve.

Ham-wrapped Shrimp

Prep time: 15 minutes
Cooking time: 15 minutes
Servings: 4

Ingredients:
- 1 pound shrimp
- 14 ounces ham
- Salt
- Ground black pepper

Directions:
Preheat the air fryer to 350°F. Peel and devein the shrimp and slice the ham thinly. Cover every of shrimp with ham. Put in the refrigerator for 20 minutes. Cook in the air fryer for 10-12 minutes and serve.

Swiss and Ham Patties

Prep time: 20 minutes
Cooking time: 30 minutes
Servings: 6

Ingredients:
- 14 ounces Swiss cheese
- 15 ounces ham
- 3 tablespoons vegetable oil
- A cup of flour
- 1 egg
- ¾ cup bread crumbs

Directions:
Preheat the air fryer to 350°F. Slice the ham thinly and cut the cheese into six cubes. Cover the cheese with two slices of ham each cube of cheese. Put in the refrigerator for 5 minutes to firm. Combine the oil with bread crumbs. Beat the egg in a separate bowl. Dip the wrapped cheese into the flour and then the egg. Cover the cheese with the bread crumbs. Put the patties in the air fryer basket. Cook for 10-15 minutes until crispy.

Squab Spring Rolls

Prep time: 10 minutes
Cooking time: 15 minutes
Servings: 4

Ingredients:

- 4 ounces squab breast
- 1 dill stalk
- 1 carrot, peeled
- 2 mushrooms
- ½ teaspoon coriander
- 1 tablespoon chicken broth
- 1 egg

- 1 teaspoon potato starch
- 8 spring roll papers
- 1 tablespoon olive oil
- Salt
- Ground black pepper
- Sugar

Directions:

Cook the squab breast in hot water, boiling for 10 minutes. Shred the squab into small pieces. Slice the dill, carrot and mushrooms. Combine the squab with the celery, carrot and mushrooms into a separate bowl and mix well. Sprinkle with the coriander, sugar, salt, and pepper. Add chicken broth and mix well. Beat an egg and mix with the potato starch to make a sticky dough. Wrap the stuffing into each spring roll and fill it with the starch mixture. Preheat the air fryer to 360°F. Sprinkle the spring rolls with the olive oil. Out the spring rolls in the cooking basket. Cook for 3-4 minutes or until golden brown. Serve with soy sauce.

Shrimp Patties

Prep time: 15 minutes
Cooking time: 20 minutes
Servings: 6

Ingredients:

- 14 ounces shrimp, peeled, deveined, and
opped
- 2 egg whites, beaten
- 2 tablespoons vegetable oil
- 1 white onion, peeled
- ½ red bell pepper, seeded
- 1 dill stalk
- ¼ teaspoon fresh tarragon

- 1 chive stalk
- 1 parsley stalk
- 1 cup mayonnaise (or sour cream)
- 3 eggs
- 1 cup flour
- 1½ cup bread crumbs scallions
- ½ teaspoon sea salt
- Ground black pepper

Directions:

Dice the onion, cucumber, dill, tarragon, chive and parsley. Sauté the greens and vegetables in the olive oil for 5-6 minutes. Remove from the heat and set aside. Combine the bread crumbs, vegetable oil, and sea salt and stir. Whisk an egg in a separate bowl. In a separate bowl, add flour and set aside. Mix the shrimp, egg white, mayonnaise, pepper, tarragon, and vegetables in a large pan. Preheat the air fryer to 360°F. Divide the shrimp mixture into pieces the size of a walnut and roll into balls. Coat the balls with first in flour, then in eggs, and finally in bread crumbs. Transfer the patties to the basket of the air fryer. Fry the patties for 8-10 minutes.

Ricotta Triangles

Prep time: 10 minutes
Cooking time: 20 minutes
Servings: 5

Ingredients:
- 1 egg
- 4 ounces ricotta cheese
- 1 dill stalk, diced
- 1 shallot, peeled and diced
- 1 pita bread
- 2 tablespoons vegetable oil
- Ground black pepper

Directions:

In a bowl, add the ricotta cheese and egg and mix well, then add the dill, shallot, and pepper and mix well. Cut the pita bread in half and then into strips. Add a teaspoon of the ricotta mixture onto the bread. Lay down the tip of the pita bread the filling to form a triangle. Repeat until all the pita and ricotta mixture have been used. Preheat the air fryer to 350°F. Sprinkle the pita with vegetable oil and put triangles in the air fryer pan. Cook for 3-4 minutes or until golden brown and serve.

Grilled Turkey Skewers with Satay Sauce

Prep time: 15 minutes
Cooking time: 15 minutes
Servings: 3

Ingredients:
- 12 ounces turkey breast, cut into chunks
- ½ cup soy sauce
- ½ cup peach juice
- 5 tablespoons olive oil
- 3 garlic cloves, peeled and chopped
- 4 shallots, peeled and chopped
- 1 tablespoon turmeric
- 2 tablespoons caraway seeds
- Cayenne pepper

Directions:

Place the turkey breast in a bowl. In a mixing bowl combine the soy sauce, peach juice, olive oil, garlic, shallots, turmeric, caraway seeds, and cayenne pepper and mix well. Cover the turkey breast with the marinade, cover the bowl, and let rest in the refrigerator for at least two hours. Preheat the air fryer to 350°F. Remove the turkey from the marinade and pat dry with paper towel. Put the turkey on oven-safe skewers into the air fryer pan. Cook for 5-7 minutes. Serve with a spiced sauce that contains peanuts.

Spicy Turkey Wings

Prep time: 15 minutes
Cooking time: 20 minutes
Servings: 5

Ingredients:

- 10 turkey wings
- 2 tablespoons sunflower oil
- 2 tablespoons balsamic vinegar
- 4 cloves garlic, peeled and minced
- 1 tablespoon allspice
- 1 teaspoon cinnamon
- 1 teaspoon salt
- 2 tablespoons sugar
- 1 tablespoon fresh dill, minced
- 4 shallots, peeled and minced
- 5 tablespoons lemon juice

Directions:

Split the wings at the joints, discarding the tips. Mix the oil, vinegar, garlic, allspice, cinnamon, salt, sugar, dill, shallots, and lemon juice in a bowl. Add the wings and cover. Marinate the wings for at least 2 hours in the refrigerator. Preheat the air fryer to 350°F. Drain the wings and pat them dry with paper towel. Put the wings in the air fryer pan. Cook for 15-20 minutes or until golden brown, turning halfway through. Serve sprinkled with shredded cheddar cheese.

Lamb Dumplings with Sour Cream Sauce

Prep time: 10 minutes
Cooking time: 25 minutes
Servings: 4

Ingredients:

- 1 pound ground lamb
- 4 ounces cooked chicken, minced
- 2 stalks dill, chopped
- 1 tbsp. sugar
- 4 teaspoons meat seasoning (cloves, marjoram, oregano, basil, cayenne pepper, and black pepper)
- 1 teaspoon tomato paste
- 2 garlic cloves, peeled and minced
- 5 tablespoons sunflower oil
- ½ tablespoon sea salt
- 1 egg white
- ½ cup sour cream
- 2 tablespoons creamed butter
- 1 teaspoon salt

Directions:

Preheat Air fryer to 350°F. Mix the lamb and chicken in a bowl. Add the dill, sugar, seasoning mix, and oil to the meat and make the dumplings. Divide the forcemeat into pieces in the size of a walnut and form into balls. Put the dumplings into the air fryer pan and cook for 6-8 minutes. While preparing dumplings, combine the egg with the sour cream, butter, and salt in a blender and whip until smooth. Serve the dumplings with sauce

Farci Mushrooms

Prep time: 10 minutes
Cooking time: 15 minutes
Servings: 4

Ingredients:
- 14 white mushrooms
- 2 tablespoons browned bread crumbs
- 1 cup cooked rabbit, minced
- 1 garlic clove, peeled and minced
- 4 stalks dill, chopped
- Ground black pepper
- 2 tablespoons vegetable oil

Directions:
Preheat the air fryer to 350°F. Add the rabbit, garlic, dill, and pepper to a blender and puree until smooth. Trim the mushroom stems and stuff the tops with the mince mixture. Dip into the bread crumbs. Sprinkle the air fryer pan with oil. Put the mushroom tops into the air fryer. Cook until the mushrooms are crispy.

Bread Rolls

Preparation time: 15 minutes
Cooking time: 20 minutes
Servings: 6

Ingredients:
- 8 bread slices
- 5 potatoes, peeled
- 2 green chilies, chopped
- 1 bunch coriander, chopped
- 2 yellow onions, peeled and chopped
- Salt and ground black pepper, to taste
- ½ teaspoon turmeric
- 1 tablespoon lime zest
- ½ teaspoon mustard seeds
- 2 tablespoons vegetable oil

Directions:
Put the potatoes in a pot, add water to cover, add Salt, and boil them. Drain the potatoes, let them cool down and mash them in a bowl using a potato masher. Heat up a pan with 1 teaspoon oil on medium heat, add the mustard seeds and toast for 1 minute. Add the onions, stir and cook for 3 minutes. Add the lime zest, turmeric, mashed potatoes, salt, and pepper, stir well and cook for 1-2 minutes. Remove from the heat and set aside to cool down. Divide this potato mix into 8 portions, wet the bread slices, press each slice well and place them all on a cutting board. Take 1 slice of bread in the palm of your hand, add 1 portion of potato mix, seal edges well and shape an oval. Repeat this with the rest of the bread. Place them into the air fryer, brush with the rest of the oil and cook at 400°F for 12 minutes. Arrange bread rolls on a platter when they're done and serve with the favorite chutney.

Banana Chips

Preparation time: 10 minutes
Cooking time: 10 minutes
Servings: 3

Ingredients:

- 4 bananas, peeled and sliced into thin pieces
- Salt
- Vegetable oil
- Ground black pepper

Directions:

Put the banana slices in the air fryer, add a drizzle of oil, salt, and pepper, toss to coat gently, and cook at 360°F for 10 minutes. Put them in a bowl and serve.

Spring Rolls

Preparation time: 10 minutes
Cooking time: 25 minutes
Servings: 8

Ingredients:

- 2 cups cabbage, chopped
- 2 yellow onions, peeled and chopped
- 1 carrot, peeled and chopped
- ½ bell pepper, seeded and chopped
- 2-inch piece ginger, peeled and grated
- 8 garlic cloves, peeled and minced
- Salt and ground black pepper, to taste
- Sugar
- 1 teaspoon soy sauce
- 2 tablespoons cooking oil
- 2 green onions, diced for serving
- 10 spring roll sheets
- Vegetable oil cooking spray
- 2 tablespoons corn flour

Directions:

Heat up a pan with the oil on medium-high heat. Add the cabbage, onions, carrot, bell pepper, ginger, garlic, salt, pepper, and sugar, stir well, and cook for 3 minutes. Add the soy sauce and green onions, stir and take off the heat. In a bowl, mix the corn flour with some water and stir until you obtain a paste. Cut each spring roll sheet and cut into 4 pieces. Place 1 tablespoons of the vegetable mix in one corner, roll the sheets, tucking in the corners as you do. Repeat this with the rest of the sheets. Place them in the air fryer's basket, spray with cooking oil and cook at 360°F for 10 minutes. Flip them and cook for 10 minutes more. Arrange on a platter and serve.

Tortilla Chips

Preparation time: 10 minutes
Cooking time: 6 minutes
Servings: 4

Ingredients:

- 8 corn tortillas
- Salt and ground black pepper, to taste
- 1 tablespoon oil
- Sour cream for serving

Directions:

Cut each tortilla into triangles and brush them with the oil. Place half of them in the fryer's basket, cook for 3 minutes at 400°F and transfer to a bowl. Repeat with the rest of the tortilla chips and season them with salt and pepper and serve with sour cream on the side.

Fried Crab Sticks

Preparation time: 5 minutes
Cooking time: 12 minutes
Servings: 6

Ingredients:

- 10 imitation crabsticks
- 2 teaspoons sesame oil
- Cajun seasoning, to taste

Directions:

Shred the crab sticks into small pieces, put them in a bowl and add sesame oil onto them. Toss to coat, transfer to the air fryer and cook at 350°F for 12 minutes. Transfer them to a bowl and sprinkle Cajun seasoning on top. Toss to coat and serve.

Cauliflower Bites

Preparation time: 10 minutes
Cooking time: 20 minutes
Servings: 6

Ingredients:

- 1 cauliflower head, florets separated into bite-size pieces
- Salt and ground black pepper, to taste
- Olive oil
- 2 teaspoons garlic powder
- 1 teaspoon butter, melted
- ½ cup hot sauce

Directions:

Put the cauliflower pieces in a bowl, add the salt, pepper, oil and garlic powder, and toss to coat. Spread on a baking sheet that fits the air fryer, cook at 450°F for 15 minutes and transfer to a bowl. Add the butter and hot sauce, toss to coat, return to the air fryer, and cook for 5 minutes more. Serve cold.

Fried Pickles

Preparation time: 10 minutes
Cooking time: 5 minutes
Servings: 4

Ingredients:

- 16 ounces jarred dill pickle wedges
- ½ cup white flour
- 1 egg
- ¼ cup milk
- Salt, to taste
- ½ teaspoon garlic powder
- ½ teaspoon paprika
- Oil for frying
- 6 drops hot sauce
- ¼ cup ranch sauce

Directions:

Pat the pickles dry and place them in a bowl. In a second bowl, mix the milk with egg and whisk well. In a third bowl, mix the flour with salt, garlic powder, and paprika and stir. Dip the pickles in flour, then in the egg mixture and again in flour, and place them in the air fryer. Cook at 400°F for 5 minutes, transfer to a bowl, and serve.

Roasted Chickpeas

Preparation time: 10 minutes
Cooking time: 20 minutes
Servings: 4

Ingredients:

- 15 ounces canned chickpeas, drained
- ½ teaspoon cumin
- 1 tablespoon olive oil
- 1 teaspoon smoked paprika
- Salt and ground black pepper, to taste
- Cayenne pepper

Directions:

In a bowl, mix the chickpeas with oil, cumin, paprika, salt, pepper, and cayenne pepper, and toss to coat. Place in the fryer's basket, cook at 390°F for 10 minutes and transfer to a bowl. Serve warm.

Sage Sausage Balls

Preparation time: 10 minutes
Cooking time: 15 minutes
Servings: 9

Ingredients:

- 3.5 ounces sausage meat
- Salt and ground black pepper, to taste
- 1 teaspoon sage
- ½ teaspoon garlic, peeled and minced
- 1 small onion, peeled and chopped
- 3 tablespoons bread crumbs

Directions:

In a bowl, mix the sausage meat with salt, pepper, sage, garlic, onion, and bread crumbs and stir well. Shape the balls from the mixture, put them in the air fryer and cook at 360°F for 15 minutes. Transfer to a platter and serve.

Jalapeño Poppers

Preparation time: 10 minutes
Cooking time: 10 minutes
Servings: 2

Ingredients:

- 1 ounce cheddar cheese, grated
- 1 egg, whisked
- 1 spring roll wrapper
- 2 jalapeños, stems cut off, sliced in halves lengthwise and patted dry

Directions:

Cut the spring roll wrapper in 4 pieces, brush each piece with the egg, and divide jalapeño halves on them. Divide the cheese, roll and seal the edges and place everything in the air fryer's cooking basket. Cook at 390°F for 10 minutes, arrange on a platter and serve.

Sun-dried Tomatoes with Rice

Preparation time: 10 minutes
Cooking time: 20 minutes
Servings: 6

Ingredients:

- 1 small yellow onion, peeled and chopped
- 1 cup Arborio rice
- 1 tablespoon extra virgin olive oil
- ¼ cup white wine
- 1½ cups water
- 1 cup vegetable stock
- Salt and ground black pepper, to taste
- 2 eggs, whisked
- ⅓ cup Parmesan cheese, grated
- 2 ounces Mozzarella cheese, shredded
- ¼ cup sun-dried tomatoes, chopped
- 1½ cups bread crumbs
- Olive oil
- Marinara sauce for serving

Directions:

Heat up a pan with 1 tablespoon oil on medium heat, add the onion, stir and cook for 5 minutes. Add the rice, wine, stock, and water, stir and cook on a low heat for 20 minutes. Add the salt, pepper and parmesan, stir well, spread on a baking sheet and set aside to cool down. Transfer the rice to a bowl, add the eggs, tomatoes, and half of the bread crumbs and stir well. Shape into 12 balls, press a hole in each ball, stuff with mozzarella pieces and mold into balls again. Dredge them in the rest of the bread crumbs, arrange the balls in the air fryer, drizzle some oil onto them and cook at 380°F for 10 minutes. Flip them and cook for 5 minutes. Arrange them on a platter and serve with marinara sauce on the side.

Chicken Dip with Naan Bread

Preparation time: 10 minutes
Cooking time: 30 minutes
Servings: 10

Ingredients:

- 3 tablespoons butter, melted
- 4 naan bread loaves, cut in strips
- 1 cup yogurt
- 12 ounces cream cheese, soft
- 2 cups chicken meat, already cooked and shredded
- 2 teaspoons curry powder
- 4 scallions, chopped
- 6 ounces Monterey jack cheese, grated
- ⅓ cup raisins
- ¼ cup fresh cilantro, chopped
- ½ cup almonds, sliced
- Salt and ground black pepper, to taste
- ½ cup chutney

Directions:

Put naan bread strips in a bowl, add butter and toss to coat. Put strips in the air fryer's basket and cook at 400°F for 5 minutes. In a bowl, mix the cream cheese with yogurt and blend using a hand mixer. Add the curry powder, scallions, chicken meat, raisins, cheese, cilantro, salt, and pepper and stir well. Spread into a baking dish that fits the air fryer, sprinkle almonds on top, place in the air fryer and bake at 300°F for 25 minutes. Transfer dip to a bowl, top with chutney and serve with naan bread strips.

Air-fried Turkey Strips

Preparation time: 10 minutes
Cooking time: 10 minutes
Servings: 4

Ingredients:

- 3.5 ounces turkey breast, cut into strips
- 1 tablespoon cheddar cheese, grated
- 1½ tablespoon bread crumbs
- ½ tablespoon rolled oats
- 1 egg, whisked
- 1 tablespoon white flour
- Salt and ground black pepper, to taste
- 1 teaspoon fresh thyme
- 1 teaspoon fresh parsley
- 1 red chile pepper, chopped
- 2 tablespoons garlic, peeled and minced
- 3.5 ounces sugar

Directions:

In a bowl, mix the bread crumbs with the oats and cheese. Put the egg in a second bowl and the flour in a third bowl. Season the turkey strips with salt and pepper, dredge them in flour, dip them in egg and then in the bread crumbs mix. Place them in the air fryer. Cook at 360°F for 8 minutes. Meanwhile, put the sugar in a pot and add some cold water. Heat to high heat, bring to a boil, and stir until the sugar dissolves. Add the chile pepper, salt, pepper, garlic, thyme, and parsley and stir well. Arrange the turkey strips on a platter and serve with the chile dip on the side.

Endives with Yogurt

Preparation time: 30 minutes
Cooking time: 10 minutes
Servings: 4

Ingredients:

- 6 endives, cut in halves lengthwise
- Salt and ground black pepper, to taste
- ½ cup yogurt
- 1 teaspoon garlic powder
- ½ teaspoon curry powder
- 3 tablespoons lemon juice

Directions:

In a bowl, mix the yogurt with salt, pepper, garlic powder, curry powder, and lemon juice and whisk well. Add the endive halves, toss to coat, and let marinate in the refrigerator for 30 minutes. Place them in the air fryer's basket and cook at 360°F for 10 minutes. Arrange them on a platter and serve.

Tofu Balls

Preparation time: 30 minutes
Cooking time: 20 minutes
Servings: 4

Ingredients:
- 12 ounces firm tofu, cubed
- 1 teaspoon paprika
- 1 teaspoon sesame oil
- 1 tablespoon coriander paste
- 2 tablespoons soy sauce
- 1 teaspoon duck fat
- 2 tablespoons fish sauce

Directions:

In a bowl, mix the paprika with sesame oil, coriander paste, fish sauce, and soy sauce and whisk well. Add the tofu cubes, toss to coat and let marinate in the refrigerator for 30 minutes. Transfer the tofu cubes to the air fryer's basket, add the duck fat and cook at 350°F for 20 minutes, shaking halfway through. Transfer them to a bowl and serve.

Caramel Popcorn

Preparation time: 5 minutes
Cooking time: 10 minutes
Servings: 4

Ingredients:
- 2 tablespoons corn kernels
- 2½ tablespoons butter
- 2 ounces brown sugar

Directions:

Put the corn kernels in the air fryer and cook at 400°F for 6 minutes. Transfer them to a tray, spread and set aside. Heat up a pan on low heat, add the butter and melt it. Add the sugar, stir, and cook until it dissolves. Add the popcorn, toss to coat, take off the heat and spread on the tray again. Let the popcorn cool down completely, transfer to a bowl, and serve.

Apple Chips

Preparation time: 10 minutes
Cooking time: 15 minutes
Servings: 2

Ingredients:
- 1 apple, cored and thinly sliced
- Salt
- ½ teaspoon ground cinnamon
- 1 tablespoon white sugar

Directions:

Arrange the apple slices on an aluminum foil-lined baking sheet and sprinkle with the salt, sugar and cinnamon. Transfer the apple slices to the air fryer's basket and cook at 390°F for 10 minutes turning them halfway. Transfer to a bowl and serve with a dip.

Zucchini Patties

Preparation time: 10 minutes
Cooking time: 10 minutes
Servings: 4

Ingredients:

- 1 carrot, peeled and grated
- 1 zucchini, grated
- 2 slices toasted bread, crumbled
- 1 egg
- Salt and ground black pepper, to taste
- ½ teaspoon paprika
- 1 teaspoon garlic, minced
- 2 tablespoons Parmesan cheese, grated
- 1 tablespoon corn flour

Directions:

Put the zucchini in a bowl, add the salt and set aside for 10 minutes. Squeeze the water and transfer zucchini to another bowl. Add the carrots, salt, pepper paprika, garlic, egg, and bread crumbs and stir well. Shape 8 patties, place them in the air fryer, and cook at 360°F for 10 minutes. Arrange on a platter and serve.

Macaroni and Cheese Balls

Preparation time: 10 minutes
Cooking time: 10 minutes
Servings: 2

Ingredients:

- 2 cups leftover macaroni and cheese
- 3 eggs
- ½ cup cheddar cheese, grated
- 1 cup flour
- 2 cups milk
- 1 cup bread crumbs

Directions:

In a bowl, mix the macaroni and cheese with cheddar cheese, stir, and leave aside. Put the bread crumbs in a bowl, the flour in another bowl, and mix the milk and egg in a third bowl. Shape the balls of macaroni and cheese mix using an ice cream scoop, dredge them in flour, then dip in egg and then in bread crumbs at the end. Place the macaroni and cheese balls in the air fryer's basket and cook at 360°F for 10 minutes, flipping them halfway. Arrange on a platter and serve.

French Toast Sticks

Preparation time: 10 minutes
Cooking time: 10 minutes
Servings: 2

Ingredients:

- 4 whole meal bread slices, each cut in 4 sticks
- 2 eggs
- ¼ cup milk
- 1 teaspoon ground cinnamon
- 1 tablespoon honey
- ¼ cup brown sugar
- Icing sugar
- Ground nutmeg

Directions:

In a bowl, mix the eggs with the milk, brown sugar, cinnamon, nutmeg, and honey and whisk well. Dip each bread stick in this mix, place them in the air fryer and cook at 360°F for 10 minutes. Transfer bread stick to a bowl and sprinkle icing sugar over them.

Fish and Seafood

Mackerel Fillets

Prep time: 15 minutes
Cooking time: 20 minutes
Servings: 4

Ingredients:
- 4 mackerel fillets
- 3 red bell peppers
- 1 red onion
- 1 tablespoon vinegar
- 1 zucchini
- ¼ cup parsley
- 4 garlic cloves
- 2 tablespoons olive oil
- 1 lemon
- ½ teaspoon chile flakes

Directions:
Peel the garlic cloves and mince them. Peel the onion and dice it. Remove the seeds from the sweet peppers and slice them. In a mixing bowl, combine all the vegetables together. Sprinkle the mixture with the vinegar and olive oil, stirring well. Take the mackerel fillets and rub it with the chile flakes. Make the lemon zest from the lemon and squeeze the juice. Combine the mixture and rub the mackerel with it. Chop the zucchini and parsley. Combine the zucchini with the vegetable mixture and stir well. Take the air fryer form and put the vegetable mixture. Add the mackerel fillets and transfer the dish to the air fryer basket. Close the lid and cook for 20 minutes. When it is cooked, all the ingredients should be soft. Remove the fish from the air fryer and serve.

Asian-style Flounder

Prep time: 15 minutes
Cooking time: 15 minutes
Servings: 4

Ingredients:
- 2 teaspoons hoisin sauce
- 1 flounder fillet
- ⅓ cup chives
- 1 teaspoon ground black pepper
- 1 teaspoon ground white pepper
- ½ tablespoon ginger
- 1 teaspoon salt
- 1 teaspoon canola oil
- 1 small white onion
- 2 tablespoons soy sauce
- 1 teaspoon fresh rosemary

Directions:
In a mixing bowl, combine the black pepper, ginger, salt, and rosemary and stir well. Take the flounder and rub it with the spicy mixture. Peel the onion and chop it. Combine the onion and soy sauce. Add the canola oil and hoisin sauce. Stir until smooth. Sprinkle the flounder with this mixture. Chop the chives. Take the air fryer tray and transfer the flounder to it. Sprinkle it with the chopped chives on all the sides. Transfer the fish in the air fryer and cook for 15 minutes. When the dish is cooked, let it cool briefly and then transfer the fish to a serving plate.

Squid with Spicy Tomato Sauce

Prep time: 15 minutes
Cooking time: 10 minutes
Servings: 2

Ingredients:
- 1 cup butter beans
- 2 garlic cloves
- 1 red onion
- 1 teaspoon fresh ginger, grated
- 1 teaspoon smoked paprika
- 3 tomatoes
- ⅓ cup green olives
- 1 jalapeño pepper
- 1 tablespoon tomato juice
- 1 cup fish stock
- 1 teaspoon salt
- 3 lemon wedges for serving
- 1 tablespoon orange zest
- 1 tablespoon grated parsley root
- 14 ounces squid

Directions:
In a mixing bowl, combine the grated parsley root, orange zest, salt, paprika, and ginger and stir well. Add the tomato juice. Dice the green olives and add them to the mixture. Remove the seeds from the jalapeño pepper and slice it. Add the jalapeño pepper in the spice mixture and add the fish stock. Peel the garlic and red onion. Mince the vegetables and combine them with the butter beans. Chop the tomatoes and add them to the spice mixture. Transfer the squid to the spice mixture. Add the butter beans and stir well. Leave the squid for 5 minutes. Transfer it to the air fryer basket and all the liquid from the squid. Close the lid and cook it for 10 minutes. When the dish is cooked, stir well and serve with the lemon wedges.

Crispy Trout

Prep time: 15 minutes
Cooking time: 15 minutes
Servings: 4

Ingredients:
- 2 eggs
- 15 ounces trout
- ⅓ cup heavy cream
- 1 cup bread crumbs
- 1 tablespoon lemon juice
- 3 tablespoons fresh ginger
- 1 teaspoon ground white pepper
- ½ teaspoon cayenne pepper
- 1 tablespoon butter
- 1 teaspoon lemon zest
- ½ teaspoon fresh rosemary

Directions:
Chop the trout into the pieces. In a large mixing bowl, beat the eggs. Add the cream and bread crumbs. Stir the mixture until smooth. Peel the ginger and grate it. Combine the ginger with the lemon zest, rosemary, lemon juice and white pepper and stir well. Melt the butter and add it to the ginger mixture and stir again. Pour the liquid into the bowl with chopped trout and stir well. Set aside for at least 5 minutes. Dip the trout in the egg mixture and transfer it to the air fryer tray. Transfer the tray to the air fryer and close it. Cook the fish for 15 minutes or until it becomes crispy. When the fish is cooked, remove it from the air fryer, let it cool briefly, and serve.

Fish Sticks

Prep time: 15 minutes
Cooking time: 8 minutes
Servings: 4

Ingredients:

- 1 pound cod
- 1 teaspoon salt
- 1 teaspoon minced garlic
- 3 slices white bread
- 1 teaspoon fresh rosemary
- 1 teaspoon fresh oregano
- 1 teaspoon fresh thyme
- 1 teaspoon paprika
- 1 teaspoon fresh cilantro
- 1 egg
- 3 tablespoons flour

Directions:

Chop the white bread slices roughly and combine them with the garlic. Stir well and transfer the mixture to the blender. Blend until smooth. Slice the cod into sticks. In a mixing bowl, combine the cilantro, paprika, thyme, oregano, and rosemary. Stir well, add the flour and stir again. Beat the egg in the mixing bowl. Take the cod sticks and dip them in the flour mixture, then dip them in the egg mixture. Finally, dip the cod sticks in the bread mixture. Transfer the fish sticks in the air fryer basket and close the lid. Cook for 8 minutes. When the fish sticks are cooked, remove them from the air fryer and rest briefly before serving.

Indian-style Sweet Salmon

Prep time: 20 minutes
Cooking time: 15 minutes
Servings: 4

Ingredients:

- 1 tablespoon tomato sauce
- 15 ounces salmon
- 1 onion
- 1 tablespoon honey
- 1 teaspoon orange juice
- 1 teaspoon lemon juice
- 1 tablespoon soy sauce
- ½ teaspoon sea salt
- 1 teaspoon olive oil
- 1 teaspoon fresh rosemary
- 1 teaspoon fresh ginger
- ½ teaspoon coriander

Directions:

Slice the salmon into the portion pieces and rub the fish with the salt and ginger. Then In a mixing bowl, combine the honey, orange juice, lemon juice, soy sauce, and tomato paste. Stir until all the ingredients are dissolved and the mixture is smooth. Pour the liquid onto the salmon, stir well, Set it aside and set aside to marinate. Peel the onion and chop it. Add the onion to the mixing bowl with the salmon. Sprinkle the mixture with the coriander. Transfer the salmon in the air fryer basket and sprinkle it with the olive oil. Close the lid and cook for 15 minutes. When the fish cooked, remove it and let it rest briefly is cooked, remove it from the air fryer, let it cool briefly, and serve.

Fish Cutlets

Prep time: 15 minutes
Cooking time: 12 minutes
Servings: 5

Ingredients:

- 14 ounces minced cod
- 1 teaspoon turmeric
- 1 teaspoon fresh oregano
- 1 teaspoon fresh basil
- 1 teaspoon salt
- 1 teaspoon sour cream
- 4 slices whole grain bread
- ½ teaspoon ground white pepper
- 1 tablespoon lemon juice
- 1 teaspoon garlic powder
- 1 egg white

Directions:

In a mixing bowl, combine the minced cod and egg white and stir well. Sprinkle the mixture with the turmeric, oregano, basil, salt, garlic powder, and ground white pepper and stir well. Add the lemon juice and sour cream. Stir again and transfer it in the refrigerator for at least 5 minutes. Meanwhile, chop the whole grain bread roughly and transfer it to the food processor and process into bread crumbs. Remove the minced fish mixture from the refrigerator and make medium-sized cutlets from the mixture and flatten them slightly. Transfer the cutlets to the air fryer basket and close the lid. Cook for 12 minutes. When the cutlets are cooked, remove them from the air fryer, let them rest briefly and serve.

Sweet and Sour Curry Fish

Prep time: 15 minutes
Cooking time: 15 minutes
Servings: 3

Ingredients:

- 14 ounces trout
- 1 green chile
- 2 tablespoons curry paste
- 4 cups fish stock
- 1 teaspoon lime zest
- 1 teaspoon salt
- 1 teaspoon cayenne pepper
- ½ lemon
- ½ tablespoon garlic, minced
- 1½ teaspoon grated ginger
- 1 teaspoon turmeric
- 1 tablespoon chili powder
- 1 teaspoon sugar

Directions:

Wash the trout and chop the fish roughly. In a mixing bowl, combine the curry paste, salt, cayenne pepper, ginger garlic paste, turmeric, sugar, and chili powder and stir well. Pour the fish stock into the mixing bowl with the curry paste mixture and stir until smooth. Add the trout to the liquid and coat the fish well. Chop the lemon and add it and the lime zest to the curry paste mass and stir. Open the air fryer and transfer the fish to the air fryer basket. Close the lid and cook for 15 minutes. When it is cooked, remove it from the air fryer and serve.

Snapper with Shallot and Tamarind Sauce

Prep time: 15 minutes
Cooking time: 17 minutes
Servings: 4

Ingredients:

- 5 -ounce snapper fillet
- 1 cup shallots
- 1 tablespoon honey
- 2 ounces cilantro
- 1 tablespoon fish sauce
- 1 red chile pepper
- 1 tablespoon tamarind
- 1 tablespoon water
- 1 teaspoon salt
- 1 lime
- ½ cup parsley
- 1 teaspoon ground ginger
- 4 garlic cloves
- 1 green onion

Directions:

Rub the snapper filet with salt and set it aside. Combine the water and tamarind in the mixing bowl and stir well until the tamarind is dissolved. Peel the garlic cloves and onion and mince them. Mince the cilantro. Remove the seeds from the chile pepper and slice it. Take a large mixing bowl and combine the ingredients. Add the fish sauce and ground ginger. Add the honey and chop the shallot and parsley. Add these ingredients to the chili mixture. Transfer the snapper fillet in the air fryer basket and sprinkle with the chili mixture. Add the tamarind mixture. Close the lid and cook for 17 minutes. Remove the fish from the air fryer and let it rest briefly and let it rest briefly. Serve with lime wedges.

Ginger Tilapia

Prep time: 10 minutes
Cooking time: 12 minutes
Servings: 4

Ingredients:

- 1 ounces fresh ginger
- 4 tilapia fillets
- 1 teaspoon thyme
- ½ teaspoon coriander
- 1 egg white
- 1 teaspoon kosher salt
- 1 tablespoon sesame oil
- 1 teaspoon garlic, minced
- 2 tablespoons soy sauce

Directions:

Take a small mixing bowl and combine the soy sauce and sesame oil and stir well. Add the minced garlic and mix well. Take the tilapia fillets and put them in a mixing bowl. Pour the ginger mixture and stir. Let the fish rest for at least 5 minutes. Combine the thyme, coriander, and kosher salt together in a mixing bowl. Peel the ginger and grate it. Add the ginger in the spice mixture. Whisk the egg white until you get stiff peaks and add the spice mixture. Stir well until smooth. Transfer the tilapia fillet in the air fryer basket and cover it with the egg white mixture. Close the lid and cook for 12 minutes. When the tilapia is done, remove it from the air fryer and let it rest briefly and serve.

Seasoned Sea Scallops

Prep time: 10 minutes
Cooking time: 7 minutes
Servings: 4

Ingredients:
- 1 pound sea scallops
- 5 garlic cloves
- 1 tablespoon lemon juice
- ½ cup butter
- 1 teaspoon paprika
- ¼ cup fresh parsley
- 1 tablespoon lemon zest
- 1 teaspoon ground black pepper

Directions:

Peel the garlic and mince it. Combine the garlic and lemon juice together. Stir the mixture and add the lemon zest. Combine the sea scallops and lemon mixture in a large bowl. Mix well and sand set aside for 5 minutes. Chop the parsley and combine it with the paprika and pepper and stir well. Add the chopped parsley to the scallops and stir well again. Take the butter and transfer it to the air fryer basket. Add the scallops and stir well. Close the lid and cook for 7 minutes. When the scallops are cooked, remove them from the air fryer let it rest briefly and serve.

Salmon Pie

Prep time: 20 minutes
Cooking time: 30 minutes
Servings: 6

Ingredients:
- 10 ounces salmon
- 1 cup spinach
- 14 ounces puff pastry
- 1 teaspoon paprika
- 1 teaspoon salt
- 1 cup broccoli
- 1 teaspoon fresh oregano
- 1 teaspoon basil
- 1 cup heavy cream
- ½ teaspoon chile flakes
- ⅓ cup dill
- 1 teaspoon lemon juice
- 3 potatoes

Directions:

Take the salmon and mince it. Sprinkle the mixture with the salt, oregano, and basil and stir well. Chop the spinach and dill. Combine the mixture together in the mixing bowl, add the cream and chile flakes and stir well. Cut the broccoli into florets and dice them. Peel the potatoes and grate them. Sprinkle the potato with the lemon juice and stir well. Add the paprika and stir well. Roll out the puff pastry and transfer it in the air fryer basket. Add the salmon, spinach, and broccoli to the puff pastry. Add the potato and cover the pie with the remaining puff pastry and transfer the pie to the air fryer. Cook for 30 minutes. When the pie is cooked, remove it from the air fryer and let it rest briefly before cutting into slices and serving.

Halibut Steak

Prep time: 20 minutes
Cooking time: 14 minutes
Servings: 2

Ingredients:

- 2 halibut fillets
- 1 tablespoon lime juice
- ½ cup cashews
- ½ cup fresh basil
- 1 teaspoon fresh oregano
- 1 teaspoon olive oil
- 4 garlic cloves
- 1 teaspoon ground ginger
- 1 white onion
- 1 teaspoon sugar
- 1 teaspoon fresh thyme
- 1 teaspoon fish sauce

Directions:

Take the halibut fillets and sprinkle them with the fish sauce. Sprinkle the fish with the thyme and set the fish aside. In a mixing bowl, combine the cashews, oregano, and ginger. Add the olive oil and stir well. Chop the basil and add it to the mixture. Peel the onion and garlic cloves. Dice the vegetables and add them to the spice mixture and stir. Sprinkle the fish with the lemon juice and sugar. Open the air fryer lid and transfer the fillets to the air fryer. Add the cashews and close the lid and cook for 14 minutes. When the fish is done, remove it from the air fryer, let it rest briefly and serve.

Fish Casserole

Prep time: 20 minutes
Cooking time: 18 minutes
Servings: 2

Ingredients:

- 7 ounces tilapia
- 1 egg
- ½ cup chives
- 1 white onion
- 1 cup bread crumbs
- 1 teaspoon salt
- 1 teaspoon paprika
- 1 teaspoon olive oil
- 2 potatoes
- ⅓ cup hard cheese

Directions:

Mince the tilapia and combine it with the bread crumbs in a mixing bowl. Beat the egg in with the fish mixture, add the olive oil and stir well. Sprinkle the fish with the paprika and salt and stir again. Peel the onion and chop it. Add the onion in the fish mixture. Peel the potatoes and grate them. Add the potato to the fish mixture. Grate the cheese. Chop the chives and sprinkle the fish mixture with it. Place the fish into the air fryer tray. Sprinkle it with the cheese and transfer the tray in the air fryer. Close the lid and cook for 18 minutes. Remove the casserole from the air fryer and let it cool briefly before serving.

Tilapia with Tomato Garlic Sauce

Prep time: 15 minutes
Cooking time: 15 minutes
Servings: 2

Ingredients:

- 7-ounce tilapia
- 6 garlic cloves
- 4 tomatoes
- 1 cup tomato juice
- 1 tablespoon fresh rosemary
- 1 teaspoon salt
- 1 teaspoon paprika
- 1 onion
- 1 teaspoon cayenne pepper
- 1 teaspoon ground ginger
- 1 teaspoon soy sauce

Directions:

Cut the tilapia into the large pieces and sprinkle the fish with the ginger and cayenne pepper. Chop the tomatoes and combine them with the tomato juice together and transfer to a food processor. Add the paprika, salt, and soy sauce. Blend for 2 minutes or until smooth. Peel the onion and garlic cloves. Mince the vegetables and add them to the tomato mixture. Add the rosemary and stir well. Transfer the tilapia in the air fryer basket and top the tomato garlic sauce. Close the lid and cook for 15 minutes. When the dish is cooked, remove it from the air fryer. Serve the fish with the tomato garlic sauce.

Sriracha Shrimp

Prep time: 15 minutes
Cooking time: 9 minutes
Servings: 3

Ingredients:

- 1 pound shrimp
- 4 tablespoons sriracha
- ¼ cup fresh mint
- ¼ cup fresh rosemary
- ½ cup butter
- 1 teaspoon ground white pepper
- 1 teaspoon salt
- ½ teaspoon brown sugar
- 1 tablespoon soy sauce

Directions:

Melt the butter, combine it with the soy sauce and stir well. Chop the rosemary and mince the mint. Combine the ingredients and add them in the butter mixture. Peel and devein the shrimp and sprinkle them with the brown sugar and salt. Add the white pepper and stir well. Add the sriracha and stir well again. Open the air fryer lid and transfer the shrimp mixture inside. Add the butter sauce and stir. Close the lid and cook for 9 minutes. Remove the seafood from the air fryer and transfer it to a serving plate. Ladle the fish sauce on top and serve.

Cod Fish with Rosemary

Prep time: 15 minutes
Cooking time: 15 minutes
Servings: 4

Ingredients:
- 1 pound cod
- ½ cup fresh rosemary
- 1 teaspoon ground white pepper
- 1 cup heavy cream
- 1 cup fish stock
- 1 teaspoon salt
- 1 teaspoon lemon zest
- 1 teaspoon lemon juice
- 1 tablespoon fish sauce
- 1 teaspoon fresh oregano
- 1 teaspoon basil

Directions:
Chop the cod into 4 fillets and sprinkle them with the lemon juice. Rub the fish with the basil and oregano and set aside for 10 minutes. Meanwhile, chop the rosemary and combine it with salt, cream, and fish stock and stir well. Add the lemon zest. Sprinkle the mixture with white pepper and transfer it to the blender. Blend until smooth. Transfer the cod fillets in the air fryer basket and pour the cream mixture on top. Close the lid and cook for 15 minutes. Remove the cod from the air fryer and transfer it to the serving plate. Sprinkle it with the cream mixture and serve.

Bacon-wrapped Tilapia with Prunes

Prep time: 15 minutes
Cooking time: 17 minutes
Servings: 3

Ingredients:
- 3 tilapia fillets
- 3 bacon strips
- ½ cup dates, pitted
- ¼ cup fresh rosemary
- 1 teaspoon fresh basil
- 1 teaspoon fresh oregano
- 1 teaspoon turmeric
- ¼ cup water
- 1 teaspoon salt
- 1 teaspoon ground black pepper

Directions:
Take the bacon strips, sprinkle them with the pepper and stir well. Rub the tilapia fillets with the basil, oregano, rosemary, and salt. Sprinkle it with the turmeric. Chop the dates into the small pieces and stuff the tilapia fillets with the dates. Roll the tilapia fillets in the bacon strips. Chop the rosemary and sprinkle the fish with it. Transfer the tilapia in the air fryer and add the water. Close the lid and cook for 17 minutes. Remove it from the air fryer and serve.

Mackerel with Pecan and Bread Crumbs

Prep time: 15 minutes
Cooking time: 15 minutes
Servings: 3

Ingredients:

- 3 mackerel fillets
- ½ cup pecans
- 1 cup bread crumbs
- ¼ cup garlic
- 1 teaspoon olive oil
- 1 onion
- 6 ounces hard cheese
- 1 teaspoon thyme
- 3 lemon wedges

Directions:

Mince the garlic and rub the mackerel fillets with the garlic. Crush the pecans and combine them with the olive oil. Sprinkle the mixture with the bread crumbs. Peel the onion and dice it. Grate the hard cheese, combine it with the thyme and stir well. Transfer the mackerel fillets to the air fryer basket and sprinkle them with the diced onion. Add the grated cheese and sprinkle the dish with the bread crumbs. Close the lid and cook for 15 minutes. Remove the dish from the air fryer and let it cool. Serve the fish with the lemon wedges.

Stuffed Trout

Prep time: 15 minutes
Cooking time: 18 minutes
Servings: 3

Ingredients:

- 1 large trout
- 2 limes
- 1 green bell pepper
- 1½ teaspoon fresh thyme
- 1 tablespoon lemon juice
- 1 teaspoon sour cream
- 1 tablespoon garlic, minced
- 1 teaspoon nutmeg
- 1 red onion
- 1 teaspoon sugar
- 1 teaspoon salt
- ¼ cup fish stock

Dir_ctions:

Rub the trout with the garlic, nutmeg, and thyme and set it aside. Peel the onion and chop it. Transfer the onion in a mixing bowl, sprinkle it with the salt and sugar and stir well. Slice the lime into wedges. Remove the seeds from the bell pepper and chop it. Add the pepper to the onion mixture. Add the sour cream. In a mixing bowl, combine the fish stock and lemon juice and stir well. Fill the trout with the onion mixture. Add the lime wedges and transfer it to the air fryer basket. Pour the fish stock mixture and close the lid. Cook the fish for 18 minutes. When it is done, remove the dish from the air fryer and serve.

Tuna Rice Casserole

Prep time: 15 minutes
Cooking time: 18 minutes
Servings: 3

Ingredients:

- 1 pound tuna
- 1 cup basmati rice
- 1 teaspoon fresh basil
- 1 cup heavy cream
- 1 tablespoon starch
- 1 white onion
- 1 teaspoon ground ginger
- 2 garlic cloves
- 1 teaspoon salt
- ½ cup mushrooms
- 1 tablespoon olive oil
- 1 teaspoon apple cider vinegar
- ⅓ cup hard cheese
- 2 tablespoons flour
- 1 cup fish stock

Directions:

Take the tuna and mince it. Transfer the tuna in the mixing bowl, sprinkle it with the salt and ginger and stir well. Peel the onion and garlic cloves. Dice the vegetables and add them to the tuna mixture. Sprinkle the tuna with the flour and starch. In a separate bowl and transfer the rice to the bowl. Pour the fish stock into the bowl and set it aside. Slice the mushrooms and grate the hard cheese. Sprinkle the mushrooms with the apple cider vinegar and olive oil and stir well. Chop the basil. Combine the tuna mixture, mushroom mixture, and rice together in the mixing bowl, stirring well. Open the air fryer lid and transfer the mixture to the air fryer basket. Pour the cream into it and close the lid. Cook for 18 minutes. When the dish is done, remove it from the air fryer and let it cool briefly before serving.

Salmon Warm Salad

Prep time: 15 minutes
Cooking time: 14 minutes
Servings: 3

Ingredients:

- 1 cup green peas
- 1 pound salmon
- ½ cup fresh dill
- ¼ cup fresh celery root
- 1 tablespoon soy sauce
- 1 teaspoon lemon juice
- ⅓ cup lentils
- 2 tablespoons sour cream
- 4 tablespoons mayonnaise, for serving
- 1 cup chicken stock

Directions:

Chop the salmon into medium-sized pieces, sprinkle the fish with the lemon juice and soy sauce and stir well. Combine the lentils and peas in a mixing bowl. Add the sour cream and stir well. Grate the celery root and chop the fresh dill and combine the ingredients and transfer to the lentils and stir well. Combine the lentils and salmon together in a mixing bowl. Stir well and transfer the dish to the air fryer and add the chicken stock. Stir again, close the lid and cook for 14 minutes. Remove it from the air fryer and let it rest briefly. Serve with the mayonnaise.

Shrimp Stew

Prep time: 10 minutes
Cooking time: 12 minutes
Servings: 4

Ingredients:
- 5 garlic cloves
- 1 tablespoon fresh ginger
- 1 teaspoon cayenne pepper
- 9 ounces shrimp
- 1 teaspoon ground white pepper
- ½ teaspoon chile flakes
- 1 cup fresh basil
- 1 cup milk
- 1 tablespoon turmeric
- 1 teaspoon paprika
- 1 teaspoon salt
- 2 yellow onions

Directions:
Peel the onions and garlic cloves and chop them. Peel and devein the shrimp. Grate the ginger, combine it with the shrimp and stir well. Chop the basil and combine it with chile flakes, white pepper, cayenne pepper, turmeric, paprika, and salt and stir well. Add milk to the basil mixture and stir again. Open the air fryer lid and add the basil mixture. Add the shrimp and stir well. Close the lid and cook for 12 minutes. When the stew is cooked, remove it from the air fryer, stir and serve.

Couscous Lobster

Prep time: 15 minutes
Cooking time: 18 minutes
Servings: 2

Ingredients:
- 1 lobster
- 1 cup fresh dill
- 2 garlic cloves
- 1 cup millet
- 2 tablespoons butter
- 1 teaspoon ground black pepper
- 1 teaspoon salt
- 1 teaspoon fresh oregano
- 1 teaspoon fresh cilantro
- 2 cups fish stock

Directions:
Cut the lobster across the bottom, remove the meat from the shell and chop it. In a mixing bowl, combine the lobster and millet. Stir well and sprinkle the mixture with the salt, oregano, cilantro, and pepper. Add the butter and stir it well. Peel the garlic cloves and chop them. Fill the lobster with the millet mixture and sprinkle it with the chopped garlic. Transfer the lobster meat to the air fryer and pour the fish stock on top. Close the lid and cook for 18 minutes. When the dish is cooked, remove the dish from the air fryer and transfer it to a serving plate.

Crunchy Cheesy Halibut

Prep time: 15 minutes
Cooking time: 15 minutes
Servings: 4

Ingredients:
- 4 halibut fillets
- 2 tablespoons lemon juice
- 1 teaspoon olive oil
- 1 teaspoon fresh basil
- 1 teaspoon fresh cilantro
- 1 teaspoon ground ginger
- 1 teaspoon black pepper
- 1 tablespoon paprika
- 1 egg
- ¼ cup flour
- 1 teaspoon salt
- 1 cup bread crumbs

Directions:

Rub the halibut fillets with the salt, pepper, and ginger. Sprinkle the fish with the lemon juice. Combine the bread crumbs, paprika, cilantro, and basil in a mixing bowl and stir well. Beat the egg in a separate bowl and whisk it. Add the flour and olive oil and continue to whisk it until smooth. Take the halibut fillets and dip them in the egg mixture. Sprinkle the fish with the bread crumbs mixture well. Transfer the fish fillets to the air fryer and close the lid. Cook for 15 minutes. When the fish is cooked, remove it from the air fryer and let it rest briefly before serving.

Mackerel with Lentils Sauce

Prep time: 20 minutes
Cooking time: 17 minutes
Servings: 3

Ingredients:
- 3 mackerel fillets
- 1 tablespoon lemon juice
- 1 tablespoon minced garlic
- 1 teaspoon fresh thyme
- 1 teaspoon salt
- 1 cup heavy cream
- ½ cup lentils
- 1 teaspoon dried dill
- 1 tablespoon fresh parsley
- 1 egg

Directions:

Chop the mackerel roughly and transfer it to the mixing bowl. Sprinkle the fish with the lemon juice and minced garlic. Stir well and leave the mixture. Then combine the cream with the thyme, lentils, and dry dill and stir well. In a separate bowl, add the egg and salt and whisk. Chop the parsley and add it to the egg. Pour the egg mixture on the fish and stir well. Transfer the fish in the air fryer and add the cream mixture. Close the air fryer lid and cook for 17 minutes. When the fish is cooked, remove it from the air fryer and serve.

Salmon Fritters

Prep time: 15 minutes
Cooking time: 13 minutes
Servings: 4

Ingredients:

- 3 cups minced salmon
- 1½ cups spinach
- 1 egg
- 1 teaspoon salt
- 1 teaspoon fresh oregano
- 1 tablespoon fresh basil
- ½ tablespoon cornstarch
- 1 tablespoon heavy cream
- 1 tablespoon minced garlic
- 1 teaspoon paprika

Directions:

Beat the egg in a mixing bowl. Whisk until smooth. Sprinkle the egg with the salt, oregano, cornstarch, and minced garlic and stir well. Add the paprika and cream and stir well. Chop the spinach, add it to the egg mixture and stir well. Add the salmon and knead the dough for fritters. Make round fritters and press them flat. Transfer the fritters in the air fryer and close the lid. Cook for 13 minutes. Remove the fritters from the air fryer, let them rest briefly before serving.

Seafood Pizza

Prep time: 15 minutes
Cooking time: 20 minutes
Servings: 3

Ingredients:

- 7 ounces pizza dough
- 1 cup shrimp
- ½ cup clams
- ½ cup fresh dill
- 1 tablespoon sour cream
- 1 tablespoon tomato sauce
- 1 teaspoon minced garlic
- 1 teaspoon salt
- 1 teaspoon soy sauce
- 2 ounces salmon
- 1 tablespoon lemon juice

Directions:

Peel and devein the shrimp. In a mixing bowl, combine the shrimp and clams. Sprinkle it with the soy sauce and stir. Chop the salmon roughly and add to the seafood mixture. Sprinkle the seafood with the minced garlic, salt, and lemon juice and stir well. Chop the dill. Roll the pizza dough using a rolling pin. Combine the tomato sauce and sour cream together in a mixing bowl and stir well. Spread the pizza dough with the tomato sauce and sprinkle it with half of the dill. Transfer the seafood mixture to the pizza dough and sprinkle it with the remaining dill. Transfer the pizza to the air fryer basket and close the lid. Cook for 20 minutes, then cut into slices and serve.

Seafood Salad with Noodles

Prep time: 15 minutes
Cooking time: 14 minutes
Servings: 4

Ingredients:

- 8 ounces rice noodles
- 3 cup chicken stock
- 1 cup scallops
- 1 cup shrimp
- 1 tablespoon lemon juice
- 1 teaspoon soy sauce
- 1 teaspoon salt
- 1 teaspoon fresh oregano
- 1 teaspoon fresh basil
- 1 teaspoon paprika
- ½ teaspoon cayenne pepper
- 1 tablespoon apple cider vinegar
- 1 carrot
- 1 cucumber, for serving

Directions:

Transfer the rice noodles in the air fryer basket. Peel the carrot and make the spirals using a spiralizer. Peel and devein the shrimp and chop them. Add the spiraled carrot and seafood to the air fryer. Combine the apple cider vinegar, cayenne pepper, paprika, basil, salt, soy sauce, and lemon juice in a mixing bowl. Add the chicken stock and stir well. Pour the liquid into the air fryer and close the lid. Cook for 14 minutes. Slice the cucumber. When the dish is cooked, remove it from the air fryer and top it with the sliced cucumber and serve.

Seafood Pie

Prep time: 10 minutes
Cooking time: 30 minutes
Servings: 3

Ingredients:

- ½ cup salmon
- ⅓ cup halibut
- 1 egg
- 1 cup heavy cream
- 1 cup flour
- 1 teaspoon salt
- 1 teaspoon paprika
- 1 teaspoon baking soda
- ½ teaspoon fresh basil
- ½ teaspoon fresh oregano
- 1 teaspoon fresh cilantro
- 1 onion
- ½ teaspoon turmeric

Directions:

Peel the onion and dice it. Dice the halibut and salmon and combine in a mixing bowl with the onion. Sprinkle the mixture with the salt, paprika, basil, oregano, cilantro, and turmeric. Stir well again. In another bowl, beat the egg and add the cream, flour, and baking soda. Mix well. Take the air fryer form and pour the 1 of the batter. Add the fish mixture. Add the remainder of the batter. Transfer the form to the air fryer and close the lid. Cook it for 30 minutes. When the pie is cooked, remove it from the air fryer, let it rest briefly, let them rest briefly before slicing and serving.

Paella

Preparation time: 10 minutes
Cooking time: 30 minutes
Servings: 4

Ingredients:

- 5 ounces paella rice
- 2 ounces peas
- 1 red bell pepper, seeded and chopped
- 14 ounces dry white wine
- 3.5 ounces water
- 2 sachets herbs
- 2 ounces squid
- 7 ounces mussels
- 3.5 ounces sea bass fillet, chopped
- 6 scallops
- 3.5 ounces clams
- 4 shrimp
- 4 crawfish
- Salt and ground black pepper, to taste
- Olive oil
- 1 lemon, sliced

Directions:

In a heatproof dish that fits the air fryer, mix the sea bass with shrimp, mussels, scallops, crawfish, clams, and squid. Add the oil, salt, and pepper and toss to coat. In a bowl, mix the peas with the herbs, salt, pepper, bell pepper, and rice and stir. Combine this with the seafood and add the wine and water. Place the dish in the air fryer at 400°F and cook for 30 minutes, stirring halfway. Serve with a lemon slice on the side.

Crunchy Shrimp

Preparation time: 10 minutes
Cooking time: 5 minutes
Servings: 4

Ingredients:

- 12 large shrimp, deveined and peeled
- 1 egg white
- 1 cup coconut, dry
- 1 cup panko bread crumbs
- 1 tablespoon cornstarch
- 1 cup white flour
- Salt and ground black pepper, to taste

Directions:

Pat the shrimp dry and place them on a cutting board. In a bowl, mix the bread crumbs with the coconut. In a second bowl, mix the flour with cornstarch. In a third bowl, whisk the egg whites. Dip the shrimp in the flour, the then egg whites and then the coconut mix and place them all in the air fryer's basket. Cook at 350°F for 10 minutes, turning them after 5 minutes.

Cajun Shrimp

Preparation time: 10 minutes
Cooking time: 5 minutes
Servings: 2

Ingredients:

- 20 tiger shrimp, peeled and deveined
- Salt and ground black pepper, to taste
- ½ teaspoon Old Bay Seasoning
- 1 tablespoon extra virgin olive oil
- Cayenne pepper
- ¼ teaspoon smoked paprika
- White rice, already cooked, for serving

Directions:

In a bowl, mix the shrimp with the oil, salt, pepper, Old Bay Seasoning, cayenne pepper, and paprika and toss to coat. Place the shrimp in the air fryer's basket and cook at 390°F for 5 minutes. Serve them with the rice.

Spicy Shrimp

Preparation time: 4 hours
Cooking time: 10 minutes
Servings: 4

Ingredients:

- 1 pound large shrimp, peeled and deveined
- 1 teaspoon red pepper flakes
- 2 tablespoons olive oil
- 1 teaspoon Tabasco sauce
- 2 tablespoons water
- 1 teaspoon oregano, dried
- Salt and ground black pepper, to taste
- ½ teaspoon parsley, dried
- ½ teaspoon garlic powder
- ½ teaspoon smoked paprika

Directions:

In a bowl, mix the oil with water, Tabasco sauce, pepper flakes, oregano, parsley, salt, pepper, garlic powder, and paprika and stir well. Add the shrimp, toss to coat, cover, and keep refrigerated for 4 hours. Drain the shrimp, place them in the air fryer's basket and cook at 370°F for 10 minutes. Divide shrimp on plates and serve with a side salad.

Garlic Shrimp

Preparation time: 1 hour
Cooking time: 6 minutes
Servings: 4

Ingredients:
- 8 large shrimp, peeled and deveined
- 4 garlic cloves, peeled and minced
- Salt and ground black pepper, to taste
- 8 green bell pepper slices
- 1 rosemary sprig, chopped
- ½ tablespoon butter, melted

Directions:

In a bowl, mix the shrimp with garlic, butter, salt, pepper, rosemary, and bell pepper, toss to coat and set aside for 1 hour. Arrange 2 shrimp and 2 bell pepper slices on a skewer. Repeat with the other shrimp and bell pepper slices. Place them in the air fryer and cook at 360°F for 7 minutes. Arrange on plates and serve.

Crispy Fish Fillets

Preparation time: 10 minutes
Cooking time: 12 minutes
Servings: 2

Ingredients:
- 3.5 ounces bread crumbs
- 4 tablespoons vegetable oil
- 1 egg
- 4 white fish fillets, boneless
- 1 lemon, sliced
- Salt and ground black pepper, to taste

Directions:

In a bowl, mix the bread crumbs with the oil and stir well. Put the egg in a bowl and whisk it. Dip the fish fillets in the egg and then in the bread crumb mix until they are covered entirely. Place them in the air fryer's basket and cook at 360°F for 12 minutes. Divide between plates and serve with chips on the side and lemon slices on top.

Fish Nuggets

Preparation time: 10 minutes
Cooking time: 12 minutes
Servings: 4

Ingredients:

- 28 ounces fish fillets, skinless and cut into medium chunks
- Salt and ground black pepper, to taste
- 5 tablespoons flour
- 1 egg
- 5 tablespoons water
- 3.5 ounces panko bread crumbs
- 1 tablespoon garlic powder
- 1 tablespoon smoked paprika
- 4 tablespoons mayonnaise
- Lemon juice from ½ lemon
- 1 teaspoon dried dill
- Vegetable oil cooking spray

Directions:

Pat the fish chunks dry and season them with salt and pepper. In a bowl, mix flour with water and stir well. Add egg and whisk the mixture again. In a second bowl, mix the bread crumbs with the garlic powder and paprika and stir well. Dip the fish pieces in the flour and egg mixture and then in bread crumbs until they are well coated. Place them in a lined baking dish, spray them with some cooking oil and place them into the air fryer. Cook at 400°F for 12 minutes. In a bowl mix the mayonnaise with the dill and lemon juice, stir well and keep refrigerated until the fish is done. Serve fish nuggets with the seasoned mayonnaise.

Glazed Salmon

Preparation time: 2 hours
Cooking time: 15 minutes
Servings: 2

Ingredients:

- 2 medium salmon fillets
- 6 tablespoons soy sauce
- 3 teaspoons mirin
- 1 teaspoon water
- 6 tablespoons honey

Directions:

Mix the soy sauce with honey, water, and mirin in a bowl and whisk well. Add the salmon fillets, toss to coat and let marinate in the refrigerator for 2 hours. Place the salmon fillets in the air fryer and cook at 360°F for 8 minutes. Flip and cook for 5 minutes. Pour the marinade into a pan and heat up on medium heat. Cook for 2 minutes and take off heat. Divide salmon between plates and serve with the sauce drizzled on top.

Crispy Fish Steak with Plum Sauce

Preparation time: 10 minutes
Cooking time: 20 minutes
Servings: 2

Ingredients:
- 2 large cod steaks
- Salt and ground black pepper, to taste
- ½ teaspoon garlic powder
- ½ teaspoon ground ginger
- ¼ teaspoon turmeric
- 1 tablespoon plum sauce
- ½ cup seasoned flour
- ½ cup corn flour
- Ginger slices for serving
- Vegetable oil cooking spray

Directions:
Pat the cod steaks dry and season them with salt and pepper. In a bowl, mix the ginger with turmeric and garlic powder and stir. In another bowl, combine the flours. Add the cod steaks and toss to coat. Dredge the cod in the flour mixture and coat evenly. Place the cod steaks in the air fryer and cook at 360°F for 15 minutes. Increase heat to 400°F and cook for 5 minutes. Heat up a pan on medium-high heat, add the ginger and brown for a few minutes. Add the plum sauce, take off the heat and stir well. Place the cod steaks on plates and serve with plum sauce on top.

Lemony Salmon

Preparation time: 2 hours
Cooking time: 8 minutes
Servings: 2

Ingredients:
- 2 salmon fillets, 7 ounces each
- Juice of 1 lemon
- Salt and ground black pepper, to taste
- Garlic powder
- ⅓ cup water
- ⅓ cup soy sauce
- Scallion slices, for serving
- ⅓ cup brown sugar
- 2 tablespoons olive oil
- Cherry tomatoes, for serving

Directions:
Pat the salmon fillets dry and season them with salt, pepper and garlic powder. In a bowl, mix the sugar with water, soy sauce, oil, and lemon juice and whisk well. Add the salmon fillets, toss to coat and let marinate in the refrigerator for 2 hours. Place the salmon fillets in the fryer's basket and cook at 360°F for 8 minutes. Serve with cherry tomatoes and scallion slices on top.

Salmon with Lemon and Capers

Preparation time: 10 minutes
Cooking time: 20 minutes
Servings: 4

Ingredients:

- 4 salmon fillets, 6 ounces each
- 1 tablespoon capers, drained
- Salt and ground black pepper, to taste
- Juice of 1 lemon
- 2 teaspoons olive oil
- 2 tablespoons olive oil
- 1 tablespoon dill, dried
- 21 ounces potatoes, chopped
- ½ cup milk
- Salt and pepper, to taste

Directions:

Put some water in a pot, add the potatoes and salt, bring to a boil on medium-high heat, cook for 15 minutes, drain them, transfer to a bowl and reserve a ½ cup cooking liquid. Mash the potatoes using a potato masher, add milk, 2 tablespoons oil, dill, salt and pepper, to taste and stir well. Add the reserved liquid, stir again and set aside. Season the salmon with salt and pepper, drizzle 2 teaspoons oil on them and rub. Place the salmon on the air fryer's grill skin side down, add the capers on top, cook at 360°F for 8 minutes and transfer to plates. Drizzle the lemon juice on them and serve with mashed potatoes on the side.

Fish and Tomatoes

Preparation time: 10 minutes
Cooking time: 30 minutes
Servings: 4

Ingredients:

- 12 ounces cherry tomatoes, cut in halves
- 8 garlic cloves, minced
- 1 tablespoon lemon zest, grated
- ⅓ cup extra virgin olive oil
- 4 medium snapper fillets
- 1½ tablespoons capers, drained
- Lemon juice from 1 lemon
- Salt and ground black pepper, to taste

Directions:

Put the tomatoes in a baking dish that fits the air fryer. Add the garlic, capers, lemon zest, half of the oil, some salt and pepper, toss to coat, Place the dish in the air fryer and cook at 350°F for 15 minutes. Add the fish, the rest of the oil, more salt and pepper and bake for 15 minutes. Divide the fish and tomato mix on plates, drizzle the lemon juice, and serve.

Saba Fish with Garlic and Lemon

Preparation time: 10 minutes
Cooking time: 8 minutes
Servings: 1

Ingredients:
- 1 saba fish fillets
- Salt and ground black pepper, to taste
- 1 red chile pepper, chopped
- Lemon juice
- 1 tablespoon olive oil
- 1 tablespoon garlic, minced

Directions:
Pat the fish dry, season it with salt and pepper and place on a piece of aluminum foil, skin side down. Add some lemon juice, oil, chile pepper and garlic toss to coat, transfer to the air fryer and cook at 360°F for 8 minutes. Serve with potato chips.

Halibut Steak

Preparation time: 20 minutes
Cooking time: 10 minutes
Servings: 3

Ingredients:
- 1 pound halibut steak
- ⅔ cup soy sauce
- ¼ cup sugar
- 2 tablespoons lime juice
- ½ cup mirin
- ¼ teaspoon red pepper flakes, crushed
- ¼ cup orange juice
- ¼ teaspoon ginger, grated
- 1 garlic clove, minced

Directions:
Put the soy sauce in a pan and heat up on medium heat. Add the mirin, sugar, lime juice, orange juice, pepper flakes, ginger, and garlic. Stir well, bring to a boil, and take off heat. Transfer half of the marinade to a container, add the halibut, toss to coat and let marinate in the refrigerator for 30 minutes. Place the halibut in the air fryer and cook at 390°F for 10 minutes. Brush fish with the rest of the marinade, divide between plates, and serve on white rice.

Salmon Cakes

Preparation time: 1 hour
Cooking time: 7 minutes
Servings: 4

Ingredients:
- 9 ounces cooked salmon, flaked
- Salt and ground black pepper, to taste
- 14 ounces mashed potatoes
- ½ cup parsley, chopped
- Zest from 1 lemon
- 2 tablespoons flour
- Vegetable oil cooking spray
- ½ cup capers, drained

Directions:
In a bowl, mix the salmon with mashed potato, parsley, zest, flour, capers, salt and pepper and stir well. Shape patties, dust them with some flour and keep in the fridge for 1 hour. Place cakes in the air fryer's basket and cook at 360°F for 7 minutes. Divide between plates and serve with a side dish.

Cod with Tomato Vinaigrette

Preparation time: 10 minutes
Cooking time: 15 minutes
Servings: 4

Ingredients:

- 4 cod steaks
- 12 cherry tomatoes, cut in halves
- 8 black olives, pitted and roughly chopped
- Juice of ½ lemon
- Salt and ground black pepper, to taste
- 2 tablespoons olive oil
- Vegetable oil cooking spray
- 1 bunch basil, torn

Directions:

Season the cod with salt and pepper, to taste, place the fish in the air fryer's basket and cook at 360°F for 10 minutes. Heat up a pan with the olive oil on medium heat, add the tomatoes, olives, and lemon juice, stir, and bring to a simmer. Take off the heat, add the basil, salt and pepper, stir well, and keep warm until fish is done. Divide the fish between plates and serve with the tomato vinaigrette on top.

Shrimp Rolls

Preparation time: 10 minutes
Cooking time: 15 minutes
Servings: 4

Ingredients:

- ½ pound already cooked shrimp, chopped
- 8 ounces water chestnuts, chopped
- ½ pounds shiitake mushrooms, chopped
- 2 cups cabbage, finely chopped
- 2 tablespoons grape seed oil
- 1 garlic clove, minced
- 1 teaspoon ginger, minced
- 3 scallions, chopped
- Salt and ground black pepper, to taste
- 1 tablespoon water
- 1 egg yolk
- 6 spring roll wrappers

Directions:

Heat up a pan with half of the oil on medium-high heat, add cabbage, stir, cook for 2-3 minutes and transfer to a bowl. Place pan on the heat again, add the mushrooms, garlic, ginger, and scallions, stir, cook for 3 minutes, and transfer to another bowl. In a bowl, mix the egg with water and stir well. Arrange the roll wrappers on a working surface, divide the shrimp and add the vegetables on them, season with salt and pepper, roll, seal edges with egg wash and place all in the air fryer's basket. Cook at 360°F for 15 minutes. Serve hot.

Baked Seafood Casserole

Preparation time: 10 minutes
Cooking time: 30 minutes
Servings: 6

Ingredients:

- 1 pound shrimp, deveined and peeled
- 1 pound scallops
- 1 pound crabmeat, flaked
- 12 ounces Mozzarella cheese, grated
- 2 pounds haddock, boneless and cut into small pieces
- 2½ cups crackers, crumbled
- ½ cup butter, melted
- Salt and ground black pepper, to taste
- 1½ teaspoon Worcestershire sauce
- 1 teaspoon garlic powder

Directions:

Butter a baking dish that fits the air fryer. Add the scallops, shrimp, crabmeat, and haddock. Sprinkle the cheese onto seafood. In a bowl, mix the Worcestershire sauce with salt, pepper, butter, garlic powder, and cracker crumbs and stir. Spread this onto the cheese, Place the dish in the air fryer and cook at 320°F for 30 minutes, shaking halfway through. Divide between plates and serve.

Seafood Salad

Preparation time: 10 minutes
Cooking time: 25 minutes
Servings: 4

Ingredients:

- ½ cup yellow onion, peeled and chopped
- 1 cup green bell pepper, seeded and chopped
- 1 cup celery, chopped
- 1 cup baby shrimp, peeled and deveined
- 1 cup crabmeat, flaked
- 1 cup mayonnaise
- 1 teaspoon Worcestershire sauce
- Salt and ground black pepper, to taste
- 2 tablespoons bread crumbs
- 1 tablespoon butter
- 1 teaspoon paprika
- 4 lemon wedges

Directions:

In a bowl, mix the shrimp with crabmeat, bell pepper, onion, mayonnaise, celery, salt, and pepper and stir. Add the Worcestershire sauce, stir again and pour everything into a baking dish that fits the air fryer. Sprinkle bread crumbs and add butter, put the dish Place the dish in the air fryer and cook at 320°F for 25 minutes, shaking halfway through. Divide between plates and serve with paprika sprinkled on top and with lemon wedges on the side.

Seafood Casserole

Preparation time: 10 minutes
Cooking time: 40 minutes
Servings: 6

Ingredients:

- 6 tablespoons butter
- 2 ounces mushrooms, chopped
- 1 green bell pepper, seeded and chopped
- 1 celery stalk, chopped
- 2 garlic cloves, peeled and minced
- 1 small yellow onion, peeled and chopped
- Salt and ground black pepper, to taste
- 4 tablespoons flour
- ½ cup white wine
- 1½ cups milk
- ½ cup heavy cream
- 4 sea scallops, sliced
- 4 ounces haddock, skinless, boneless, and cut in small pieces
- 4 ounces lobster meat, cooked and cut into small pieces
- ½ teaspoon mustard powder
- 1 tablespoon lemon juice
- ⅓ cup bread crumbs
- Salt and ground black pepper, to taste
- 3 tablespoons cheddar cheese, grated
- ½ cup fresh parsley, chopped
- 1 teaspoon sweet paprika

Directions:

Heat up a pan with 4 tablespoons butter on medium-high heat, add the bell pepper, mushrooms, celery, garlic, and onion, stir, and cook for 8 minutes. Add the wine, stir, and cook for 3 minutes. Add the flour, stir well, and cook for 2 minutes. Add the cream and milk, stir, bring to a simmer, and cook for 4 minutes. Add the lemon juice, salt, pepper, mustard powder, scallops, lobster meat, and haddock, stir well, cook for 1 minute, take off the heat and divide this mix into 6 ramekins. In a bowl, mix the rest of the butter with bread crumbs, paprika, and cheese. Sprinkle this atop the seafood mixture, place the ramekins in the air fryer's basket and cook at 370°F for 16 minutes. Serve with parsley sprinkled on top.

Mahi Mahi Strips

Preparation time: 10 minutes
Cooking time: 10 minutes
Servings: 5

Ingredients:

- 20 ounces mahi-mahi, cut in medium sticks
- Vegetable oil cooking spray
- Salt and ground black pepper, to taste
- 1 cup almonds, chopped
- 2 eggs
- ½ cup bread crumbs
- 1 cup almond butter
- 4 teaspoons soy sauce
- ¼ cup lemon juice
- 1 teaspoon almond oil
- ¼ cup water

Directions:

In a blender, mix the almonds with the bread crumbs, pulse well and transfer to a bowl. In another bowl, whisk the eggs with salt and pepper. Dip the fish sticks in egg mixture, then in crumb mixture, place them all in the air fryer's basket, spray some cooking oil on them, and cook at 400°F for 10 minutes, flipping them halfway through. In the blender, combine the almond butter with the soy sauce, lemon juice, almond oil, and water and blend well. Transfer this to a bowl and serve with the fish sticks.

Baked Catfish

Preparation time: 10 minutes
Cooking time: 16 minutes
Servings: 4

Ingredients:

- 4 catfish fillets
- Salt and ground black pepper, to taste
- 2 tablespoons fresh parsley, chopped
- ¾ teaspoon paprika
- ½ teaspoon dried oregano
- ½ teaspoon dried thyme
- ½ teaspoon dried basil
- Juice of 1 lemon
- 2 tablespoons butter, melted
- Vegetable oil cooking spray
- ¼ teaspoon garlic powder

Directions:

In a bowl, mix the parsley with the salt, pepper, oregano, thyme, paprika and basil and stir. Add the fish fillets and toss to coat. Place fillets in a baking dish that fits the air fryer's basket and spray cooking oil on them. In a bowl, mix the lemon juice with the garlic powder and lemon juice and stir well. Pour this on fish and cook at 320°F for 16 minutes, turning halfway through.

Salt-crusted Salmon

Preparation time: 15 minutes
Cooking time: 15 minutes
Servings: 4

Ingredients:

- 1 pound salmon fillets, skin on
- 1 tablespoon honey
- 2 egg whites, whisked
- 1½ pounds rock salt
- 1 cilantro sprig, chopped
- 6 tablespoons vinegar
- 1 shallot, chopped
- 6 tablespoons water
- 1 cup Greek yogurt
- ½ cup fresh cilantro, chopped
- Olive oil
- Salt and pepper, to taste

Directions:

Pat the salmon fillets dry and place them on a cutting board. In a bowl, mix the salt with the egg whites, cilantro, and honey. Spread ⅓ of this mix into a baking dish that fits the air fryer. Add the salmon fillets and spread the rest of the salt mixture on them. Place dish in the air fryer and cook at 420°F for 15 minutes. Heat a pan on medium-high heat, add the shallot, water, and vinegar, stir and cook for a couple of minutes. Add the cilantro, yogurt, salt, and pepper, stir well, take off heat, and transfer to a bowl. Take the salmon out of the air fryer, discard the salt crust and divide fish between plates. Drizzle yogurt sauce onto the fish and serve.

Cod Curry

Preparation time: 10 minutes
Cooking time: 16 minutes
Servings: 4

Ingredients:

- 4 cod fillets
- 1½ cups coconut milk
- 2 teaspoons curry paste
- A handful cilantro, chopped
- Salt and ground black pepper, to taste
- 2 teaspoons ginger, grated

Directions:

Heat a pan on medium-high heat, add the coconut milk, curry paste, and ginger, stir well, and cook for 3-4 minutes. Pour some of the sauce in a baking dish that fits the air fryer. Add the fish, season with salt and pepper and top with the rest of the curry mix. Place the dish in the air fryer at 470°F and bake for 16 minutes, shaking halfway through. Divide on plates, sprinkle with cilantro and drizzle the sauce onto the fish.

Tuscan-style Baked Tilapia

Preparation time: 10 minutes
Cooking time: 10 minutes
Servings: 4

Ingredients:

- Zest from 1 lime, grated
- Juice from 1 lime
- 4 medium tilapia fillets
- 2 tablespoons butter
- Salt and ground black pepper, to taste
- Vegetable oil cooking spray

Directions:

Pat the tilapia fillets dry, season with salt and pepper to taste, and mix with the lime juice and lime zest. Place the fish fillets in you air fryer's basket, spray them with cooking oil, add butter on top, and cook at 350°F for 10 minutes, turning them halfway through. Arrange on a platter and serve.

Pesto Salmon

Preparation time: 10 minutes
Cooking time: 16 minutes
Servings: 2

Ingredients:

- 2 salmon fillets, boneless
- ¾ cup pecans
- 1½ cups fresh basil
- ¼ cup olive oil
- ¼ cup Pecorino cheese, shredded
- 4 garlic cloves, peeled
- Salt and ground black pepper, to taste
- Vegetable oil cooking spray

Directions:

Pat the salmon dry, season the fillets with salt and pepper, place them in the air fryer's basket, spray some cooking oil on them, and cook at 370°F for 16 minutes, turning once. In a food processor, mix the basil with the pecans, cheese, olive oil, garlic, some salt and pepper and blend well. Divide the salmon fillets between plates and serve with the pesto drizzled on top.

Salmon Meatballs with Avocado Sauce

Preparation time: 10 minutes
Cooking time: 12 minutes
Servings: 4

Ingredients:

- 3 tablespoons cilantro, minced
- 1 pound salmon, skinless and chopped
- 1 small yellow onion, peeled and chopped
- 1 egg white
- Salt and ground black pepper, to taste
- 2 garlic cloves, peeled and minced
- ½ teaspoon paprika
- ¼ cup panko bread crumbs
- ½ teaspoon dried oregano
- Vegetable oil cooking spray
- 1 avocado, pitted and peeled
- 1 garlic clove, peeled and minced
- 3 tablespoons yogurt
- 2 tablespoons fresh cilantro, minced
- Juice of ½ lime
- 5 tablespoons water
- Salt and ground black pepper, to taste
- ½ teaspoon chili powder

Directions:

In a food processor, mix the salmon with the onion, cilantro, egg white, garlic, salt, pepper, paprika, and oregano, and stir well. Add the bread crumbs, blend again and shape meatballs from this mixture using your hands. Place them in the air fryer's basket, spray them with cooking spray and cook at 320°F for 12 minutes, shaking the fryer halfway through. In a blender, mix the avocado with the yogurt, garlic, lime juice, water, cilantro, chili powder, salt, and pepper and blend well. Divide salmon meatballs between plates and serve with avocado sauce drizzled on top.

Sole Fillets

Preparation time: 10 minutes
Cooking time: 12 minutes
Servings: 6

Ingredients:

- 10 small sole fillets
- 1 lime, sliced
- Juice from 1 lime
- ½ cup butter, melted
- ½ cup olive oil
- 3 garlic cloves, peeled and minced
- 2 shallots, peeled and chopped
- 2 tablespoons capers
- Salt and ground black pepper, to taste
- 1 teaspoon garlic powder
- 1 teaspoon cumin
- 6 green onions, chopped
- ¾ cup fresh dill, chopped

Directions:

In a bowl, mix the oil with butter, salt, pepper, lime juice, garlic, capers and shallots and stir well. In another bowl, mix the cumin with the garlic powder. Add this spice mixture to the fish fillets, place them in a baking dish that fits the air fryer, add the butter mixture, lime slices, and green onions. Place in the air fryer and cook at 360°F for 12 minutes. Divide the fish between plates, sprinkle with dill and serve.

Salmon with Strawberries and Lemon

Preparation time: 15 minutes
Cooking time: 12 minutes
Servings: 2

Ingredients:
- 2 medium salmon fillets
- 1 tablespoon honey
- ½ cup strawberries, hulled and chopped
- 1 tablespoon olive oil
- Juice of ½ lemon
- Lemon slices for serving
- Black pepper, to taste
- Vegetable oil cooking spray

Directions:
Put the strawberries in a blender and puree until smooth. Transfer the puree to a bowl, add the honey, oil, a pinch of black pepper, and lemon juice and whisk well. Add the salmon fillets and let marinate in the refrigerator for 15 minutes. Transfer the salmon in a baking dish that fits the air fryer, brush the fish with strawberry marinade, spray some cooking oil on top, and cook at 400°F for 12 minutes. Serve with lemon slices on top.

Whitefish with Vegetables

Preparation time: 10 minutes
Cooking time: 18 minutes
Servings: 4

Ingredients:
- 2 red onions, peeled and cut into chunks
- 2 zucchinis, cut into medium chunks
- 3 tomatoes, cored and cut into wedges
- ¼ cup black olives, pitted and cut in halves
- 4 medium white fish fillets
- ¼ cup olive oil
- Salt and ground black pepper, to taste
- 1 garlic clove, peeled and minced
- 1 tablespoon mustard
- 1 tablespoon lemon juice
- ½ cup fresh parsley, chopped

Directions:
In a baking dish that fits the air fryer, mix the onion with the zucchini, olives, and tomatoes. Add 1 tablespoon of the oil and toss to coat. Brush the fish with another tablespoon of the oil and add on top of the vegetables. Place the dish in the air fryer at 370°F and bake for 18 minutes. In a bowl, mix the rest of the oil with the lemon juice, mustard and garlic and whisk well. Divide fish and vegetables on plates, drizzle with the lemon dressing, and serve.

Poultry

Chicken Casserole

Prep time: 20 minutes
Cooking time: 20 minutes
Servings: 6

Ingredients:

- 9 ounces boneless and skinless chicken breast
- 2 white onions
- 1 teaspoon fresh thyme
- 1 teaspoon coriander
- 1 teaspoon fresh basil
- 2 carrots
- ½ cup celery
- ⅓ cup bread crumbs
- 1 teaspoon salt
- 2 sweet potatoes
- ½ cup broccoli
- 1 cup heavy cream
- 1 cup chicken stock

Directions:

Take the chicken fillet and cut it into strips. Sprinkle the chicken strips with the salt and basil. Wash the carrot, peel and slice it. Peel the onions and dice them. Peel the sweet potatoes and chop them. Chop the celery. Wash the broccoli. In a mixing bowl, combine all the vegetables. Stir the mixture and add the coriander and thyme and stir. Transfer the chicken strips into the air fryer basket and add the vegetables. Pour the mixture with cream on top. Sprinkle the casserole with the bread crumbs. Add the chicken stock and close the lid. Cook for 20 minutes. When the dish is cooked, serve immediately.

Chicken Neck Soup with Dumplings

Prep time: 20 minutes
Cooking time: 18 minutes
Servings: 6

Ingredients:

- 5 cups chicken stock
- 1 cup flour
- 14 ounces chicken necks
- 1 onion
- 1 egg
- 1 teaspoon salt
- ½ teaspoon baking soda
- ½ cup water
- 1 carrot
- 1 cup fresh dill
- 1 bay leaf
- ½ teaspoon fresh rosemary
- 1 tablespoon sour cream
- 1 teaspoon paprika

Directions:

In a mixing bowl, beat the egg. Add the water and stir well. Combine the flour and baking soda and add this to the egg. Sprinkle it with salt and knead the dough and set aside. Peel the onion and carrot and chop them. Chop the dill and combine it with the vegetables. Place the chicken necks into the air fryer and add the vegetable mixture. Pour the chicken stock on top and add the dill, bay leaf, rosemary, paprika, and sour cream. Make the small dumplings from the dough and add them to the air fryer basket. Close the lid and cook for 18 minutes. When the soup is done, transfer it to the serving bowls and serve.

Chicken Marsala

Prep time: 10 minutes
Cooking time: 20 minutes
Servings: 4

Ingredients:

- ¾ cup marsala
- 1 cup mushrooms
- 2 chicken breast, boneless and skinless
- 2 cup chicken stock
- ½ cup flour
- 2 tablespoons butter
- 1 teaspoon salt
- 1 teaspoon ground black pepper
- 1 teaspoon garlic powder
- ½ teaspoon onion powder
- 1 teaspoon fresh thyme
- 1 bay leaf
- ½ teaspoon cayenne pepper

Directions:

Chop the chicken breasts. In a mixing bowl, combine flour, garlic powder, onion powder, thyme, and cayenne pepper. Add the chopped chicken and stir well. Remove the chicken from the flour and add them to the air fryer basket. Slice the mushrooms and sprinkle them with the salt, ground black pepper, and butter and stir well. Add the mushrooms in the air fryer basket. Add the bay leaf, marsala, and chicken stock and stir well. Close the lid and cook for 20 minutes. When it is cooked, remove the dish from the air fryer and serve.

Chicken Stew with Gnocchi

Prep time: 15 minutes
Cooking time: 20 minutes
Servings: 4

Ingredients:

- 2 carrots
- 1 cup mashed potatoes
- 3 tablespoons flour
- 1 egg
- 1 teaspoon salt
- 4 boneless and skinless chicken breasts
- 1 onion
- ½ cup fresh dill
- 1 teaspoon fresh oregano
- 1 teaspoon fresh cilantro
- 1 teaspoon minced garlic
- 1 teaspoon grated ginger
- 2 cups chicken stock

Directions:

Combine the flour and potatoes together to make the gnocchi. Beat the egg in a bowl, season with the salt and add to the potato mixture. Knead the dough. Chop the chicken into medium-sized pieces. Sprinkle the meat with the cilantro, oregano, garlic, and ginger and stir well. Peel the onion and carrot and dice the vegetables. Add the vegetables to the chicken and add to the air fryer. Add the chicken stock. Make the gnocchi and transfer them in the air fryer basket. Close the lid and cook for 20 minutes. Remove the dish from the air fryer, let it cool briefly, and serve, let it rest briefly.

Hot and Spicy Chicken with BBQ Sauce

Prep time: 10 minutes
Cooking time: 14 minutes
Servings: 3

Ingredients:

- 3 tablespoons barbecue sauce
- 3 boneless and skinless chicken breasts
- ½ cup black olives
- 1 onion
- 1 tablespoon tomato sauce
- 1½ teaspoons cayenne pepper
- 1 teaspoon olive oil
- 1 teaspoon salt
- 2 tablespoons minced garlic
- ¾ cup soy sauce
- ¾ cup chicken stock

Directions:

In a mixing bowl, combine the soy sauce and chicken stock and stir well. Take the chicken breasts and rub them with the cayenne pepper and salt. Sprinkle the meat with the olive oil. Slice the black olives. Take a small mixing bowl and combine the barbecue sauce and tomato sauce and stir well. Peel the onion and dice it. Combine the onion and garlic with sauces and add the chicken. Transfer the chicken to the air fryer basket and add the soy sauce mixture. Sprinkle the meat with the olives. Close the lid and cook for 14 minutes. When the meat is cooked, remove it from the air fryer. Serve immediately with sauce from the air fryer.

Thai-style Chicken with Teriyaki Sauce

Prep time: 15 minutes
Cooking time: 20 minutes
Servings: 4

Ingredients:

- 4 chicken thighs
- 1 cup soy sauce
- 1 tablespoon sugar
- 1 tablespoon cooking sake
- 1 teaspoon sesame seeds
- 1 tablespoon tomato sauce
- 1 teaspoon honey
- 4 tablespoons chicken stock

Directions:

Pour the chicken stock into the air fryer basket. In a mixing bowl, combine the soy sauce, sugar, honey, sake, and tomato sauce. Stir the mixture until smooth. Transfer the chicken to the sauce and coat well. Sprinkle the chicken with the sesame seeds and stir again. Let the chicken rest for at least 5 minutes. Transfer the meat to the air fryer basket and pour the sauce on top. Close the lid and cook for 20 minutes. Remove the dish from the air fryer and serve.

Butter Chicken

Prep time: 15 minutes
Cooking time: 18 minutes
Servings: 4

Ingredients:

- 14 ounces chicken
- 1 teaspoon salt
- 1 teaspoon cayenne pepper
- 1 tablespoon lemon juice
- ½ teaspoon turmeric
- 1 teaspoon garam masala
- 1 teaspoon olive oil
- ½ teaspoon grated ginger
- ½ teaspoon minced garlic
- ⅓ cup Greek yogurt
- 3 tablespoons butter
- 1 teaspoon cardamom
- 1 clove
- 1 coriander leaf
- 1 teaspoon sugar
- ½ cup heavy cream

Directions:

Chop the chicken roughly and transfer it to a mixing bowl. Sprinkle the chicken with the salt, cayenne pepper, and lemon juice and stir well. Add turmeric, garam masala, and olive oil. Stir the mixture again. Add ginger, garlic, and cardamom. Take a separate bowl and combine Greek yogurt and butter. Stir until smooth. Add the coriander leaf, sugar, and clove and stir. Add the cream and stir again. Transfer the chicken to the air fryer basket and top it with the yogurt mixture. Close the lid and cook for 18 minutes. When the dish is done, stir well and transfer it to serving plates.

Chicken Enchiladas

Prep time: 20 minutes
Cooking time: 16 minutes
Servings: 4

Ingredients:

- 4 boneless and skinless chicken breasts
- 4 tortillas
- 2 white onions
- 1 cup heavy cream
- 1 tablespoon Greek yogurt
- 2 cups Cheddar cheese
- 1 cup pickled cucumbers
- 1 teaspoon ground black pepper
- 1 teaspoon minced garlic
- 2 tablespoons tomato sauce
- 1 tablespoon sour cream
- 1 teaspoon salt
- 1 teaspoon red chile flakes
- 1 cup lettuce
- 1 teaspoon fresh parsley

Directions:

Cut the chicken into strips. Cut the chicken into halves. Transfer the meat to the mixing bowl and sprinkle it with the parsley, salt, pepper, and garlic and stir well. In a separate bowl and combine yogurt, sour cream, tomato sauce, and chile flakes. Stir until smooth. Grate the Cheddar cheese and dice the pickled cucumber. Peel the onion and chop it. Take the tortillas and spread them with the yogurt mixture. Transfer the chicken to the tortillas, add the cucumber and onion, and top with the Cheddar cheese. Roll the tortillas and transfer them to the air fryer basket. Top with the cream. Close the lid and cook for 16 minutes. When the dish is cooked, remove it from the air fryer basket and serve.

Chicken with Artichokes

Prep time: 15 minutes
Cooking time: 17 minutes
Servings: 4

Ingredients:

- 8 boneless and skinless chicken thighs
- 2 white onions
- 10 ounces artichoke hearts
- ⅓ cup fresh parsley
- 1 teaspoon ground black pepper
- 1 teaspoon ground white pepper
- ⅓ cup sour cream
- ¾ cup mayonnaise
- 1 cup chicken stock
- 1 teaspoon turmeric
- 1 tablespoon grated ginger
- 1 teaspoon paprika
- 1 teaspoon butter

Directions:

Chop the chicken thighs roughly and transfer them to a mixing bowl. Sprinkle it with the black pepper, white pepper, turmeric, and ginger and stir well. In a separate bowl, combine the chicken stock, butter, mayonnaise, and sour cream. Stir until smooth. Combine the stock and chicken and set it aside. Chop the artichokes hearts. Peel the onion and chop it. Chop the parsley and combine it with the paprika and chopped onion. Combine the meat, chopped artichokes, and onion mixture and transfer it to the air fryer basket. Close the lid and cook it for 17 minutes. When the dish is cooked, remove the dish from the air fryer and serve.

Chicken Cordon Bleu

Prep time: 15 minutes
Cooking time: 18 minutes
Servings: 4

Ingredients:

- 4 boneless and skinless chicken breasts
- 5 ounces hard cheese
- 4 eggs
- ½ cup flour
- 1 cup bread crumbs
- 4 slices of ham
- 4 teaspoons butter
- 1 teaspoon salt
- 1 teaspoon paprika

Directions:

In a mixing bowl, sift the flour. Add the eggs and stir until smooth. Take the chicken breasts and tenderize them. Rub the chicken with the salt and paprika. Add the ham and hard cheese to the top of every breast. Add the butter and seal the chicken closed with toothpicks. Dip them in the egg mixture, then dip them in the bread crumbs. Transfer the chicken in the air fryer and close the lid. Cook for 18 minutes. When it is cooked, remove it from the air fryer, remove the toothpicks and serve.

Honey Chicken Wings

Prep time: 15 minutes
Cooking time: 15 minutes
Servings: 4

Ingredients:

- 16 chicken wings
- 1 tablespoon honey
- 2 teaspoons soy sauce
- 1 tablespoon tomato sauce
- 1 teaspoon minced garlic
- 1 tablespoon brown sugar
- 3 tablespoons butter
- 1 teaspoon salt
- ½ cup cilantro
- 1 tablespoon lemon juice
- 1 teaspoon apple cider vinegar

Directions:

In a mixing bowl, combine honey, soy sauce, tomato sauce, and minced garlic and stir well. Add the chicken wings to the mixing bowl, mix well and set aside. Wash the cilantro and chop it roughly. Transfer the cilantro to a food processor and blend until smooth. Add the lemon juice, salt, and vinegar. Add the butter and brown sugar. Blend for 30 seconds. Ladle the mixture on the wings and toss to coat. Transfer the chicken wings to the air fryer basket and close the lid. Cook for 15 minutes. When the chicken is cooked, remove it from the air fryer basket and let it cool briefly before serving.

Chicken Breasts with Prunes and Cilantro

Prep time: 15 minutes
Cooking time: 15 minutes
Servings: 2

Ingredients:

- 2 boneless and skinless chicken breasts
- ½ cup prunes
- 1 cup cilantro
- ½ cup sun-dried tomatoes
- 1 tablespoon butter
- 1 teaspoon salt
- 1 teaspoon paprika
- 1 teaspoon fresh basil
- 1 tablespoon olive oil
- 1 cup heavy cream

Directions:

Take the chicken breasts and cut them in half crossways. Rub the meat with the basil, paprika, and salt. Chop the prunes and tomatoes. Chop the cilantro and combine all the chopped ingredients. Transfer the mixture to the top of the chicken. Add the butter and seal the chicken closed with toothpicks. Coat the chicken with the olive oil. Transfer the chicken breasts to the air fryer basket and top with the cream. Cook for 15 minutes. When it is cooked, remove it from the air fryer basket and let it cool briefly before serving.

Stuffed Chicken Breast with Herbs and Mushrooms

Prep time: 15 minutes
Cooking time: 17 minutes
Servings: 2

Ingredients:

- 1 cup cremini mushrooms
- 1 yellow onion
- ½ cup butter
- 1 teaspoon thyme
- 1 teaspoon coriander
- 1 teaspoon fresh oregano
- 2 tablespoons heavy cream
- 1 teaspoon minced garlic
- 1 tablespoon minced ginger
- 1 teaspoon dried dill
- 1 cup chicken stock
- 1 skinless and boneless chicken breast

Directions:

In a mixing bowl, add the butter, thyme, oregano, coriander, and garlic and mix until smooth. Combine the cream with the dill and ginger, stirring well. Peel the onion and chop it. Wash the mushrooms and slice them. Cut the chicken breast in half crossways and top with the mushrooms and butter mixtures. Seal the breasts closed with toothpicks. Transfer the chicken breast in the air fryer basket and top with the cream mixture. Close the lid and cook for 17 minutes. When the chicken is cooked, remove it from the air fryer and let it rest briefly. Cut into slices and serve.

Chicken Divan

Prep time: 15 minutes
Cooking time: 16 minutes
Servings: 2

Ingredients:

- 1 cup quinoa
- 1 carrot
- 1 cup broccoli
- 10 ounces chicken
- 1 cup shallots
- 2 cups chicken stock
- 1 cup water
- ½ cup hard cheese
- 1 tablespoon white wine
- 1 teaspoon nutmeg
- 1 teaspoon salt
- ½ teaspoon sugar
- 1 onion

Directions:

Chop the chicken into medium-sized pieces. Add it to a bowl and sprinkle it with the salt and nutmeg. Peel the onion and chop it. Peel the shallots and slice them. Wash the broccoli, separate into florets, and dice. In a mixing bowl, add the broccoli, shallots, and onions. Add the quinoa. Grate the cheese. Transfer the quinoa mixture to the chicken mixture and add the cheese. Stir well and transfer the mixture to the air fryer basket. Pour the chicken stock, wine, and water into the air fryer basket and close the lid. Cook for 16 minutes. When it is done, remove it from the air fryer, stir well and serve.

Curry Chicken

Prep time: 15 minutes
Cooking time: 15 minutes
Servings: 4

Ingredients:

- 1 cup chives
- 12 ounces boneless and skinless chicken breasts
- 1 cup chicken stock
- 1 tablespoon curry paste
- ½ tablespoon garam masala
- 1 onion
- 1 tablespoon heavy cream
- 1 tablespoon flour
- 1 teaspoon minced garlic
- 1 tablespoon minced ginger
- 1 teaspoon dried celery root

Directions:

Cut the chicken breast into strips and combine it with the garam masala and curry paste in a bowl and stir. In a separate bowl, combine the celery root, ginger, and garlic. Stir well and add the flour and cream. Add the chicken stock and mix well until smooth. Chop the chives. Transfer the chicken strips in the air fryer, sprinkle the mixture with the chives and pour the chicken stock on top. Close the lid and cook for 15 minutes. When the chicken is cooked, remove it from the air fryer and transfer it to the serving bowls, ladle the liquid from the air fryer onto the chicken and serve.

Buffalo Chicken

Prep time: 15 minutes
Cooking time: 15 minutes
Servings: 5

Ingredients:

- 12 ounces boneless and skinless chicken breasts
- 2 tablespoons hot sauce
- 1 teaspoon olive oil
- 1 tablespoon onion powder
- 1 teaspoon garlic powder
- 1 teaspoon salt
- ½ teaspoon cayenne pepper
- 1 teaspoon turmeric
- 1 teaspoon paprika
- 4 tablespoons chicken stock

Directions:

Wash the chicken and chop it coarsely. Add the chicken to a bowl and sprinkle it with the salt, cayenne pepper, onion powder, garlic powder, paprika, and turmeric and stir well. In a shallow bowl, combine the olive oil, hot sauce, and chicken stock and stir. Pour the hot sauce liquid on the chicken mixture and stir again. Transfer the chicken to the air fryer and close the lid. Cook for 15 minutes. When the chicken is cooked, let it rest briefly and serve.

Chicken Nuggets

Prep time: 10 minutes
Cooking time: 8 minutes
Servings: 2

Ingredients:

- 10 ounces boneless and skinless chicken breasts
- 1 cup bread crumbs
- 1 egg
- 1 teaspoon salt
- 1 teaspoon fresh basil
- 1 teaspoon turmeric
- 1 tablespoon heavy cream
- 1 tablespoon flour

Directions:

Wash the chicken, chop it coarsely, and add it to a bowl. Sprinkle the chicken with the salt. In another bowl, combine the turmeric and basil and stir. In a third bowl, beat the egg and add the cream and flour, stirring until smooth. In another bowl, combine the bread crumbs and turmeric and mix well. Dip the chicken in the batter, the into the bread crumbs. Transfer the chicken nuggets to the air fryer and close the lid. Cook for 8 minutes. Remove the chicken nuggets from the air fryer and serve.

Chicken Legs with Spicy Lemon Sauce

Prep time: 15 minutes
Cooking time: 15 minutes
Servings: 2

Ingredients

- 4 chicken legs
- 2 lemons
- 1 tablespoon lemon zest
- 1½ teaspoon cayenne pepper
- 1 teaspoon hot sauce
- 1 teaspoon fresh parsley, chopped
- 1 teaspoon fresh oregano
- 1 teaspoon honey

Directions:

Cut one lemon in half and squeeze the juice into a bowl. Combine the lemon juice and lemon zest and the cayenne pepper, hot sauce, oregano, and honey and stir well. Slice the other lemon into wedges and transfer them to the lemon mixture. Add the chicken legs and stir well. Transfer the chicken legs with all the liquid in the air fryer and close the lid. Cook for 15 minutes. When the chicken legs are cooked, remove them from the air fryer and serve.

Crunchy Chicken Fillet

Prep time: 15 minutes
Cooking time: 9 minutes
Servings: 4

Ingredients:

- 2 skinless and boneless chicken breasts
- 10 ounces Parmesan cheese
- 1 tablespoon soy sauce
- 1 teaspoon honey
- 1 teaspoon ground ginger
- 1 teaspoon paprika
- 1 tablespoon dried parsley

Directions:

Take the chicken breasts and slice them inhale. Rub the fillets with the ginger and paprika, and then add them to a bowl with the soy sauce and honey and stir. Set the chicken aside for 10 minutes. Grate the Parmesan cheese. Sprinkle the chicken with the parsley and transfer it in the air fryer basket. Sprinkle the meat with the cheese. Cook for 9 minutes. When the dish is cooked, remove it from the air fryer and let it rest briefly before serving.

Garlic Chicken Wings

Prep time: 15 minutes
Cooking time: 14 minutes
Servings: 4

Ingredients:

- 8 chicken wings
- ½ cup garlic cloves
- 1 tablespoon sour cream
- 1 tablespoon lime zest
- 1 teaspoon curry powder
- 1 tablespoon fish sauce
- 1 teaspoon butter

Directions:

Combine the fish sauce and butter together in a bowl and whisk. Add the curry powder and sour cream and stir until smooth. Transfer the chicken wings to the mixture, sprinkle it with the lemon zest and toss to coat. Peel the garlic cloves and slice them. Transfer the sliced garlic to the chicken wings mixture and stir well. Set aside for at least 5 minutes. Transfer the chicken mixture to the air fryer and close the lid. Cook for 14 minutes. When the dish is cooked, remove it from the air fryer and discard the liquid from the chicken wings before serving.

Chicken Piccata

Prep time: 15 minutes
Cooking time: 15 minutes
Servings: 4

Ingredients:

- 4 boneless and skinless chicken breasts
- 1 lemon
- ½ cup fresh parsley
- ½ cup heavy cream
- ¾ cup white wine
- 1 teaspoon nutmeg
- 1 teaspoon ground black pepper
- ⅓ cup capers
- ⅓ cup flour
- 2 eggs
- ¾ cup chicken stock
- 2 teaspoons paprika

Directions:

Take the large mixing bowl and beat the eggs in it. Add the cream and stir well. Sprinkle the mixture with the paprika and stir it. Tenderize the chicken and transfer them to the egg mixture. Dip the chicken in the flour. In a separate bowl, combine the capers, ground black pepper, white wine, and chicken stock and stir. Pour this mixture into the air fryer and then add the chicken. Close the lid and cook for 15 minutes. Chop the parsley. Transfer the chicken to serving plates and sprinkle them with capers and parsley and serve.

Sweet Duck Fillet

Prep time: 20 minutes
Cooking time: 17 minutes
Servings: 6

Ingredients:

- 2 boneless and skinless duck breasts
- 1 cup tomato juice
- 1 tablespoon apple cider vinegar
- 1 teaspoon brown sugar
- 2 tablespoons honey
- 1 teaspoon soy sauce
- 2 teaspoons minced garlic
- 1 carrot
- ½ cup green olives

Directions:

Cut the duck breasts in half. In a large mixing bowl, combine the tomato juice, apple cider vinegar, brown sugar, honey, and soy sauce. Stir until all the ingredients are dissolved. Add the garlic. Peel the carrot and make the spirals using a spiralizer. Add the carrot in the tomato mixture and stir well. Transfer the chicken breasts to the tomato mixture and mix well. Set aside for at least 5 minutes. Slice the green olives and transfer them to the air fryer and add the tomato mixture. Close the lid and cook for 17 minutes. Remove the dish from the air fryer and cut the duck into pieces. Ladle it with the tomato sauce and serve.

Garlic Duck with Pineapple-Honey Sauce

Prep time: 15 minutes
Cooking time: 18 minutes
Servings: 4

Ingredients:

- 2 tablespoons minced garlic
- 2 boneless and skinless duck breasts
- 1 tablespoon honey
- 1 tablespoon soy sauce
- 1 teaspoon ground black pepper
- ½ cup pineapple juice
- ¼ cup canned pineapple
- 1 teaspoon salt
- 1 teaspoon turmeric
- 1 teaspoon onion powder
- ⅓ cup shallots

Directions:

Combine the minced garlic and ground black pepper in a bowl and stir well. Chop the duck breast coarsely and sprinkle it with the turmeric and salt. Add the garlic mixture and stir well. Chop the shallots and pineapple and combine them with the onion powder, soy sauce, honey, pineapple juice. Mix until smooth. Transfer the mixture to a food processor and puree for 30 seconds. Transfer the duck breasts in the air fryer and pour the pineapple sauce on top. Close the lid and cook for 18 minutes. Remove the duck breast from the air fryer and discard the liquid. Serve the duck with the honey sauce.

Duck Strips with Jalapeño Pepper

Prep time: 15 minutes
Cooking time: 15 minutes
Servings: 4

Ingredients:

- 14 ounces chicken
- 1 cup tomato sauce
- 3 jalapeño peppers
- 2 teaspoons cayenne pepper
- 1 cup chicken stock
- 1 teaspoon turmeric
- 1 teaspoon fresh basil
- 1 teaspoon fresh oregano
- 1 teaspoon apple cider vinegar
- ½ teaspoon ground ginger
- 1 teaspoon cinnamon
- 1 white onion

Directions:

Chop the chicken roughly, add it to a bowl, sprinkle it with the ginger and cinnamon and stir well. Peel the onion and slice it into thin circles. Chop the jalapeño peppers. Combine the ingredients, then add the basil, oregano, apple cider vinegar, turmeric, and tomato sauce. Mix well. Transfer the chicken to the tomato mixture and stir well. Set aside for at least 5 minutes. Transfer the chicken in the air fryer and top it with the tomato mixture. Cook it for 15 minutes. Remove it from the air fryer and serve.

Duck Roll with Chickpeas

Prep time: 20 minutes
Cooking time: 20 minutes
Servings: 4

Ingredients:

- 3 duck breast fillets
- 1 cup chickpeas
- 1 onion
- 1 carrot
- ⅓ cup sweet corn
- 1 teaspoon butter
- 1 tablespoon soy sauce
- 1 teaspoon honey
- 1 teaspoon basil
- ½ cup fresh dill
- 1 teaspoon apple cider vinegar
- 1 tablespoon paprika
- 5 garlic cloves

Directions:

Peel the garlic cloves, onion, and carrot. Dice the vegetables and transfer the ingredients to a mixing bowl and add the basil, honey, and paprika and stir well. Add chickpea, sweet corn, and butter. Mix well again. Tenderize the duck fillet and put them into the air fryer tray. Transfer the filling from the chickpeas to the fillets and roll it. Sprinkle the roll with the soy sauce and apple cider vinegar. Cover the roll in the baking paper. Transfer the roll in the air fryer and cook it for 20 minutes. Remove the roll from the air fryer and discard the baking paper. Slice it into thin slices and serve.

Duck with Plums and Dried Fruits

Prep time: 20 minutes
Cooking time: 18 minutes
Servings: 4

Ingredients:

- 2 duck breasts
- 3 anise stars
- 1 teaspoon cardamom
- ¼ cup dried apricots
- 1 cup plums, pitted
- ¾ cup prunes
- 1 orange
- 1 cup chicken stock
- 1 teaspoon salt
- 1 teaspoon paprika

Directions:

Take the duck breasts and chop them roughly. Transfer the meat to a mixing bowl and sprinkle it with salt, paprika, and cardamom. Add the anise and mix well. Chop the apricots, plums, and prunes. Cut the orange in half and slice it. Add the fruit in the mixing bowl with the meat and stir well. Transfer the mixture to the air fryer basket and add the chicken stock. Close the lid and cook for 18 minutes. When the duck is cooked, remove it from the air fryer and serve with the juice from the air fryer.

Stuffed Rosemary Chicken

Prep time: 20 minutes
Cooking time: 30 minutes
Servings: 6

Ingredients:

- 1 large chicken
- 2 cups rice, cooked
- 1 bell pepper
- 1 red onion
- ⅓ cup fresh rosemary
- 1 teaspoon fresh basil
- 1 cup fresh dill
- 1 teaspoon chile pepper
- 1 teaspoon tomato sauce
- 2 cup heavy cream
- 1 teaspoon salt
- 1 tablespoon ground ginger

Directions:

Wash the chicken and add the meat to a mixing bowl with the ginger, chile pepper, basil, and salt and set aside. In a mixing bowl, add the rice. Peel the onion and remove the seeds from the bell pepper. Chop the vegetables and add them to the rice. Chop the dill and rosemary and add them to the rice and stir. Add the tomato sauce and stir well. Fill the chicken with the rice mixture. Transfer the chicken to the air fryer basket and pour the cream. Close the lid. Cook for 30 minutes. Remove the chicken from the air fryer, place on a serving platter, and add the liquid from the air fryer and serve.

Battered Chicken

Prep time: 10 minutes
Cooking time: 20 minutes
Servings: 4

Ingredients:

- 16 ounces chicken
- 1 tablespoon sriracha
- 2 eggs
- ½ cup heavy cream
- 4 tablespoon flour
- 1 teaspoon ground black pepper
- 1 teaspoon paprika
- 1 teaspoon minced garlic

Directions:

In a mixing bowl, and beat the eggs. Whisk the mixture, add the cream and stir well. Add the flour and stir the mixture until smooth. Take the chicken and add it to the mixing bowl. Sprinkle it with the sriracha, pepper, paprika, and garlic and stir. Dip the chicken in the batter and set it aside set the pieces aside for 2 minutes. Dip the meat in the batter again and transfer the chicken to the air fryer basket and close the lid. Cook for 20 minutes. Remove the dish from the air fryer and let it rest briefly before serving.

Autumn Poultry Stew

Prep time: 20 minutes
Cooking time: 20 minutes
Servings: 6

Ingredients:

- 3 sweet potatoes
- 2 red onions
- 1 duck breast
- 1 chicken breast
- 2 teaspoons red wine
- 1 teaspoon brown sugar
- 1 carrot
- 2 red bell peppers
- 1 teaspoon chile flakes
- 1 chile pepper
- 3 cups chicken stock
- 1 teaspoon salt

Directions:

Chop the chicken breast and duck breast roughly, add to a bowl, season the meat with the salt and chili flakes and stir well. Add the wine and let the meat marinate for a few minutes. Remove the seeds from the bell peppers and slice them. Chop the chile pepper and combine it with the bell pepper. Peel the potatoes and onions and chop them coarsely. Combine the chopped vegetables and peppers and mix with the brown sugar. Peel the carrots and chop coarsely. Transfer all the vegetables and meat to the air fryer basket. Pour the chicken stock into the air fryer basket and close the lid. Cook for 20 minutes. When the stew is cooked, remove it from the air fryer, let it rest briefly and serve.

Chicken Pasta Casserole

Prep time: 15 minutes
Cooking time: 18 minutes
Servings: 6

Ingredients:

- 10 ounces dried pasta
- 2 tomatoes
- 14 ounces boneless and skinless chicken breast, boiled
- 2 cups Parmesan cheese
- 2 cups heavy cream
- 1 cup green peas
- 1 teaspoon ground black pepper
- 1 teaspoon ground white pepper
- 1 tablespoon paprika
- 1 onion

Directions:

Peel the onion and dice it. Chop the tomatoes and combine them with the onion in a bowl. Sprinkle the mixture with the white pepper and black pepper and stir well. Add the peas. Chop the chicken breast into medium-sized pieces and add it to the mixing bowl. Grate the Parmesan cheese. Transfer the chicken mixture to the air fryer form and add the pasta. Pour the cream onto the chicken and sprinkle it with the grated cheese. Transfer the form in the air fryer and close the lid. Cook for 18 minutes. Remove it from the air fryer and let it cool briefly before serving.

Chicken Wings

Preparation time: 10 minutes
Cooking time: 40 minutes
Servings: 4

Ingredients:
- 1 egg
- ¼ cup flour
- ¼ cup cornstarch
- Salt and ground black pepper, to taste
- 1 tablespoon vegetable oil
- 10 chicken wings, each cut in 2 pieces
- ½ cup water
- Ginger, peeled and sliced
- ½ cup brown sugar
- 1½ tablespoons soy sauce
- 3 tablespoons rice vinegar
- ½ cup corn syrup
- ⅓ cup peanuts, roasted and chopped
- 1 teaspoon chile flakes
- 2 tablespoons sesame seeds, toasted

Directions:
In a bowl, mix the cornstarch with flour, salt, pepper and egg and whisk well. Add the wings and mix to coat well. Transfer the chicken pieces to the air fryer, drizzle the vegetable oil and cook at 350°F for 35 minutes. Transfer the chicken wings to paper towels to drain the excess oil and set them aside. Put the water in a pot and bring it to a boil on medium heat, add the ginger, brown sugar, soy sauce, corn syrup and vinegar and whisk until it thickens. Add the chicken pieces to this mix. Add the sesame seeds, chile flakes and peanuts, toss to coat, and serve.

Chicken Tikkas

Preparation time: 2 hours
Cooking time: 15 minutes
Servings: 4

Ingredients:
- 17 ounces chicken meat, boneless and cut into small pieces
- 3 colored bell peppers, cut into chunks
- 14 ounces yogurt
- Salt and ground black pepper, to taste
- 3.5 ounces cherry tomatoes, cut in halves
- ½ tablespoon fresh ginger
- ½ tablespoon garlic, minced
- 2 tablespoons chili powder
- 2 tablespoons coriander
- 2 teaspoons olive oil
- 1 teaspoon turmeric
- 2 tablespoons cumin powder
- 1 teaspoon garam masala
- ⅓ cup coriander, chopped
- 1 yellow onion, thinly sliced
- 3 mint leaves, torn
- 1 lemon, cut in half

Directions:
In a bowl, mix the chicken with the yogurt, bell peppers, tomatoes, ginger, garlic, chili powder, turmeric, cumin, coriander, olive oil, garam masala, salt, and pepper, toss to coat, and let marinate in the refrigerator for 2 hours. Place the chicken, bell peppers and tomatoes on skewers, place them in the lined air fryer and cook at 400°F for 15 minutes, turning them halfway through. Divide the skewers on plates, sprinkle with the coriander, mint and onions, and serve them with lemon on the side.

Simple Fried Chicken Wings

Preparation time: 10 minutes
Cooking time: 30 minutes
Servings: 2

Ingredients:

- 16 pieces chicken wings
- Salt and ground black pepper, to taste
- ¼ cup butter
- ¾ cup potato starch
- ¼ cup honey
- 4 tablespoons garlic, minced

Directions:

Pat the chicken wings dry and put them in a bowl. Add the starch, salt and pepper, toss to coat well, and transfer to the air fryer. Cook at 380°F for 25 minutes and at 400°F for 5 minutes. Heat up a pan with the butter on medium high heat, melt it and add the garlic. Stir and cook for 2 minutes. Add the salt, pepper and honey, stir and simmer on low heat for 20 minutes. Divide chicken on plates and serve with the honey sauce.

Coconut Chicken

Preparation time: 4 hours
Cooking time: 25 minutes
Servings: 3

Ingredients:

- 3 chicken legs
- 5 teaspoons turmeric
- 2 tablespoons ground ginger
- 1½ tablespoon galangal
- Salt, to taste
- 1.5 ounces coconut paste

Directions:

In a bowl, mix the coconut paste with the turmeric, ginger, galangal and salt and stir well. Cut some slits into chicken legs, add them to coconut mix and toss to coat well. Let the chicken marinate for 4 hours in the refrigerator. Transfer the chicken to the preheated air fryer and cook at 370°F for 25 minutes. Serve the chicken with a delicious side salad.

Lime Chicken Wings

Preparation time: 6 hours and 30 minutes
Cooking time: 15 minutes
Servings: 6

Ingredients:

- 16 chicken wings, cut into 2 pieces
- 2 tablespoons honey
- 2 tablespoons soy sauce
- Salt and ground black pepper, to taste
- ¼ teaspoon ground white pepper
- 2 tablespoons lime juice

Directions:

In a bowl, mix the honey with the soy sauce, salt, black pepper, white pepper, lime juice and whisk well. Add the chicken pieces, toss to coat and keep in refrigerated for 6 hours. Take the chicken out of the refrigerator and leave at room temperature for 30 minutes. Transfer chicken to the air fryer, cook at 370°F for 6 minutes, flip, cook for 6 more, increase heat to 400°F and cook for 3 minutes. Serve with lime wedges.

Chicken with Herbs

Preparation time: 45 minutes
Cooking time: 40 minutes
Servings: 4

Ingredients:

- 1 whole chicken
- Salt and ground black pepper, to taste
- 1 teaspoon garlic powder
- 1 teaspoon onion powder
- ½ teaspoon fresh thyme
- 2 tablespoons olive oil

Directions:

Season the chicken with salt and pepper, drizzle the oil and rub the bird all over with it. Add the thyme, garlic powder, and onion powder and rub again well. Let the chicken aside for 45 minutes, place it in the air fryer's baking pan, cook at 360°F for 20 minutes, turn and cook for 20 minutes. Let the chicken rest for 10 minutes, carve and serve.

Stuffed Chicken

Preparation time: 10 minutes
Cooking time: 22 minutes
Servings: 4

Ingredients:

- 2 cups baby spinach
- 4 chicken breasts, boneless and skinless
- 1 cup sun-dried tomatoes, chopped
- Salt and ground black pepper, to taste
- 1½ tablespoons Italian seasoning
- 4 Mozzarella cheese slices
- Olive oil

Directions:

Cut a pocket in each chicken breast, stuff with the tomatoes, mozzarella, and spinach. Season with the salt, pepper, and Italian seasoning and seal the chicken pockets with toothpicks. Heat up a pan with olive oil on medium heat, add the chicken, sear for 3 minutes on each side and place them in a pan that fits the air fryer. Cook at 380°F for 12 minutes. Divide between plates and serve.

Chicken Parmesan

Preparation time: 10 minutes
Cooking time: 15 minutes
Servings: 4

Ingredients:

- 2 cups panko bread crumbs
- ¼ cup Parmesan cheese, grated
- ½ teaspoon garlic powder
- 2 cups white flour
- 1 egg, whisked with 1 tablespoon water
- 1½ pounds chicken cutlets, skinless and boneless
- Vegetable oil for frying
- Salt and ground black pepper, to taste
- 1 cup Mozzarella cheese, grated
- 2 cups marinara sauce
- 3 tablespoons basil, chopped

Directions:

In a bowl, mix the bread crumbs with the Parmesan cheese and garlic powder and stir. Put flour in a second bowl and the egg mixture in a third bowl. Season the chicken with salt and pepper, dip the chicken in the flour, then in the egg and finally in the bread crumbs. Heat up a pan with the oil on medium-high heat, add the chicken, cook for 5 minutes and transfer to paper towels. Place the chicken in a baking dish that fits the air fryer, add warm marinara sauce to the chicken and top with Mozzarella cheese. Place the dish in the air fryer and cook at 380°F for 5 minutes. Divide on plates, sprinkle with basil and serve.

Salsa Verde Chicken

Preparation time: 10 minutes
Cooking time: 20 minutes
Servings: 4

Ingredients:
- 16 ounces salsa verde
- 1 tablespoon olive oil
- Salt and ground black pepper, to taste
- 1 pound chicken breast, boneless and skinless
- 1½ cup Monterey Jack cheese, grated
- ¼ cup fresh cilantro, chopped
- 1 teaspoon garlic powder
- Lime, cut into wedges for serving
- White rice, already cooked, for serving

Directions:
Pour the salsa verde in a baking dish that fits the air fryer. Season the chicken with salt, pepper, garlic powder and brush with olive oil. Place chicken on top of sauce. Place the dish in the air fryer and cook at 380°F for 20 minutes. Sprinkle the cheese on top and cook for 2 minutes. Divide between plates and serve with white rice and lime wedges on the side.

Chicken and Rice

Preparation time: 10 minutes
Cooking time: 30 minutes
Servings: 4

Ingredients:
- 1 pound chicken breasts, skinless, boneless and cut into quarters
- 1 cup white rice, already cooked
- Salt and ground black pepper, to taste
- Olive oil
- 3 garlic cloves, minced
- 1 yellow onion, chopped
- ½ cup white wine
- ¼ cup heavy cream
- 1 cup chicken stock
- ¼ cup parsley, chopped
- 2 cups peas, frozen
- 1½ cups parmesan, grated

Directions:
Heat up a pan with a drizzle of oil on medium-high heat, add the chicken pieces, season them with salt and pepper, cook for 6 minutes on each side and transfer to a plate. Heat the pan again on medium heat, add the onions and garlic, stir and cook for 3 minutes. Add the heavy cream, wine, stock, salt, and pepper, stir, bring to a boil and simmer for 5 minutes. Transfer this to a baking dish that fits the air fryer, add the chicken, rice, peas, Parmesan cheese, and parsley. Place the dish in the air fryer and cook at 420°F for 10 minutes. Divide between plates and serve.

Sicilian Chicken

Preparation time: 10 minutes
Cooking time: 22 minutes
Servings: 4

Ingredients:

- 5 chicken thighs
- 1 tablespoon olive oil
- 2 garlic cloves, minced
- 1 tablespoon fresh thyme, chopped
- ½ cup heavy cream
- ¾ cup chicken stock
- 1 teaspoon red pepper flakes, crushed
- ¼ cup Parmesan cheese, grated
- ½ cup sun-dried tomatoes
- ½ cup fresh basil, chopped for serving
- Salt and ground black pepper, to taste

Directions:

Heat up a pan with the oil on medium-high heat, add the chicken, season with salt and pepper, cook for 3 minutes on each side, and transfer to a plate. Return the pan to heat, add the thyme, garlic, and pepper flakes, stir and cook for 1 minute. Add the tomatoes, stock, cream, Parmesan cheese, salt, and pepper, stir, bring to a simmer, then take off the heat. Transfer the mixture to a baking dish that fits the air fryer, add the chicken to the dish and cook at 320°F for 12 minutes. Divide between plates and serve with basil sprinkled on top.

Roasted Turkey Legs

Preparation time: 10 minutes
Cooking time: 1 hour
Servings: 3

Ingredients:

- 3 turkey legs
- Salt and ground black pepper, to taste
- 6 tablespoons butter
- ½ cup water
- 3 celery stalks, cut into thirds

Directions:

Pat the turkey legs dry, season with salt and pepper and make 3 pockets in each. Press a celery piece in each pocket, rub the turkey legs with the butter and place in the air fryer's pan. Add the water, place the pan in the air fryer and cook for 1 hour at 350°F. Turn the turkey legs halfway through and serve.

Crispy Duck Legs

Preparation time: 10 minutes
Cooking time: 30 minutes
Servings: 2

Ingredients:

- 2 duck legs
- Salt and ground black pepper, to taste
- 1 teaspoon five spice powder
- 1 tablespoon fresh parsley, chopped
- 1 tablespoon fresh thyme, chopped

Directions:

Rub the duck legs with the salt, pepper, and five spice powder. Rub them with the parsley and thyme and place them in the air fryer's basket. Cook at 330°F for 25 minutes and at 400°F for 5 minutes and serve.

Smoked Duck Breast

Preparation time: 10 minutes
Cooking time: 20 minutes
Servings: 2

Ingredients:

- 1 smoked duck breast
- 1 teaspoon honey
- 1 teaspoon tomato paste
- 1 tablespoon mustard
- ½ teaspoon apple cider vinegar

Directions:

Put the honey in a bowl. Add the tomato paste, vinegar, and mustard and whisk well. Add the duck breast, toss to coat, transfer to the air fryer, and cook at 370°F for 15 minutes. Take the duck breast out of the fryer, coat with more of the sauce from the bowl again and cook at 360°F for 5 minutes. Cut the breast in half and serve.

Baked Duck Legs

Preparation time: 10 minutes
Cooking time: 30 minutes
Servings: 2

Ingredients:

- 2 duck legs
- 2 dried chilies, chopped
- 1 tablespoon vegetable oil
- 1 cinnamon stick
- 2 star anise
- 1 bunch green onions, chopped
- 4 ginger slices
- 1 tablespoon oyster sauce
- 1 tablespoon soy sauce
- 1 teaspoon sesame oil
- ½ chicken bouillon cube
- 14 ounces water
- 1 tablespoon Chinese rice wine

Directions:

Heat up a baking dish that fits the air fryer with the vegetable oil on medium-high heat. Add the cinnamon, chili, star anise, sesame oil, rice wine and ginger. Stir and cook for 2 minutes. Add the oyster sauce, soy sauce, water, and chicken bouillon cube, stir again, and cook for 2 minutes. Add the green onions and duck legs, toss to coat, Place the dish in the air fryer and cook at 370°F for 30 minutes. Transfer the duck legs to plates and serve.

Beggar Chicken

Preparation time: 10 minutes
Cooking time: 40 minutes
Servings: 6

Ingredients:

- 3 pounds whole chicken
- 10 wolfberries
- 8 longan pieces, dried
- 3 solomonseal rhizome slices
- 4 Tong Kwai slices
- 3 Chinese yam slices
- 1-quart water
- 1 teaspoon soy sauce
- Salt and white pepper, to taste
- 1 teaspoon sesame oil

Directions:

Season the chicken with the salt, pepper, soy sauce and sesame oil and coat the chicken well. Put the water in a pot, bring to a boil on medium heat, add the longan, wolfberries, solomonseal rhizome, yam, and Tong Kwai, stir, and boil for a few minutes. Stuff the chicken with Chinese herbs, place it in the air fryer, cover the chicken with some aluminum foil, and bake at 400°F for 25 minutes. Uncover the chicken and bake at 360°F for 15 minutes. Serve chicken with some soy sauce.

Crispy Chicken Breasts

Preparation time: 10 minutes
Cooking time: 16 minutes
Servings: 4

Ingredients:

- ¾ cup white flour
- 1 pound chicken breast, skinless, boneless and cut lengthwise
- 1 teaspoon paprika
- 1 cup panko
- 1 egg, whisked
- Salt and ground black pepper, to taste
- ½ tablespoon olive oil
- Zest from 1 lemon, finely grated
- 2 tablespoons fresh parsley, chopped

Directions:

In a bowl, mix the paprika with the flour, salt, pepper, and lemon zest and stir. Put the whisked egg in another bowl and the panko bread crumbs in a third bowl. Dredge the chicken pieces in the flour, egg, and bread crumbs and place them in the lined air fryer's basket. Drizzle the oil onto them. Cook at 400°F for 8 minutes, turn, and cook for 8 more minutes. Serve them with parsley sprinkled on top.

BBQ Chicken

Preparation time: 1 hour
Cooking time: 30 minutes
Servings: 4

Ingredients:

- 4 chicken breast halves
- 2 tablespoons lemon juice
- 1½ teaspoon smoked paprika
- 3 tablespoons olive oil
- Salt and ground black pepper, to taste
- 3 garlic cloves, minced
- 1 cup barbecue sauce

Directions:

Place the chicken breast halves in a bowl, season with salt and pepper and mix with olive oil, lemon juice, paprika, and garlic. Toss to coat and let the chicken marinate in the refrigerator for 1 hour. Place the chicken breast halves in the air fryer's basket and cook for 15 minutes at 350°F. Transfer the chicken pieces to a lined baking sheet that fits the air fryer, add the barbecue sauce on them and cook at 350°F for 15 minutes and serve.

Chicken and Potatoes

Preparation time: 10 minutes
Cooking time: 30 minutes
Servings: 4

Ingredients:

- 8 chicken thighs
- 2 tablespoons olive oil
- 1 pound baby potatoes, cut in halves
- 2 teaspoons fresh oregano
- 2 garlic cloves, peeled and minced
- 1 red onion, peeled and chopped
- 2 teaspoons fresh thyme, chopped
- Salt and ground black pepper, to taste
- ½ teaspoon paprika

Directions:

In a bowl, mix the chicken pieces with potatoes, salt, pepper, thyme, paprika, onion, garlic, oregano and oil. Toss to coat, spread everything on a lined baking sheet that fits the air fryer, and cook at 400°F for 30 minutes, shaking halfway through. Divide between plates and serve.

Ranch Chicken

Preparation time: 10 minutes
Cooking time: 35 minutes
Servings: 4

Ingredients:

- 4 chicken breasts, boneless and skinless
- 1 ounce ranch seasoning mix
- ¼ cup butter, melted
- ½ cup Parmesan cheese, grated
- 1 cup corn flakes, crushed
- Salt and ground black pepper, to taste
- Vegetable oil cooking spray

Directions:

In a bowl, mix the ranch seasoning with the corn flakes, salt, pepper, and Parmesan cheese and stir. Dip chicken in the melted butter and then in the ranch seasoning mix. Place the chicken in the air fryer's basket, spray with cooking spray and cook at 360°F for 35 minutes. Divide between plates and serve.

Chicken Piccata

Preparation time: 10 minutes
Cooking time: 20 minutes
Servings: 2

Ingredients:
- 4 chicken thighs
- 3 tablespoons capers
- 4 garlic cloves, minced
- 3 tablespoons butter, melted
- Salt and ground black pepper, to taste
- ½ cup chicken stock
- 1 lemon, sliced
- 4 green onions, chopped

Directions:
Brush the chicken with the butter, sprinkle with salt and pepper, to taste and place them in a baking dish that fits the air fryer. Add the capers, garlic, chicken stock, and lemon slices, toss to coat and place the dish in the air fryer. Cook at 370°F for 20 minutes, shaking halfway through. Sprinkle green onions onto chicken, divide between plates and serve.

Chicken and Mushrooms

Preparation time: 10 minutes
Cooking time: 30 minutes
Servings: 8

Ingredients:
- 8 chicken thighs
- Salt and ground black pepper, to taste
- 8 ounces cremini mushrooms, cut in halves
- 3 garlic cloves, minced
- 3 tablespoons butter, melted
- 1 cup chicken stock
- ¼ cup heavy cream
- ½ teaspoon dried basil
- ½ teaspoon dried thyme
- ½ teaspoon dried oregano
- 1 tablespoon mustard
- ¼ cup Parmesan cheese, grated

Directions:
Heat up a pan with 2 tablespoons butter on medium-high heat, add the chicken, season with salt and pepper, to taste, brown for 3 minutes on each side, and transfer to a bowl. Return pan to heat, add the rest of the butter and melt it. Add the mushrooms and garlic, stir and cook for 5 minutes. Add salt, pepper, stock, oregano, thyme and basil and stir well. Add the chicken, stir to coat, and place the dish in the air fryer. Cook at 370°F for 20 minutes. Take the pan with the chicken out of the air fryer and place on the stove on medium heat. Add the mustard, Parmesan cheese, and heavy cream, stir, bring to a simmer, cook for 5 minutes and divide between plates and serve.

Goose Breasts with Orange Sauce

Preparation time: 10 minutes
Cooking time: 25 minutes
Servings: 4

Ingredients:

- 4 goose breasts
- A splash of dry vermouth
- Salt and ground black pepper, to taste
- Juice from 1 orange
- 1 teaspoon lemon juice
- 1 tablespoon orange zest, grated
- ¼ teaspoon caraway seeds
- 1 tablespoon soy sauce
- 1 garlic clove, minced
- ½ teaspoon dry mustard
- 1 teaspoon brown sugar

Directions:

Put the goose breasts in a baking dish that fits the air fryer, season with salt and pepper and set aside. In a bowl, mix the orange juice with orange zest, sugar, lemon juice, soy sauce, garlic, caraway, and mustard and whisk well. Pour this onto the goose breasts, place the dish in the air fryer at 330°F, and bake for 25 minutes. Divide the goose breasts on plates, drizzle the sauce onto them and serve.

Duck Breasts with Plum Sauce

Preparation time: 10 minutes
Cooking time: 15 minutes
Servings: 2

Ingredients:

- 2 duck breasts
- 1 tablespoon butter
- 1 star anise
- 1 thyme sprig
- 1 tablespoon olive oil
- 1 shallot, peeled and chopped
- 9 ounces red plums, pitted, cut into small wedges
- 2 tablespoons sugar
- 2 tablespoons red wine
- 10 ounces beef stock

Directions:

Heat up a pan with the olive oil on medium heat, add the shallot, stir and cook for 5 minutes. Add the sugar and plums, stir and cook until sugar dissolves. Add the stock and wine, stir, cook for 15 minutes, take off the heat and keep warm. Score the duck breasts and season with salt and pepper. Heat up a pan on medium-high heat, add the duck breasts, skin side down, cook for 6 minutes, flip, add the butter, thyme, and star anise and toss to coat. Transfer this to a baking dish that fits the air fryer, place into the air fryer at 360°F and bake for 7 minutes. Slice the duck breasts, divide between plates and serve with the plum sauce on top.

Roasted Duck with Hoisin Sauce

Preparation time: 10 minutes
Cooking time: 25 minutes
Servings: 6

Ingredients:

- 6 duck breasts, boneless
- 4 tablespoons soy sauce
- 1½ teaspoons five spice powder
- 2 tablespoons honey
- Salt and ground black pepper, to taste
- 20 ounces chicken stock
- 4 ginger slices
- 4 tablespoons hoisin sauce
- 1 teaspoon sesame oil

Directions:

In a bowl, mix the five spice powder with soy sauce and honey and whisk well. Add the duck breasts, toss to coat, and set aside for now. Heat up a pan with the stock on medium-high heat. Add the hoisin sauce, ginger and sesame oil, stir well, cook for 2-3 minutes, take off the heat, and leave aside. Transfer the duck from the marinade to the steamer basket of the air fryer and cook at 400°F for 16 minutes. Divide the duck breasts on plates, drizzle with hoisin sauce on them and serve.

Braised Duck Breasts

Preparation time: 10 minutes
Cooking time: 40 minutes
Servings: 6

Ingredients:

- 6 boneless and skinless duck breasts, cut in halves
- Salt and ground black pepper, to taste
- 3 tablespoons flour
- 6 tablespoons butter
- 2 cups chicken stock
- ½ cup wine
- ¼ cup parsley, chopped
- 2 cups canned chopped mushrooms

Directions:

Season the duck breasts with salt and pepper, place them in a heated pan with the butter. Brown the meat for 3-4 minutes, take out of the pan, and set aside for now. Add the flour to the butter and stir well. Add the wine, salt, pepper and chicken stock and stir well. Arrange the duck breasts in a baking dish that fits the air fryer, pour the sauce on them, add the parsley and mushrooms, place the dish in the air fryer and cook at 350°F for 40 minutes. Divide between plates and serve.

Duck Breasts with Endives and Sauce

Preparation time: 10 minutes
Cooking time: 25 minutes
Servings: 4

Ingredients:

- 2 duck breasts
- 2 tablespoons duck fat
- Salt and ground black pepper, to taste
- 1 tablespoon sugar
- 6 endives, julienned
- 2 tablespoons cranberries
- 8 ounces demi-glace
- 1 tablespoons garlic, minced
- 2 tablespoons cream

Directions:

Score the duck breasts and season them with salt and pepper. Heat up a pan on medium heat, add the duck breasts, cook for 6 minutes, flip and cook for 4 minutes more and transfer to the air fryer's basket. Cook at 350°F for 6 minutes. Heat up the pan with duck fat on medium heat, add the sugar and endives, stir and cook for 2 minutes. Add the salt, pepper, demi-glace, garlic, and cranberries, stir and cook for 3 minutes. Divide the duck breasts on plates after slicing them, spoon cranberry sauce and endives on them and serve.

Duck Breasts and Leeks

Preparation time: 10 minutes
Cooking time: 16 minutes
Servings: 2

Ingredients:

- 1 duck breast, cut in halves
- 1 leek, chopped
- 1 potato, chopped
- Salt and ground black pepper, to taste
- 2 tablespoons butter
- 1 ounce red wine
- A splash of water
- Nutmeg

Directions:

Score the duck halves with a knife, season with salt and pepper, to taste put it in a pan, and heat up on medium-high heat. Cook for 3 minutes on each side and transfer to the air fryer's basket. Cook at 360°F for 8 minutes. Heat up a pan with the butter on medium heat, add the leeks, water, salt, pepper, wine, and nutmeg, stir and cook for 2-3 minutes. Put the potatoes in a pot, add the water to cover, bring to a boil on medium-high heat, cook for 5 minutes, drain, and fry them in the pan where you browned the duck breast halves. Divide the leeks mix on plates. Take the duck breast out of the air fryer, slice and divide it between plates on top of leeks. Serve with potatoes on the side.

Simple Tomato Chicken Breast

Preparation time: 10 minutes
Cooking time: 20 minutes
Servings: 4

Ingredients:

- 1 red onion, peeled and chopped
- 4 chicken breasts, skinless and boneless
- ¼ cup balsamic vinaigrette dressing
- 14 ounces canned tomatoes, chopped
- Salt and ground black pepper, to taste
- ¼ cup Parmesan cheese, grated
- ¼ teaspoon garlic powder
- Vegetable oil cooking spray

Directions:

Spray a baking dish that fits the air fryer with some cooking oil. Add the chicken, season with salt, pepper, balsamic dressing, and garlic powder. Add the tomatoes and cheese, place the dish in the air fryer, and cook at 400°F for 20 minutes. Divide between plates and serve.

Chicken with Asparagus

Preparation time: 10 minutes
Cooking time: 30 minutes
Servings: 4

Ingredients:

- 8 chicken wings
- Bunch of asparagus spears
- Salt and ground black pepper, to taste
- 1 tablespoon fresh rosemary, chopped

Directions:

Pat the chicken wings, season with salt, pepper, and rosemary, and put them in the air fryer's basket. Cook at 360°F for 20 minutes. Heat up a pan with some water on medium heat, add asparagus, cook until tender, transfer to a bowl filled with ice water, drain and arrange on plates. Add the chicken wings on the side and serve.

Meat

Ground Beef with Spinach Leaves

Prep time: 6 minutes
Cooking time: 35 minutes
Servings: 2

Ingredients:

- 1 pound ground beef.
- 1 onion, peeled and chopped
- 2 garlic cloves, peeled and minced2 cups tomato sauce
- 1 tablespoon Worcestershire sauce2 cups beef broth

- 2 tomatoes, cored and diced
- 1 bunch spinach, chopped
- Salt and ground black pepper, to taste
- Cheddar cheese, grated

Directions:

Add the beef broth to the air fryer, preheated to 300°F. Mix the onion, garlic, tomato sauce, Worcestershire sauce, and tomatoes. Add the beef and let it cook for 15 minutes. Mix the spinach leaves with salt and pepper. Cook for 20 minutes. When ready, serve with grated cheese on top.

Beef with Beans

Prep time: 5 minutes
Cooking time: 20 minutes
Servings: 4

Ingredients:

- 2 cups canned white beans, drained
- 2 cups beef stock
- 4 cups ground beef
- 2 cups yellow mustard
- 1 onion, peeled and minced

- 1 tablespoon chili powder –
- 1 tablespoon cumin1 tablespoon white vinegar
- Salt and ground black pepper, to taste

Directions:

Add the beans to the air fryer. Mix the beef stock, yellow mustard, onion, chili powder, salt, and pepper. Add the beef and cumin and mix well. Cook at 300°F for 20 minutes. When cooked, remove the dish from the air fryer and serve.

Steak with Mustard

Prep time: 4 minutes
Cooking time: 15 minutes
Servings: 3

Ingredients:

- ½ cup soy sauce
- ¼ cup red wine vinegar
- ¼ cup brown sugar
- ¼ cup green onions, sliced
- 1 tablespoon garlic, chopped
- 1 tablespoon mustard powder
- 2 pounds beef steak
- 2 tablespoons sesame seeds

Directions:

Add the garlic to the air fryer. Mix the soy sauce, wine vinegar, sugar, mustard powder, and sesame seeds into the bowl. Add the mixture into a bowl with beef steaks. Sprinkle the dish with green onions. Cook at 300°F for 15 minutes and serve.

Beef Worcestershire

Prep time: 4 minutes
Cooking time: 20 minutes
Servings: 2

Ingredients:

- ½ cup balsamic vinegar
- ¼ cup soy sauce
- 3 tablespoons garlic, chopped
- 2 tablespoons honey
- Salt and ground black pepper, to taste
- 1 teaspoon Worcestershire sauce
- 1 teaspoon onion powder
- 1 teaspoon Smoke flavor liquid
- Cayenne pepper
- 2½ pounds beef steaks

Directions:

Add the garlic and soy sauce to the air fryer. Mix the balsamic vinegar, soy sauce, honey, salt, pepper, Worcestershire sauce, onion powder, and cayenne pepper and stir well. Add the beef steak. Pour the mixture onto it and cook at 350°F for 20 minutes. When ready, take it out, and serve!

Beef with Maple Syrup

Prep time: 5 minutes
Cooking time: 15 minutes
Servings: 2

Ingredients:

- ½ cup soy sauce
- ¼ cup maple syrup
- 6 garlic cloves, chopped
- 1 tablespoon ginger, grated
- 1 teaspoon mustard powder
- 1 teaspoon sesame oil
- ¼ teaspoon hot pepper sauce
- ½ cup beer
- 4 10-ounce beef steak

Directions:

Add the sesame oil to the air fryer. Mix the soy sauce, garlic, ginger, mustard powder, hot pepper sauce, maple syrup, and beer into the bowl. Add the beef steak into the pan. Pour the mixture onto it. Cook at 400°F for 15 minutes and serve.

Slow-roasted Steak

Prep time: 6 minutes
Cooking time: 30 minutes
Servings: 3

Ingredients:

- ½ cup vegetable oil
- ¼ cup Worcestershire sauce
- 6 tablespoons soy sauce
- ¼ cup garlic cloves, chopped
- 1 onion, peeled and chopped
- Salt and ground black pepper, to taste
- 1 tablespoon dried rosemary
- 2 tablespoons steak seasoning
- 2 tablespoons steak sauce
- 4 10-ounce Delmonico beef steaks

Directions:

Add the oil in the air fryer pan. Place the beef steaks inside. Cook at 300°F for 15 minutes. Mix the onion, garlic, and rosemary. Add the Worcestershire sauce, soy sauce, steak seasoning, steak sauce, salt, and pepper and stir well. Cook for another 15 minutes. Remove the dish when done and serve.

Quick Ground Beef and Rice

Prep time: 4 minutes
Cooking time: 20 minutes
Servings: 2

Ingredients:

- 1 tablespoon canola oil
- ¼ cup ground beef
- 1 green onion, green and white parts separated
- 3 cups short grain rice, cooked
- 1 teaspoon sesame oil
- 1 teaspoon butter
- 1 egg

Directions:

Add the canola oil to the air fryer. Mix the green onion, sesame oil, butter, and egg. Add the ground beef and rice. Cook at 300°F for 20 minutes and serve.

Beef and Pork Mix

Prep time: 4 minutes
Cooking time: 30 minutes
Servings: 2

Ingredients:

- 1 onion, chopped
- ⅔ pound ground beef
- ⅓ pound ground pork
- Salt and ground black pepper, to taste
- ¼ teaspoon nutmeg
- ¼ teaspoon ground ginger2 cups beef broth
- ½ cup sour cream

Directions:

Add the beef broth to the air fryer. Mix the ginger, nutmeg, salt, pepper, and onion. Add the beef and pork. Cook at 400°F for 30 minutes. When ready, serve with sour cream.

Beef and Carrots

Prep time: 5 minutes
Cooking time: 25 minutes
Servings: 3

Ingredients:

- 2 pounds ground beef
- ½ cup onion, peeled and chopped
- 1 teaspoon ground ginger
- Salt and ground black pepper, to taste
- 2 teaspoons sugar
- 3 tablespoons vinegar
- 1 tablespoon soy sauce
- 1 carrot
- 1 green bell pepper

Directions:

Add the beef to the air fryer. Mix the soy sauce, vinegar, ginger, salt, and pepper and toss to coat. Cook at 300°F for 15 minutes. Add the green bell pepper and carrots. Cook for another 10 minutes. When cooked, remove the dish from the air fryer and serve.

Ground Meat Trio

Prep time: 5 minutes
Cooking time: 15 minutes
Servings: 2

Ingredients:

- 1 pound ground beef
- ½ pound ground veal
- ½ pound ground pork
- Salt and ground black pepper, to taste
- ⅓ cup onion, peeled and chopped
- 2 cups sour cream
- ¼ cup fresh dill

Directions:

Add the onion to the air fryer. Mix the dill, flour, butter, cream, onion, pork, veal, and beef. Cook at 300°F for 15 minutes. When ready, serve with sour cream and enjoy.

Pork Tenderloin

Prep time: 15 minutes
Cooking time: 35 minutes
Servings: 3

Ingredients:

- 14 ounces pork tenderloins
- 1 large white onion
- 1 teaspoon cayenne pepper
- 1 teaspoon oregano
- 3 teaspoons tomato sauce
- 1 cup pork stock
- 1 teaspoon salt
- 1 carrot
- 1 teaspoon soy sauce
- 1 tablespoon lemon juice

Directions:

Take the pork tenderloin and tenderize it. Take a shallow bowl and combine the salt, oregano, and cayenne pepper and stir well. Take another bowl and combine tomato sauce and pork stock and stir well. Rub the meat with the spice mixture and then pour the tomato mixture onto the meat and set aside. Peel the onion and carrot. Grate the carrot and dice the onion. Combine the vegetables together and stir well. Add the lemon juice and mix well. Transfer the mixture to the meat mixture and stir well again. Preheat the air fryer to 360°F and transfer the meat mixture. Cook for 35 minutes. Remove the meat from the air fryer and serve.

Sour Beef Strips

Prep time: 25 minutes
Cooking time: 35 minutes
Servings: 4

Ingredients:

- 20 ounces beef
- 2 yellow onions
- 1 tablespoon honey
- 1 teaspoon salt
- 1 tablespoon oregano
- 1 cup celery root
- 1 tablespoon apple cider vinegar
- 1 teaspoon sriracha
- 1 cup heavy cream
- 1 teaspoon flour
- 1 teaspoon ground black pepper
- 1 teaspoon chopped parsley

Directions:

Take the beef and cut it into strips. Sprinkle the beef strips with the black pepper, salt, and sriracha. Add the honey and stir well. Let it marinate for at least a couple of hours. Peel the onions and dice them. Combine the onions with the oregano and vinegar and stir well. Grate the celery root and combine it with the onion. In a separate bowl, combine the cream and flour. Stir the mixture until smooth. Transfer the onion mixture to the beef strips mixture and stir again. Set aside for 5 minutes. Preheat the air fryer to 360°F and transfer the meat to the air fryer basket. Pour the cream mixture and stir. Close the lid and cook for 35 minutes. When the dish is cooked, remove it from the air fryer, stir it again, and sprinkle with the chopped parsley.

Lamb Roll with Bacon

Prep time: 20 minutes
Cooking time: 35 minutes
Servings: 6

Ingredients:

- 19 ounces lamb
- 13 ounces bacon strips
- 2 tablespoons butter
- 1 tablespoon garlic powder
- 1 teaspoon onion powder
- 1 teaspoon Dijon mustard
- 1 cup spinach
- ½ cup chicken stock
- 1 carrot
- ⅓ cup kale
- 1 teaspoon fresh rosemary
- 1 teaspoon fresh thyme
- 1 tablespoon apple cider vinegar

Directions:

Beat the lamb meat gently and rub it with the garlic powder and onion powder. Add the vinegar and set the meat aside. Chop the spinach and kale. Combine the ingredients together in the mixing bowl. Add the Dijon mustard and butter and stir well. Peel the carrot and grate it. Add the carrot to the spinach mixture. Take the bacon strips and sprinkle them with the rosemary and thyme. Take the lamb meat and add the spinach mixture o the meat. Roll the meat. Wrap the lamb meat in the bacon strips. Preheat the air fryer to 360°F and transfer the meat to the air fryer basket. Pour the chicken stock on top and cook for 35 minutes. When the dish is cooked, remove it from the air fryer and let it rest for 2 minutes before serving.

Korean-style Pork

Prep time: 10 minutes
Cooking time: 15 minutes
Servings: 3

Ingredients:

- 21 ounces pork tenderloin
- 1 tablespoon sesame seeds
- 3 tablespoons soy sauce
- 1 teaspoon olive oil
- 1 tablespoon tomato sauce
- 3 medium white onions
- 1 tablespoon fresh ginger, peeled
- 1 teaspoon brown sugar
- 1 teaspoon fresh thyme
- 1 teaspoon coriander
- 1 teaspoon fresh oregano
- 1 teaspoon fresh mint
- 1 tablespoon honey

Directions:

Chop the pork tenderloin roughly. In a mixing bowl, combine soy sauce, olive oil, tomato sauce, and brown sugar. Stir until the sugar is dissolved. Add the thyme, coriander, mint, and oregano. Stir the mixture again. Peel the white onion and chop it. Chop the fresh ginger. Add the ingredients in the soy sauce mixture and add the honey Stir again. Combine the honey mixture and meat mixture together and stir well. Set aside for at least 10 minutes. Preheat the air fryer to 400°F and transfer the meat to the basket. Cook for 10 minutes, then stir well and sprinkle it with the sesame seeds. Cook the meat for 5 minutes and serve.

Stuffed Lamb Rack

Prep time: 20 minutes
Cooking time: 40 minutes
Servings: 6

Ingredients:

- 26 ounces lamb rack
- 1 cup millet
- 1 cup fresh parsley
- 1 teaspoon ground black pepper
- 1 teaspoon olive oil
- 1 teaspoon paprika
- 1 carrot
- 1 red onion
- 2 tomatoes
- 1 teaspoon salt
- 2 tablespoons lemon juice
- 1 tablespoon apple cider vinegar
- 1 cup beef broth

Directions:

Make the small cuts across the lamb rack. Rub the meat with olive oil, paprika, salt, lemon juice, ground black pepper, and apple cider vinegar. Let the meat marinate in the refrigerator for a couple of hours. Peel the carrot and onion and chop them. In a mixing bowl, combine the chopped vegetables and millet. Chop the parsley and tomatoes. Add the ingredients in the vegetable mixture and stir well. Preheat the air fryer to 350°F. Fill the lamb rack with the vegetable mixture and transfer the meat in the air fryer. Pour the beef broth into the air fryer. Cook for 40 minutes. Remove it from the air fryer and chill it for at least 5 minutes before serving.

Pork Roll with Eggs

Prep time: 20 minutes
Cooking time: 35 minutes
Servings: 5

Ingredients:

- 4 eggs, boiled
- 1 white onion
- 17 ounces minced pork
- 1 teaspoon ground black pepper
- 1 teaspoon paprika
- 1 teaspoon fresh thyme
- 1 teaspoon fresh oregano
- ½ cup pork broth
- 1 tablespoon butter
- 1 teaspoon fresh basil
- 1 egg

Directions:

In a mixing bowl, add the minced pork. Peel the onion and chop it. Add the onion to the meat and stir well. Beat the egg in the mixture and stir well until smooth. Sprinkle the mixture with the pepper, paprika, thyme, oregano, and basil. Mix well. Melt the butter and peel the boiled eggs. Take the air fryer tray and transfer the meat mixture to it, spread evenly. Put the eggs on the meat and sprinkle with the melted butter. Make the roll. Preheat the air fryer to 355 F and transfer the tray with the roll. Cook the dish 35 minutes. When the roll is cooked, remove it from the air fryer and let it rest. Slice it and serve.

Tender Pork and Beef Cutlets

Prep time: 15 minutes
Cooking time: 30 minutes
Servings: 4

Ingredients:

- 1 cup minced beef
- 3 cups minced pork
- 1 egg
- 1 teaspoon starch
- ½ cup minced garlic
- 1 potato
- 1 teaspoon ground black pepper
- 1 teaspoon paprika
- 1 teaspoon cayenne pepper
- 1 teaspoon turmeric
- 1 teaspoon salt
- 1 teaspoon orange juice
- 1 teaspoon fresh rosemary

Directions:

In a mixing bowl, combine the pork and beef. Take a separate bowl and combine starch, black pepper, paprika, cayenne pepper, turmeric, salt, and rosemary and stir well. Peel the potato and grate it. Add the potato to the meat mixture. Blend the egg into the mixture. Add the garlic and orange juice. Sprinkle the meat mixture with the spice mixture and mix well. Make the medium cutlets from the meat mixture. Preheat the air fryer to 360°F and transfer the cutlets to the air fryer basket. Cook for 30 minutes. When the dish is cooked, remove it from the air fryer and let the cutlets rest before serving.

Beef Stew

Prep time: 20 minutes
Cooking time: 35 minutes
Servings: 5

Ingredients:

- 1 cup red wine
- 2 red onions
- 20 ounces beef
- 2 carrots
- 2 cups beef broth
- 1 teaspoon salt
- 1 teaspoon sugar
- 1 teaspoon chile flakes
- 1 tablespoon sour cream
- 3 tablespoons tomato juice
- ½ cup celery root
- 1 tablespoon fresh oregano
- 1 cup celery stalk

Directions:

Take the beef and chop it roughly. Transfer the beef in a mixing bowl, add the red wine and stir well. Set the meat aside. Peel the onions and carrot. Chop the vegetables into medium-sized pieces and put them in a separate bowl. In another bowl, combine the sugar, salt, sour cream, and tomato juice. Stir until smooth. Chop the celery root and celery stalk. Pour the tomato liquid on the meat and stir well. Take a separate bowl and combine the chile flakes and oregano and stir. Transfer the spice mixture to the meat mixture and stir well. Take the air fryer form and put the meat mixture. Add the vegetable mixture and beef broth and stir well. Preheat the air fryer to 360°F, and transfer the stew to the air fryer. Cook for 35 minutes. Remove it from the air fryer, let it rest briefly and serve it.

Stuffed Onions

Prep time: 15 minutes
Cooking time: 30 minutes
Servings: 4

Ingredients:

- 4 large white onions
- 2 cups minced pork
- 7 garlic cloves
- 7 ounces Parmesan
- 1 teaspoon ground black pepper
- ¾ cup beef broth
- 1 teaspoon salt
- 1 tablespoon butter
- 1 teaspoon turmeric
- 1 teaspoon rosemary

Directions:

Peel the onions and garlic cloves and cut the onions into the thick circles. Grate the Parmesan cheese. In a mixing bowl, combine minced pork and pepper. Add the salt, turmeric, and rosemary and stir well. Mince the garlic and add it to the meat mixture. Take the air fryer basket and ad the beef broth. Transfer the onion to the air fryer basket. Fill the onion circles with the meat mixture and sprinkle them with the grated cheese. Close the lid and cook at 360°F for 30 minutes. When the onions are cooked, remove them from the air fryer and let them rest for 5 minutes before serving.

Lamb Casserole

Prep time: 15 minutes
Cooking time: 35 minutes
Servings: 4

Ingredients:

- 15 ounces lamb
- 4 potatoes
- 1 zucchini
- 1 cup green beans
- 1 eggplant
- 1 cup sweet corn
- 1 cup chicken stock
- 2 cups Parmesan cheese
- 1 teaspoon salt,
- 1 teaspoon paprika
- 1 teaspoon ground black pepper
- 1 teaspoon basil
- 5 ounces rice noodles
- 1 cup heavy cream

Directions:

Mince the lamb meat and put it in a bowl. Sprinkle the meat with the black pepper, basil, and paprika and stir well. Chop the zucchini and the eggplant into medium-sized pieces and add sweet corn and green beans. Grate the Parmesan cheese. Combine the cream with salt and stir the mixture until salt is dissolved. Peel the potatoes and slice them. Take the large air fryer tray and add the chicken stock. Add the potato and chopped vegetables. Add the rice noodles and meat. Sprinkle the mixture with the grated cheese. Add the cream to the mixture. Preheat the air fryer to 360°F and transfer the casserole in the air fryer. Cook for 35 minutes. When the casserole is cooked, let it rest briefly and serve.

Pork Fillets with Cheese

Prep time: 15 minutes
Cooking time: 35 minutes
Servings: 3

Ingredients:

- 17 ounces pork fillet
- 8 ounces Cheddar cheese
- 1 cup pineapple
- 2 red, white onions
- 1 teaspoon black pepper
- 4 tomatoes

- 1 cup chicken stock
- 3 tablespoons mayonnaise
- 1 teaspoon tomato sauce
- 1 teaspoon basil
- 1 teaspoon turmeric
- 1 teaspoon salt

Directions:

Take the pork fillet and tenderize it. Sprinkle the meat with the black pepper, basil, salt, and turmeric. Set the meat aside. Chop the pineapple. Peel the onions and slice them. Slice the tomatoes. In a shallow bowl and combine the mayonnaise and tomato sauce in the bowl and stir well. Rub the meat with the mayonnaise mixture. Grate the Cheddar cheese. Take the air fryer tray and pour chicken stock. Transfer the meat fillets in the tray. Add the onions and tomatoes. Sprinkle the mixture with the chopped pineapple and top with the grated cheese. Preheat the air fryer to 350°F and transfer to the air fryer basket. Cook for 35 minutes. When the meat is cooked, remove it from the air fryer and let it cool briefly before serving.

Tender Meat Wraps

Prep time: 15 minutes
Cooking time: 18 minutes
Servings: 4

Ingredients:

- 17 ounces pork fillet
- 8 ounces Cheddar cheese
- 1 cup pineapple
- 2 white onions
- 1 teaspoon black pepper
- 4 tomatoes

- 1 cup chicken stock
- 3 tablespoons mayonnaise
- 1 teaspoon tomato sauce
- 1 teaspoon basil
- 1 teaspoon turmeric
- 1 teaspoon salt

Directions:

Tenderize the pork fillet and rub them with the black pepper and mayonnaise. Chop the pineapple and white onions. Slice the tomatoes. In a shallow bowl and combine the tomato sauce, basil, turmeric, and salt and stir well. Combine the spice mixture and the chopped pineapple and white onions together. Add the tomatoes. Grate the Cheddar cheese. Take the pork fillets and put the pineapple mixture in the bowl. Add the cheese and wrap the meat. Preheat the air fryer to 350°F. Pour the chicken stock and add pork rolls in the air fryer. Cook for 15 minutes and serve.

Egg Roll with Minced Meat

Prep time: 15 minutes
Cooking time: 20 minutes
Servings: 4

Ingredients:

- 15 ounces omelet
- 2 cups minced pork
- 1 medium white onion
- 1 large carrot
- 1 teaspoon salt
- 1 teaspoon ground black pepper
- 1 teaspoon paprika
- ⅓ cup chives, for serving
- 1 large egg
- 1 teaspoon oregano
- ½ teaspoon chile flakes

Directions:

Combine the minced pork and egg together in a mixing bowl. Sprinkle the mixture with the salt, pepper, paprika, oregano, and chile flakes and stir well. Peel the onion and carrot. Chop the onion and grate the carrot and add to a bowl. Take the omelet and spread it with meat mixture. Sprinkle it with the vegetable mixture and make the roll. Wrap the roll in the baking paper. Preheat the air fryer to 380°F. Transfer the roll in the air fryer and cook for 20 minutes. Remove the dish from the air fryer and let it rest briefly. Cut the roll into slices and sprinkle the dish with the chives and serve.

Pork with Currant Sauce

Prep time: 20 minutes
Cooking time: 18 minutes
Servings: 4

Ingredients:

- 1 cup fresh currants
- 1 tablespoon white sugar
- 1 tablespoon honey
- 1 teaspoon ground white pepper
- ½ teaspoon cayenne pepper
- 25 ounces pork fillet
- 1 yellow onion
- 1 teaspoon salt
- 1 teaspoon olive oil
- 1 tablespoon butter
- 2 tablespoons water

Directions:

Cut the pork fillet into 4 parts and sprinkle the meat with the salt, cayenne pepper, and white pepper. Stir the mixture and set aside. Transfer the currants in a blender and blend it for 1 minute or until smooth. Peel the onion and chop it. Add the onion to the currant mixture. Sprinkle the currant mixture with the sugar and honey. Add the olive oil and sugar. Stir the mixture until sugar is dissolved. Preheat the air fryer to 380°F and add the butter in the air fryer basket to melt. Transfer the meat mixture to the air fryer and cook it for 5 minutes from the both sides. Add the currant mixture and cook the meat for 8 minutes. When the dish is cooked, transfer it to serving plates.

Pork Knuckles

Prep time: 15 minutes
Cooking time: 30 minutes
Servings: 4

Ingredients:

- 25 ounces pork knuckles
- 2 onions
- 5 garlic cloves
- 1 tablespoon paprika
- 1 teaspoon cayenne pepper
- 1 teaspoon coriander
- 1 teaspoon ground ginger
- ½ teaspoon ground white pepper
- ½ teaspoon ground black pepper
- ½ cup pork stock
- 1 teaspoon fresh thyme
- 1 teaspoon orange juice
- 1 tablespoon olive oil

Directions:

Wash the pork knuckles carefully. Peel the garlic cloves and stuff the pork knuckle with it. Take the shallow bowl and combine paprika, cayenne pepper, coriander, ginger, white pepper, black pepper, and thyme. Stir the mixture and rub the pork knuckles with it. Combine the pork stock and orange juice together and stir well. . Peel the onions and blend in a blender until smooth. Sprinkle the meat with the onion. Preheat the air fryer to 380°F. Spray the air fryer with the olive oil inside and transfer the pork knuckles to the air fryer basket. Cook the meat for 10 minutes on the both sides. Pour the pork stock mixture into the air fryer, and cook the meat for 10 minutes. Remove the meat from the air fryer and let it rest before serving.

Beef Stroganoff

Prep time: 15 minutes
Cooking time: 20 minutes
Servings: 5

Ingredients:

- 25 ounces beef steak
- 1 cup fresh mushrooms
- 2 tablespoons sour cream
- 1 cup beef broth
- 1 teaspoon ground white pepper
- ½ teaspoon ground black pepper
- 1 teaspoon salt
- 1 tablespoon flour
- 3 garlic cloves
- 2 yellow onions
- 1 teaspoon tomato sauce
- ½ cup heavy cream
- 2 tablespoons butter

Directions:

Chop the beef and sprinkle the meat with the white pepper, black pepper, and salt and stir well. Peel the onion and garlic cloves. Slice the vegetables. Combine the broth with the tomato sauce, flour, cream, and sour cream. Stir the mixture until smooth. Slice the mushrooms. Preheat the air fryer to 400°F and add the butter to the air fryer basket. Add the meat and cook it for 6 minutes and stir. Add the mushrooms, onion and garlic and top the mixture with the cream. Cook for 14 minutes. Remove the dish from the air fryer, stir, and serve.

Meatballs with Herbs

Prep time: 10 minutes
Cooking time: 12 minutes
Servings: 4

Ingredients:

- 1 cup minced beef
- 1 cup minced chicken
- 1 teaspoon fresh thyme
- 1 teaspoon coriander
- 5 garlic cloves
- 1 teaspoon fresh oregano
- 1 teaspoon lemon zest
- 1 teaspoon ground ginger
- 1 teaspoon salt
- 4 tablespoons tomato sauce
- 1 cup chicken stock
- ½ teaspoon ground black pepper
- 1 egg

Directions:

In a mixing bowl, combine the chicken and beef. Peel the garlic cloves and mince them. Add the garlic to the meat mixture. Stir with the thyme, coriander, oregano, lemon zest, ginger, salt, and pepper and stir well. Beat the egg into the mixture and stir well again until smooth. Preheat the air fryer to 400°F. Make meatballs from the meat mixture and transfer them in the air fryer. Cook the meatballs for 2 minutes. Combine the tomato sauce and chicken stock and stir until smooth. Turn the meatballs onto other side and pour the chicken stock mixture into the air fryer. Cook for 10 minutes more. When the meatballs are cooked, remove them from the air fryer, place on a serving plate, sprinkle them with the liquid from the air fryer and serve.

Chili

Prep time: 15 minutes
Cooking time: 15 minutes
Servings: 4

Ingredients:

- 2 cups canned beans
- 1 cup minced beef
- 1 yellow onion
- ½ cup tomato sauce
- 1 teaspoon garlic powder
- ¼ cup garlic cloves
- 1 teaspoon sugar
- ½ teaspoon cumin
- 6 ounces celery
- 1 teaspoon basil
- 1 cup tomato juice
- 1 teaspoon salt
- 1 jalapeño pepper
- 1 bell pepper

Directions:

Take the mixing bowl and combine canned beans and beef. Stir the mixture and add the tomato sauce. Peel the garlic and slice it. Chop the celery and jalapeño pepper. Combine the celery, jalapeño, and garlic. Transfer the mixture to the meat mixture. Add the garlic powder, sugar, cumin, basil, tomato juice, and salt and stir well. Slice the bell pepper and add it to the mixture. Preheat the air fryer to 390°F. Transfer the chili mixture to the air fryer and cook for 15 minutes. Remove the chili from the air fryer and stir well. Let it cool briefly and serve.

Taco Pie

Prep time: 15 minutes
Cooking time: 18 minutes
Servings: 3

Ingredients:

- 1 cup ground beef
- 15 ounces Cheddar cheese
- 1 teaspoon oregano
- 1 teaspoon basil
- 1 teaspoon black pepper
- 1 teaspoon cayenne pepper
- 1 tomato
- 1 white onion
- 1 tablespoon minced garlic
- 1 tablespoon sour cream
- 1 teaspoon salt
- 1 teaspoon ground white pepper
- 10 ounces puff pastry
- 1 egg yolk
- 2 tablespoons butter
- 1 teaspoon taco seasoning

Directions:

In a mixing bowl, combine the beef, oregano, basil, black pepper, cayenne pepper, minced garlic, and salt and stir well. Peel the onion and chop it. Whisk the egg yolk. Take the puff pastry and roll it out. Cut the dough into 2 parts. Sprinkle the dough with the whisked egg yolk and taco seasoning. Transfer the ground beef mixture to one part of the puff pastry. Grate the cheese and sprinkle the puff pastry with it. Add the onion. Cover the mixture with the second part of the puff pastry and wrap the pie in the parchment paper. Preheat the air fryer to 400°F. Transfer the pie in the air fryer and cook for 18 minutes. When the dish is cooked, remove it from the air fryer and discard the parchment paper. Add the sour cream and serve.

Cocktail Meatballs

Prep time: 10 minutes
Cooking time: 8 minutes
Servings: 3

Ingredients:

- 1 cup ground chicken
- 1 cup ground lamb
- 1 tablespoon minced garlic
- 1 teaspoon salt
- 1 teaspoon honey
- 1 tablespoon tomato sauce
- 1 tablespoon beef broth
- 1 teaspoon fresh thyme
- ½ teaspoon cayenne pepper
- 1 teaspoon starch
- 1 teaspoon olive oil

Directions:

In a mixing bowl, combine the chicken and lamb in the bowl. Stir the mixture and sprinkle it with the minced garlic, salt, thyme, cayenne pepper, and starch. Mix well until smooth Take another bowl and combine the honey, tomato sauce, and beef broth. Stir well. Preheat the air fryer to 380°F. Spray the air fryer basket with the olive oil. Make medium-sized meatballs from the meat mixture and transfer them in the air fryer. Cook for 3 minutes from the both sides. Add the honey sauce and cook the meatballs for 2 minutes. Serve immediately.

Beef Roll

Preparation time: 10 minutes
Cooking time: 14 minutes
Servings: 4

Ingredients:

- 2 pounds beefsteak
- Salt and ground black pepper, to taste
- 1 cup baby spinach
- 3 ounces red bell pepper, roasted and chopped
- 6 slices Provolone cheese
- 3 tablespoons pesto

Directions:

Butterfly the steak and place it on a working surface. Spread pesto all over the surface, add the cheese in a single layer, and then add the bell peppers, spinach, salt, and pepper. Roll the steak and secure with toothpicks. Season again with salt and pepper, place roll in the air fryer's basket and cook at 400°F for 14 minutes, rotating the roll halfway. Transfer to a cutting board, set aside to cool for 10 minutes, slice, arrange on plates, and serve.

Beef Empanadas

Preparation time: 10 minutes
Cooking time: 25 minutes
Servings: 4

Ingredients:

- 1 package empanada shells
- 1 tablespoon olive oil
- 1 pound ground beef
- 1 yellow onion, peeled and chopped
- Salt and ground black pepper, to taste
- 2 garlic cloves, peeled and minced
- ½ teaspoon cumin
- ¼ cup tomato salsa
- 1 egg yolk whisked with 1 tablespoon water
- 1 green bell pepper, seeded and chopped

Directions:

Heat up a pan with the oil on medium-high heat, add the beef and brown on all sides. Add the onion and garlic, stir and cook for 4 minutes. Add the salt, pepper, bell pepper and tomato salsa, stir, and cook for 10 minutes. Divide the meat into empanada shells, brush them with egg wash, and seal. Brush them again with egg wash, place them in the air fryer's steamer basket and cook at 350°F for 10 minutes. Divide between plates and serve.

Rib Eye Steak

Preparation time: 10 minutes
Cooking time: 22 minutes
Servings: 4

Ingredients:

- 2 pounds rib eye steak
- Salt and ground black pepper, to taste
- 1 tablespoons olive oil
- 1 tablespoon steak rub
- 3 tablespoons smoked paprika
- 2 tablespoons onion powder
- 2 tablespoons garlic powder
- 1 tablespoon brown sugar
- 2 tablespoons dried oregano
- 1 tablespoon ground cumin

Directions:

In a bowl, mix the paprika with the onion powder, garlic powder, sugar, oregano, salt, pepper, and cumin . Rub the steak with this mixture and the oil, season with salt and pepper, to taste and place in the air fryer's basket. Cook at 400°F for 14 minutes, flip the steak and cook for 7 minutes. Transfer the steak to a cutting board, set aside for a few minutes, slice and serve.

Beef and Broccoli

Preparation time: 45 minutes
Cooking time: 12 minutes
Servings: 4

Ingredients:

- ¾ pound round steak, cut into strips
- 1 pound broccoli florets
- ⅓ cup oyster sauce
- 2 teaspoons sesame oil
- 1 teaspoon soy sauce
- 1 teaspoon cornstarch
- 1 teaspoon sugar
- ⅓ cup sherry
- 1 tablespoon olive oil
- 1 garlic clove, peeled and minced
- 1 slice ginger root

Directions:

In a bowl, mix the sesame oil with the cornstarch, oyster sauce, soy sauce, sherry, and sugar and stir well. Add the beef strips, toss to coat and set aside for 45 minutes. Add the beef to the air fryer. Add the broccoli, olive oil, garlic, and ginger and cook at 370°F for 12 minutes. Divide between plates and serve.

Pork with Bell Peppers

Preparation time: 10 minutes
Cooking time: 15 minutes
Servings: 2

Ingredients:

- 1 red onion, peeled and sliced thinly
- 1 yellow bell pepper, seeded and cut into strips
- Salt and ground black pepper, to taste
- 2 teaspoons Provencal herbs
- ½ tablespoon mustard
- 1 tablespoon olive oil
- 7 ounces pork tenderloin

Directions:

In a baking dish that fits the air fryer, mix the bell pepper with the onion, salt, pepper, and Provencal herbs. Add half of the oil and toss to coat. Rub pork with salt, pepper, mustard and mix with the rest of the oil. Place in the baking dish, introduce everything in the air fryer and cook at 370°F for 15 minutes turning meat halfway. Divide between plates and serve.

Steak Strips with Vegetables

Preparation time: 10 minutes
Cooking time: 25 minutes
Servings: 2

Ingredients:

- 2 steaks, cut into strips
- Salt and ground black pepper, to taste
- 4 potatoes, cut in quarters
- 7 ounces snow peas
- 8 ounces mushrooms, cut in quarters
- 1 yellow onion, peeled and cut in rings
- 4 tablespoons soy sauce
- Olive oil
- 1 tablespoon sugar

Directions:

In a bowl, mix the olive oil with the sugar and soy sauce and stir. Add the steak strips, toss to coat and set aside. In another bowl, mix the potatoes with the snow peas, onion rings and mushrooms with salt, pepper, and some oil. Put the vegetables in the air fryer and cook at 350°F for 20 minutes. Add the steak and cook for 6 minutes more at 400°F. Divide between plates and serve.

Lamb Chops

Preparation time: 10 minutes
Cooking time: 22 minutes
Servings: 4

Ingredients:

- 3 tablespoons olive oil
- 8 lamb chops
- Salt and ground black pepper, to taste
- 1 garlic bulb
- 1 tablespoon fresh oregano, chopped

Directions:

Coat the garlic with half of the oil and put in the air fryer's basket. Cook at 400°F for 12 minutes. In a bowl, mix the oregano with salt, pepper, the rest of the oil, and the lamb chops and toss to coat. Remove the garlic, add lamb chops and cook at 400°F for 5 minutes. Divide lamb chops on plates, squeeze garlic into a bowl and mix well with salt and pepper and add atop lamb and serve.

Meatballs with Feta Cheese

Preparation time: 10 minutes
Cooking time: 8 minutes
Servings: 10

Ingredients:

- 4 ounces lamb meat, minced
- Salt and ground black pepper, to taste
- 1 slice of bread, toasted and crumbled
- 2 tablespoons feta cheese
- ½ tablespoon lemon peel, grated
- 1 tablespoon fresh oregano, chopped

Directions:

In a bowl, mix the bread crumbs with the meat, salt, pepper, feta, oregano, and lemon peel and stir well. Divide into 10 balls, place them in the air fryer's basket and cook at 400°F for 8 minutes. Divide between plates and serve.

Meatloaf

Preparation time: 10 minutes
Cooking time: 25 minutes
Servings: 4

Ingredients:

- 14 ounces ground beef
- 3 tablespoons bread crumbs
- 1 egg, whisked
- 1 ounce chorizo, chopped
- Salt and ground black pepper, to taste
- 1 tablespoon fresh thyme, chopped
- 1 yellow onion, peeled and chopped
- 2 mushrooms, sliced
- Olive oil

Directions:

In a bowl, mix the meat with the bread crumbs, egg, chorizo, salt, pepper, onion and thyme and stir well. Transfer this mix to a pan, add the mushrooms slices on top and drizzle some olive oil on the meatloaf. Place the pan in the air fryer and cook at 400°F for 25 minutes. Let the meatloaf cool down for a few minutes before slicing and serving.

Veal Rolls

Preparation time: 10 minutes
Cooking time: 15 minutes
Servings: 4

Ingredients:

- 14 ounces beef stock
- 7 ounces white wine
- 4 veal cutlets
- Salt and ground black pepper, to taste
- 8 sage leaves
- 4 ham slices
- 1 tablespoon butter

Directions:

Heat up a pan with the stock on medium-high heat, add the wine and cook until everything is reduced. Season the cutlets with salt and pepper, cover with sage and roll them in ham. Brush the cutlets with the butter, place them in the air fryer's basket and cook at 400°F for 10 minutes. Reduce temperature to 360°F and cook for 5 minutes. Divide them between plates and serve with the wine gravy.

Toad in a Hole

Preparation time: 10 minutes
Cooking time: 30 minutes
Servings: 4

Ingredients:

- 8 sausages
- 1 tablespoon olive oil
- Salt and ground black pepper, to taste
- 4 ounces flour
- 2 eggs
- 4 ounces milk
- 3 ounces water
- 1 red onion, peeled and sliced
- 1 tablespoon fresh rosemary, chopped
- 1 garlic clove, peeled and crushed

Directions:

Spread oil in a baking dish that fits the air fryer. In a bowl, mix the eggs with the water, milk, garlic, onion, salt, and pepper and whisk well. Place the sausages in the dish, add the rosemary and pour eggs mix onto them. Cook in the air fryer at 360°F for 30 minutes. Set aside to cool down briefly, cut and serve.

Rolled Pork

Preparation time: 10 minutes
Cooking time: 40 minutes
Servings: 4

Ingredients:
- 1 pork fillet, about 15 ounces
- ½ teaspoon chili powder
- 1 teaspoon ground cinnamon
- 1 garlic clove, peeled and minced
- Salt and ground black pepper, to taste
- 2 tablespoons olive oil
- 1½ teaspoon cumin
- 1 red onion, peeled and chopped
- 3 tablespoons fresh parsley, chopped

Directions:
Put the pork fillet on a cutting board and use a meat tenderizer to flatten it. In a bowl, mix the garlic with the cinnamon, salt, pepper, chili powder, cumin and oil and stir well. Take 1 tablespoon of this mixture and transfer to another bowl. Add the onion and parsley to the first bowl and stir again. Spread this onto the meat, roll well and tie with string, rub with the reserved garlic mix. Place the pork into the air fryer and cook at 360°F for 40 minutes. Let the pork roll to cool briefly, slice and serve.

Steak Burgers

Preparation time: 10 minutes
Cooking time: 8 minutes
Servings: 4

Ingredients:
- 14 ounces beef, minced
- 2 tablespoons ham, cut in strips
- 1 leek, chopped
- 3 tablespoons bread crumbs
- Salt and ground black pepper, to taste
- A pinch of nutmeg

Directions:
In a bowl, mix the beef with the leek, salt, pepper, ham, bread crumbs and nutmeg and stir well. Shape 4 burgers from this mix, place them in the air fryer's basket and cook at 400°F for 8 minutes and serve.

Roasted Lamb Rack

Preparation time: 10 minutes
Cooking time: 30 minutes
Servings: 4

Ingredients:
- 1 tablespoon bread crumbs
- 2 tablespoons macadamia nuts, toasted and crushed
- 1 tablespoon olive oil
- 1 garlic clove, peeled and minced
- 28 ounces rack of lamb
- Salt and ground black pepper, to taste
- 1 egg, whisked
- 1 tablespoon rosemary, chopped

Directions:
In a bowl, mix the oil with garlic and stir well. Season the lamb with the salt, pepper and brush with garlic oil. In another bowl, mix the nuts with the bread crumbs and rosemary. Put the egg in a second bowl. Dip the meat in the egg, then in the macadamia mix and place them in the air fryer's basket. Cook at 360°F and cook for 25 minutes, then increase heat to 400°F and cook for 5 minutes. Divide between plates and serve.

Pork Satay

Preparation time: 35 minutes
Cooking time: 10 minutes
Servings: 4

Ingredients:

- 1 teaspoon ground ginger
- 2 teaspoons chili paste
- 2 garlic cloves, peeled and minced
- 14 ounces pork chops, cubed
- 1 shallot, peeled and chopped
- 1 teaspoon coriander
- 7 ounces coconut milk
- 2 tablespoons vegetable oil
- 3 ounces peanuts, ground
- 3 tablespoons soy sauce
- Salt and ground black pepper, to taste

Directions:

In a bowl, mix the ginger with 1 teaspoon chili paste, half of the garlic, half of the soy sauce and half of the oil and stir. Add the meat, toss to coat and leave aside for 20 minutes. Transfer the meat to the air fryer's basket and cook at 400°F for 12 minutes, turning halfway through. Heat up a pan with the rest of the oil on medium-high heat, add the shallot, the rest of the garlic and coriander and stir. Add the coconut milk, the remaining ingredients, stir and cook for 5 minutes. Divide the pork on plates, add the coconut mix on top and serve.

Coffee-rubbed Steak

Preparation time: 15 minutes
Cooking time: 1 hour and 20 minutes
Servings: 4

Ingredients:

- ¼ cup espresso powder
- ¼ cup chili powder
- 2 tablespoons brown sugar
- 1 tablespoon dry mustard
- 3 tablespoons paprika
- Salt and ground black pepper, to taste
- 2 teaspoons ground ginger
- 1 tablespoon dried oregano
- 1 tablespoon coriander
- 1 teaspoon cayenne pepper
- 4 rib eye steaks
- French fries for serving

Directions:

In a bowl, mix the chili powder with espresso, paprika, sugar, mustard powder, salt, pepper, coriander, oregano, ginger, and cayenne pepper and stir. Add the steaks, toss to coat well and set aside for 15 minutes. Transfer the steaks to the air fryer and cook at 400°F for 10 minutes. Flip the steaks and cook for 10 more. Divide between plates and serve.

Leg of Lamb with Brussels Sprouts

Preparation time: 10 minutes
Cooking time: 2 hours
Servings: 4

Ingredients:

- 2 pounds leg of lamb, scored
- 2 tablespoons peanut oil
- 1 tablespoon fresh rosemary, chopped
- 1 tablespoon lemon thyme
- 1 garlic clove, peeled minced
- 1½ pounds Brussels sprouts
- 4 potatoes, chopped
- 1 tablespoon butter
- Nutmeg
- ½ cup milk
- Salt and ground black pepper, to taste

Directions:

Season the leg of lamb with the salt, pepper, lemon thyme, and rosemary. Brush with oil, place in the air fryer's basket and cook at 300°F for 75 minutes. Transfer the leg of lamb to a plate and leave aside for now. Put the water in a pot, add the salt and potatoes, bring to a boil on medium-high heat, cook until potatoes are done. Drain the potatoes, mash them using a potato masher, add the salt, pepper, milk, butter, and nutmeg and stir well. Take spoonfuls of this mix and put in the air fryer's basket. Cook at 400°F for 15 minutes. Transfer them to a plate and set aside. Put the Brussels sprouts in the air fryer, return the lamb as well and cook at 400°F for 10 minutes. Return the potato quenelles to the fryer and cook for 5 minutes. Divide between plates and serve.

Beef Stroganoff

Preparation time: 10 minutes
Cooking time: 30 minutes
Servings: 4

Ingredients:

- 1½ pounds beef fillet
- 2 teaspoons paprika
- 2 tablespoons olive oil
- 1 tablespoon tomato paste
- ½ cup beef stock
- 1 tablespoon Worcestershire sauce
- 5 ounces mushrooms, sliced
- 1 red onion, roughly chopped
- ½ cup sour cream
- 2 tablespoons thyme, chopped
- Salt and ground black pepper, to taste

Directions:

Season the beef with the salt, pepper, paprika and rub with the oil, place in the air fryer's basket and cook at 400°F for 17 minutes. In a bowl, mix the Worcestershire sauce with tomato paste, beef stock, onion, mushroom, and thyme and stir. Take the beef out of the air fryer and transfer to a pan. Transfer the mushroom mix to the same pan that fits the air fryer and cooks at 400°F for 16 minutes. Take the pan out of the air fryer, add sour cream, toss to coat, divide the mushroom mix between plates, slice the meat and place next to vegetables and serve.

Mustard Roast Beef

Preparation time: 10 minutes
Cooking time: 40 minutes
Servings: 8

Ingredients:

- 1 garlic bulb, roasted
- 1 cup mayonnaise
- ⅓ cup sour cream
- 3 pounds beef fillet
- 2 tablespoons chives, chopped
- 2 tablespoons yellow mustard
- 2 tablespoons Dijon mustard
- ¼ cup tarragon, chopped
- Salt and ground black pepper, to taste

Directions:

Season beef with salt and pepper, to taste, place in the air fryer and cook at 370°F for 20 minutes. Take out of the air fryer and set aside for 5 minutes. Squeeze the garlic and put in a bowl. Add the sour cream, chives, mayonnaise, salt and pepper and stir well. In a bowl, mix yellow mustard, Dijon mustard, and tarragon and stir well. Rub the beef with this mixture, place in the air fryer again and cook for 20 minutes. Slice beef and arrange on plates. Add the garlic and mayonnaise mix on top and serve.

Beef with Horseradish and Mustard Marinade

Preparation time: 10 minutes
Cooking time: 55 minutes
Servings: 6

Ingredients:

- 6 bacon strips
- 2 tablespoons butter
- 3 garlic cloves, peeled and minced
- Salt and ground black pepper, to taste
- 1 tablespoon prepared horseradish
- 1 tablespoon mustard
- 3 pounds beef roast
- 1 ¾ cups beef stock
- ¾ cup red wine

Directions:

In a bowl, mix the butter with the mustard, garlic, salt, pepper and horseradish and stir well. Rub the beef roast with this marinade. Place the bacon strips on a cutting board, place the beef on top, wrap the bacon around the beef, transfer to the air fryer's basket and cook at 400°F for 15 minutes. Take beef out of the air fryer and transfer to a pan that fits the machine. Add the stock and wine. Place the pan into the air fryer, reduce heat to 360°F and cook for 40 minutes. Let the roast rest for a few minutes, carve and serve.

Vegetables

Vegetable Spice Mixture

Prep time: 10 minutes
Cooking time: 10 minutes
Servings: 4

Ingredients:
- 2 zucchinis
- 2 carrots
- 1 white onion
- 1 yellow onion
- 1 tablespoon vegetable shortening
- 1 cup green beans
- 1 teaspoon salt
- ½ teaspoon thyme
- ½ teaspoon basil
- ⅓ cup fresh dill
- ¼ cup vegetable stock
- 10 ounces asparagus

Directions:

Wash the zucchini and cut it into strips. Transfer the zucchini to a mixing bowl. Peel the carrots and onions. Chop them roughly and add the ingredients to the bowl. Cut the asparagus into 2 parts and add it to the mixture. Sprinkle the vegetables with the green beans, salt, thyme, basil, and vegetable stock. Mix well. Chop the dill and sprinkle the vegetables with it. Preheat the air fryer to 380°F. Add the shortening to the air fryer, then add the vegetables. Cook for 10 minutes. When the vegetables are cooked, stir them and serve.

Mediterranean-style Roasted Vegetables

Prep time: 10 minutes
Cooking time: 10 minutes
Servings: 4

Ingredients:
- 4 potatoes
- 1 cup fresh plums, pitted
- ⅓ cup cashews
- ½ cup sweet corn
- 3 bell peppers
- 1 cup cherry tomatoes
- 2 red onions
- 1 cup fresh basil
- ½ cup fresh oregano
- 1 teaspoon salt
- 1 tablespoon olive oil
- 7 ounces asparagus
- 1 teaspoon apple cider vinegar
- 1 cup vegetable stock

Directions:

Wash the potatoes, chop them, and put them into a mixing bowl. Sprinkle it with the salt and sweet corn. Slice the bell peppers and chop the asparagus. Add the vegetables to the mixing bowl. Peel the onions and slice them. Chop the basil and oregano. Add all of the ingredients in the mixing bowl. Sprinkle the mixture with salt, olive oil, vegetable stock, and apple cider vinegar. Stir the mixture and add the cherry tomatoes. Preheat the air fryer to 400°F and transfer the vegetable mixture to it. Cook for 5 minutes. Stir and sprinkle it with the cashews and cook the meal for 5 minutes. When the dish is cooked, remove from the pan and serve.

Sweet Potato Taquitos

Prep time: 8 minutes
Cooking time: 5 minutes
Servings: 4

Ingredients:

- 4 sweet potatoes, baked
- 4 corn tortillas
- ½ cup sweet corn
- 1 cup Cheddar cheese
- 1 tablespoon tomato sauce

- 1 tablespoon butter
- 1 teaspoon fresh oregano
- 1 teaspoon fresh basil
- 1 tablespoon sour cream

Directions:

Grate the cheese and combine it with the sweet corn. Combine the sour cream and tomato sauce and stir until smooth. Sprinkle the mashed potato with the oregano and basil. Mix up it carefully. Spread the corn tortillas with the tomato sauce mixture and then add mashed potato. After this, sprinkle it with the grated cheese and roll the tortillas. Preheat the air fryer to 400°F and put butter in the air fryer. Then transfer the taquitos in the air fryer basket and cook for 5 minutes. Serve it immediately.

Vegetable Lasagna

Prep time: 10 minutes
Cooking time: 15 minutes
Servings: 4

Ingredients:

- 4 lasagna noodles, cooked
- 1 cup marinara sauce
- 1 teaspoon salt
- 1 zucchini
- 1 cup fresh basil
- 1 cup cream cheese

- 1 teaspoon ground white pepper
- 1 white onion
- 1 cup mushrooms
- 1 cup heavy cream
- 2 cups grated Cheddar cheese

Directions:

Peel the onions and chop them. Slice the zucchini and mushrooms and put all the vegetables in a bowl with the cream cheese and mix well. Sprinkle the vegetables with the ground white pepper and stir well. Preheat the air fryer to 390°F. Chop the fresh basil. Take the air fryer form and put the 2 of the lasagna noodles in the form. Then add half of the sliced zucchini, mushrooms, and onions. Top with some of the sauce and sprinkle the mixture with half of the basil and grated cheese. After this, cover the mixture with the second part of the lasagna noodles and repeat with the remaining ingredients, topping everything with all the remaining cheese. Top with the cream and transfer the lasagna in the air fryer. Cook for 15 minutes. Remove it from the air fryer and let it rest briefly. Serve warm.

Roasted Garlic Broccoli

Prep time: 10 minutes
Cooking time: 8 minutes
Servings: 2

Ingredients:

- 2 cups broccoli
- 1 cup garlic
- 1 teaspoon salt
- 1 cup vegetable stock
- 1 cup heavy cream
- 1 teaspoon fresh thyme
- 1 teaspoon ground cinnamon
- 1 tablespoon olive oil
- 1 teaspoon butter

Directions:

Wash the broccoli and cut into florets and add to a bowl. Sprinkle the broccoli with the salt and thyme. Add the cinnamon and stir. Slice the garlic and combine it with the olive oil in another bowl and stir well. Add the garlic mixture to the broccoli and stir. Pour the cream into the mixture and set aside for 5 minutes. Preheat the air fryer to 400°F. Add the butter to the air fryer. Add broccoli mixture and cook for 8 minutes. Remove the dish from the air fryer and let it rest briefly before serving.

Tomato Cabbage Stew

Prep time: 10 minutes
Cooking time: 20 minutes
Servings: 4

Ingredients:

- 1 cup white beans
- 15 ounces cabbage
- 2 cups tomato juice
- 1 cup kale
- 1 cup chicken stock
- 1 tablespoon sour cream
- 2 red bell peppers
- 1 cup celery stalk
- 1 teaspoon ground black pepper
- 2 cups water
- 2 white onions

Directions:

Chop the cabbage and combine it with the pepper in a bowl. Add the tomato juice and stir. Chop the kale and celery stalk. Remove the seeds from the bell peppers and slice them. Preheat the air fryer to 400°F. Peel the onions and chop them. Transfer the white bean to the air fryer and add the water. Cook for 10 minutes. Add the cabbage, kale, and celery to the air fryer. Add the sour cream and stir. Add the sliced onion and pour the chicken stock onto the mixture and stir well. Cook for 10 minutes. When the stew is cooked, remove it from the air fryer, let it cool briefly, and serve.

Millet Kale Rolls

Prep time: 15 minutes
Cooking time: 18 minutes
Servings: 4

Ingredients:

- 10 ounces kale
- 1 cup millet, cooked
- 1 cup ground chicken
- 1 teaspoon ground black pepper
- 1 white onion
- 2 bell peppers
- 1 teaspoon salt
- 1 cup tomato juice
- 1 cup vegetable stock
- 1 teaspoon fresh basil
- 1 teaspoon fresh oregano

Directions:

See and chop the bell peppers and peel and dice the onion and add them to a bowl. Add the cooked millet and ground chicken. Sprinkle the mixture with the basil and oregano and stir well. Fill the kale leaves with the millet mixture and roll them. In another bowl and combine the vegetable stock and tomato juice and stir well. Preheat the air fryer to 400°F and transfer the kale rolls to the air fryer basket. Add the vegetable stock mixture and cook for 18 minutes. Remove the kale rolls from the air fryer, let them rest briefly and serve.

Creamed Corn

Prep time: 15 minutes
Cooking time: 10 minutes
Servings: 4

Ingredients:

- 18 ounces corn, frozen
- 1 cup heavy cream
- 1 cup milk
- 1 teaspoon brown sugar
- 1 teaspoon cinnamon
- $\frac{1}{3}$ teaspoon coriander
- 3 tablespoons chives, chopped
- 1 teaspoon oregano
- 1 teaspoon turmeric

Directions:

In a mixing bowl, combine cream and milk together. Sprinkle the mixture with turmeric, oregano, and coriander and stir well. Preheat the air fryer to 400°F and pour the liquid mixture into the air fryer basket. Cook for 3 minutes. Add the sweet corn, brown sugar, and cinnamon and stir. Cook for 7 minutes. Remove the corn from the air fryer and let it rest briefly. Serve in bowls.

Ratatouille

Prep time: 15 minutes
Cooking time: 15 minutes
Servings: 4

Ingredients:

- 12 ounces Feta cheese
- 4 tomatoes
- 2 zucchini
- 2 eggplants
- 1 cup fresh green basil
- 1 cup vegetable stock
- 3 tablespoons tomato sauce
- 1 teaspoon salt
- ½ teaspoon cayenne pepper
- 3 red onions
- 1 white onion
- 1 teaspoon olive oil

Directions:

Crumble the Feta cheese into a bowl and sprinkle it with the cayenne pepper. Wash the zucchini and eggplants and slice them. Peel the onions and slice them. Slice the tomatoes. Add the vegetables to the cheese and sprinkle with the salt. Chop the green basil. Preheat the air fryer to 370°F. Take the air fryer basket and spray it with the olive oil. Transfer all the ingredients to the air fryer basket in layers. Combine the tomato sauce and vegetable stock together and stir until smooth. Pour the mixture into the air fryer basket. Sprinkle the mixture with the basil, and cook for 15 minutes. Let the dish cool briefly and serve.

Candied Carrots

Prep time: 10 minutes
Cooking time: 8 minutes
Servings: 6

Ingredients:

- 5 medium carrots
- 2 tablespoons honey
- 1 teaspoon ground cinnamon
- 1 teaspoon fresh thyme
- 1 teaspoon cardamom
- ½ teaspoon chile flakes
- 2 tablespoons brown sugar
- 4 tablespoon water

Directions:

Peel the carrot and cut into medium strips. Add the carrots to a bowl and combine with the cinnamon, thyme, cardamom, and chile flakes and stir well. Sprinkle the carrot strips with the brown sugar and water. Stir well. Preheat the air fryer to 370°F. Sprinkle the carrot mixture with the spices and stir well. Transfer the carrot mixture to the air fryer and cook for 7 minutes. Add the honey and stir again. Cook for 1 minute. Remove the dish from the air fryer and let it cool briefly before serving.

Baked Cauliflower with Cheddar Cheese

Prep time: 10 minutes
Cooking time: 12 minutes
Servings: 3

Ingredients:
- 15 ounces cauliflower
- 1 cup heavy cream
- 1 cup whole milk
- 2 cup Cheddar cheese
- 1 teaspoon salt
- 2 tablespoons butter
- ½ cup fresh dill
- 2 eggs
- 1 teaspoon oregano
- 1 teaspoon turmeric

Directions:
In a mixing bowl, and beat the eggs. Add the milk and cream and stir well. Wash the cauliflower and cut into florets. Chop the dill and combine it with the cauliflower florets. Sprinkle the vegetables with the turmeric, oregano, and salt. Stir again. Chop the butter and add it to the vegetable mixture. Preheat the air fryer to 390°F and transfer the cauliflower to it. Pour the cream mixture on top and cook for 12 minutes. Remove the cauliflower from the air fryer and let it rest briefly before serving.

Tomalito

Prep time: 15 minutes
Cooking time: 12 minutes
Servings: 4

Ingredients:
- 3 tablespoons butter
- ⅓ cup masa harina flour
- 4 tablespoons brown sugar
- 1 cup corn kernels
- 6 tablespoons cornmeal
- 1 tablespoon milk
- 1 teaspoon salt
- ½ teaspoon ground black pepper
- 2 teaspoons olive oil

Directions:
In a mixing bowl, combine masa harina, brown sugar, cornmeal, and milk together. Add the corn and blend using a blender. Add the salt, pepper, and butter and stir well until smooth. Preheat the air fryer to 400°F. Spray the air fryer basket with the olive oil and transfer the mixture. Cook for 12 minutes. Remove the tomalito from the air fryer and let it cool briefly before serving.

Eggplant Balls

Prep time: 10 minutes
Cooking time: 8 minutes
Servings: 6

Ingredients:

- 3 eggplants
- 1 large white onion
- ½ cup bread crumbs
- 1 egg
- 1 tablespoon sour cream
- ½ teaspoon ground white pepper
- 7 ounces Parmesan cheese, grated
- 1 teaspoon minced garlic
- ⅓ teaspoon ground ginger

Directions:

Wash the eggplants and peel them. Peel the onion. Chop the eggplants and onion and transfer to a blender. Blend the mixture until smooth. Add to a mixing bowl and sprinkle the mixture with the pepper, ginger, and garlic. Stir well and beat the egg into the mixture. Stir the mass until smooth. Add the grated Parmesan cheese and sour cream and stir well. Preheat the air fryer to 400°F. Make balls from the eggplant mixture and dip them in the bread crumbs. Transfer them in the air fryer. Cook for 4 minutes on the both sides. When the eggplant balls are cooked, remove them from the air fryer and let them rest before serving.

Spinach-Mushroom Stew

Prep time: 10 minutes
Cooking time: 15 minutes
Servings: 2

Ingredients:

- 1 cup mushrooms
- 2 cups fresh spinach
- ½ cup whole milk
- 1 cup heavy cream
- 1 teaspoon salt
- ½ teaspoon ground black pepper
- 1 teaspoon oregano
- 1 teaspoon paprika
- 2 tablespoons butter
- 1 teaspoon olive oil
- ¼ cup celery root

Directions:

Wash the mushrooms and slice them. Add to a mixing bowl and season with the salt and pepper. Chop the spinach and combine it with the paprika, oregano, and olive oil in another bowl and mix well. Peel the celery root and grate it. Preheat the air fryer to 380°F. Add the butter to the air fryer and add the sliced mushrooms. Cook for 8 minutes and then stir. Add the spinach and grated celery root. Pour the milk and cream on top and stir. Cook for 7 minutes more. Remove the stew from the air fryer and stir again and serve.

Spinach Pie

Prep time: 20 minutes
Cooking time: 30 minutes
Servings: 6

Ingredients:

- 1 teaspoon fresh yeast
- 1 cup whey
- 2 cups whole grain flour
- 1 teaspoon sugar
- ½ teaspoon salt
- 6 eggs
- 2 cups spinach
- 1 teaspoon basil
- 1 teaspoon turmeric
- 3 tablespoons butter
- 1 tablespoon heavy cream

Directions:

In a mixing bowl, combine fresh yeast and whey together. Add the sugar and stir the mixture until everything is dissolved. Add the flour and salt and knead the dough. Chop the spinach and combine it with the butter and cream. Sprinkle the mixture with turmeric and basil and stir well. Take the air fryer form, add the dough, and transfer it to the air fryer. Transfer the spinach mixture to the dough. Beat the eggs and add to the pie. Preheat the air fryer to 390°F and add the pie to the air fryer. Cook for 30 minutes. Remove the dish from the air fryer and let it rest. Cut the pie into pieces and serve.

Vegan Pizza

Prep time: 10 minutes
Cooking time: 25 minutes
Servings: 6

Ingredients:

- 10 ounces yeast dough
- 1 cup mashed potatoes
- 1 tablespoon tomato sauce
- 1 tablespoon mayonnaise
- 1 teaspoon black pepper
- 2 white onions
- 8 cherry tomatoes
- 1 tablespoon chives, chopped
- 1 teaspoon heavy cream
- 1 jalapeño pepper
- 1 egg yolk
- 1 teaspoon olive oil

Directions:

Roll the dough into the shape of a pizza. In a mixing bowl, combine the tomato sauce and mayonnaise together and stir well. Spread the pizza dough with the sauce mixture. Add the mashed potatoes. Slice the tomatoes. Peel the onions and slice them. Chop the jalapeño pepper. In another bowl, combine the vegetables together. Add the jalapeño and stir. Top the pizza dough with the vegetable mixture. Whisk the egg yolk and spread the pizza edges with it. Preheat the air fryer to 390°F and spray the air fryer form with the olive oil. Transfer the pizza to the air fryer and cook for 25 minutes. When the pizza is cooked, remove it from the air fryer, let it cool briefly, and serve.

Lentil Stew

Prep time: 15 minutes
Cooking time: 15 minutes
Servings: 4

Ingredients:

- 1½ cup lentils
- 4 medium tomatoes
- 4 garlic cloves
- ½ cup chives
- 1 tablespoon chicken stock
- 2 cups vegetable stock
- 1 cup green beans
- 1 teaspoon salt
- 1 teaspoon coriander
- 1 teaspoon harissa

Directions:

Peel the garlic cloves and slice them. Chop the chives. Preheat the air fryer to 400°F. Add the vegetable stock and chicken stock to the air fryer's basket. Add the lentils and cook for 10 minutes. Combine the green beans, salt, coriander, and harissa. Add the garlic. Chop the tomatoes and add them to the mixture and stir. Add the mixture to the air fryer and stir well. Cook for 5 minutes. Remove the dish from the air fryer and discard the liquid from the dish. Serve immediately.

Hasselback Sweet Potato

Prep time: 10 minutes
Cooking time: 7 minutes
Servings: 4

Ingredients:

- 4 sweet potatoes
- 1 tablespoon walnuts
- 1 tablespoon parsley
- 2 ounces olive oil
- 1 teaspoon butter
- 4 garlic cloves
- ⅓ teaspoon onion powder
- 2 tablespoons water
- 4 bacon strips

Directions:

Wash the sweet potatoes and make a cut into each of them. Put a bacon strip in every sweet potato. Crush the nuts and chop the parsley. Peel the garlic and chop it. Add the butter to the sweet potatoes. Preheat the air fryer to 380°F and add the sweet potatoes to it. Cook for 5 minutes. Sprinkle the potatoes with the olive oil, add the water and sprinkle them with the parsley, garlic, nuts, and onion powder. Cook for 2 minutes. Remove the sweet potatoes from the air fryer, let the rest briefly and serve.

Butternut Squash with Apple

Prep time: 15 minutes
Cooking time: 10 minutes
Servings: 4

Ingredients:

- 2 cups butternut squash, peeled and seeded
- 4 apples
- 1 cup water
- 4 tablespoons sugar
- 1 teaspoon ground cinnamon
- ½ teaspoon vanilla sugar
- 1 teaspoon lemon zest

Directions:

Chop the squash into tiny pieces and add to a bowl. Sprinkle the squash with the sugar and cinnamon and stir well. Peel the apples and chop them into the same size pieces as the squash. Combine all the ingredients together and sprinkle them with the lemon zest and vanilla sugar. Add the water and stir. Preheat the air fryer to 390°F. Transfer the apple mixture to the air fryer and cook for 10 minutes. Remove it from the air fryer and stir well. Let it rest briefly and serve.

Sweet and Sour Bok Choy

Prep time: 10 minutes
Cooking time: 8 minutes
Servings: 4

Ingredients:

- 15 ounces bok choy
- 1 tablespoons black sesame seeds
- 1 tablespoon olive oil
- 1 teaspoon kimchi
- 2 tablespoons lime juice
- ½ teaspoon white sesame seeds
- 1 tablespoon honey
- 4 tablespoons water

Directions:

In a mixing bowl, combine the honey and kimchi. Add the olive oil and water and stir. Wash the bok choy and chop it roughly. Sprinkle it with the lime juice, black sesame seeds, and white sesame seeds. Mix well. Preheat the air fryer to 370°F and transfer the bok choy. Cook for 2 minutes and add the honey mixture. Stir well and cook for 5 minutes. When the dish is cooked, remove it from the air fryer, let it rest briefly and serve.

Potatoes with Greek Yogurt

Preparation time: 10 minutes
Cooking time: 20 minutes
Servings: 4

Ingredients:
- 1½ pounds potatoes, peeled and cubed
- 2 tablespoons olive oil
- Salt and ground black pepper, to taste
- 1 tablespoon hot paprika
- 3.5 ounces Greek yogurt

Directions:
Put the potatoes in a bowl, add enough water to cover and leave aside for 10 minutes. Drain, pat the potatoes dry them and coat them with 1 tablespoons oil, salt, pepper and paprika. Put the potatoes in the air fryer's basket and cook at 360°F for 20 minutes. In a bowl, mix the yogurt with salt, pepper and the rest of the oil and stir well. Spread the potatoes on a platter, add yogurt on top and serve.

Mushroom Croquettes

Preparation time: 10 minutes
Cooking time: 8 minutes
Servings: 8

Ingredients:
- 3.5 ounces mushrooms, chopped
- 1 small yellow onion, chopped
- Salt and ground black pepper, to taste
- Nutmeg
- 2 tablespoons vegetable oil
- 1 tablespoon butter
- 1½ tablespoon flour
- 1 tablespoon bread crumbs
- 14 ounces milk

Directions:
Heat up a pan with the butter on medium-high heat, add onion and mushrooms, stir and cook for 3 minutes. Add the flour and stir well. Add the milk gradually, along with salt, pepper and nutmeg, stir, take off heat and leave aside for 2 hours. In a bowl, mix the oil with the bread crumbs and stir well. Take 1 tablespoon mushroom filling and transfer to bread crumbs mix. Coat well and place in the air fryer's basket. Repeat with the rest of the mushroom mix and cook at 400°F for 8 minutes. Place croquettes on a platter and serve.

Bell Pepper Rolls

Preparation time: 10 minutes
Cooking time: 10 minutes
Servings: 8

Ingredients:

- 1 yellow bell pepper, cut in half
- 1 orange bell pepper, cut in half
- Salt and ground black pepper, to taste
- 3.5 ounces feta cheese
- 1 green onion, chopped
- 2 tablespoons fresh oregano, chopped

Directions:

In a bowl, mix the cheese with the onion and oregano and stir well. Add salt and ground black pepper, to taste and stir again. Place the bell pepper halves in the air fryer's basket and cook at 400°F for 10 minutes. Take the bell pepper halves out of the fryer, let them cool down, peel them and place on a cutting board. Divide cheese mix on each bell pepper half, roll, secure with toothpicks and arrange on a serving platter.

Small Bell Peppers Stuffed with Cheese

Preparation time: 10 minutes
Cooking time: 8 minutes
Servings: 8

Ingredients:

- 8 small bell peppers
- 1 tablespoon olive oil
- Salt and ground black pepper, to taste
- 3.5 ounces goat cheese, cut into 8 pieces

Directions:

Cut the tops off the bell peppers, remove the seeds, and place them on a cutting board. In a bowl, mix the oil with salt and pepper. Add the goat cheese and toss to coat. Place a piece of cheese in each bell pepper, place them in the air fryer's basket and cook at 400°F for 8 minutes. Arrange peppers on a plate and serve.

Roasted Red Pepper Salad

Preparation time: 10 minutes
Cooking time: 10 minutes
Servings: 4

Ingredients:

- 1 tablespoon lemon juice
- 1 red bell pepper
- 1 lettuce head, cut in strips
- Salt and ground black pepper, to taste
- 3 tablespoons yogurt
- 2 tablespoons olive oil
- 1 ounces arugula

Directions:

Place the bell pepper in the air fryer's basket, cook at 400°F for 10 minutes, transfer to a bowl, and set aside for 10 minutes. Peel and deseed the bell pepper and cut into thin strips. Place the bell pepper strips in a bowl, add the arugula and lettuce strips. In a bowl, mix oil with the lemon juice, yogurt, salt and pepper and whisk well. Add this to salad, toss to coat, and serve.

Spinach Quiche

Preparation time: 10 minutes
Cooking time: 15 minutes
Servings: 4

Ingredients:

- 7 ounces flour
- 2 tablespoons butter
- 7ounces spinach
- 1 tablespoon olive oil
- 2 eggs
- 2 tablespoons milk
- 3 ounces cottage cheese
- Salt and ground black pepper, to taste
- 1 yellow onion, peeled chopped

Directions:

In a food processor, mix the flour with butter, 1 egg, milk, salt, and pepper and blend well. Transfer to a bowl, knead a bit, cover and keep in the refrigerator for 10 minutes. Heat up a pan with the oil on medium-high heat, add the onion, stir and cook for 2 minutes. Add the spinach, stir and cook for 1 minute. Add the salt, pepper, the remaining egg and cottage cheese and stir well. Take off the heat and set aside for a few minutes. Divide dough into 4 pieces, roll each piece and place on the bottom of a ramekin. Add the spinach filling to the dough, place all ramekins in the air fryer's basket and cook at 360°F for 15 minutes. Let the quiches rest briefly and then serve.

Mediterranean Vegetables

Preparation time: 10 minutes
Cooking time: 45 minutes
Servings: 4

Ingredients:

- 8 ounces eggplant, sliced
- 8 ounces zucchini, sliced
- 8 ounces bell peppers, seeded and chopped
- 2 garlic cloves, peeled and minced
- 5 tablespoons olive oil
- 1 bay leaf
- 1 thyme sprig
- 2 onions, peeled and chopped
- 8 ounces tomatoes, cut in quarters
- Salt and ground black pepper, to taste

Directions:

Heat up a pan that fits the air fryer with 2 tablespoons oil on medium-high heat. Add the eggplant, stir and cook for 5 minutes. Transfer to a plate, season with salt and pepper and set aside. Heat up the pan with another tablespoon of oil, add the zucchini, cook for 3 minutes, transfer to the same plate as the eggplant, add salt and pepper and set aside. Heat up the pan again, add the bell peppers, stir, cook for 2 minutes and transfer to the plate with the vegetables. Heat up the pan with 2 tablespoons oil, add the onions, stir and cook for 3 minutes. Add the tomatoes, the rest of the veggies, bay leaf, thyme, garlic, salt and pepper, stir, transfer to the air fryer and cook at 300°F for 30 minutes. Divide between plates and serve.

Roasted Parsnips

Preparation time: 10 minutes
Cooking time: 45 minutes
Servings: 6

Ingredients:

- 2 pounds parsnips, peeled and cut into chunks
- 1 tablespoon parsley flakes
- 1 tablespoon duck fat, melted
- 2 tablespoons maple syrup

Directions:

Put the melted duck fat in a pan that fits the air fryer. Add the parsnip chunks, place the pan in the air fryer and cook at 360°F for 25 minutes. Add the parsley and maple syrup, toss to coat and cook for 5 minutes. Divide between plates and serve.

Roasted Mushrooms

Preparation time: 10 minutes
Cooking time: 30 minutes
Servings: 4

Ingredients:

- 2 pounds mushrooms, cut into halves
- 2 tablespoons white vermouth
- 2 teaspoons herbs de Provence
- ½ teaspoon garlic powder
- 1 tablespoon duck fat

Directions:

Heat up a pan with the duck fat on medium heat, add the herbs and heat them up for 2 minutes.
Add the mushrooms and garlic powder, stir, place the pan in the air fryer's basket and cook at 360°F for 25 minutes. Add the vermouth, stir and cook for 5 minutes and serve hot.

Maple-glazed Beets

Preparation time: 10 minutes
Cooking time: 50 minutes
Servings: 8

Ingredients:

- 3 pounds beetroots, peeled and cut into medium chunks
- 4 tablespoons maple syrup
- 1 tablespoon duck fat

Directions:

Add the duck fat to a pan that fits the air fryer, add the beet chunks and toss to coat. Place the pan in the air fryer and cook at 350°F for 40 minutes. Add half of the maple syrup and cook for 10 minutes. Divide on plates, drizzle the rest of the maple syrup, and serve.

Grilled Tomatoes

Preparation time: 10 minutes
Cooking time: 20 minutes
Servings: 2

Ingredients:

- 2 tomatoes, cut in halves
- Vegetable oil cooking spray
- Salt and ground black pepper, to taste
- 1 teaspoon dried parsley
- 1 teaspoon dried basil
- 1 teaspoon dried oregano
- 1 teaspoon dried rosemary

Directions:

Spray the tomato halves with cooking oil, season with salt and pepper and sprinkle the parsley, basil, oregano and rosemary on them. Place them in the air fryer's basket and cook at 320°F for 20 minutes. Divide between plates and serve.

Roasted Carrots and Rhubarb

Preparation time: 10 minutes
Cooking time: 25 minutes
Servings: 4
Ingredients:

- 1 pound heritage carrots, peeled and cut into chunks
- 1 pound rhubarb, cut into chunks
- 2 teaspoons walnut oil
- 2 tablespoons orange zest
- 1 orange, cut in sections
- ½ cup walnuts, chopped
- ½ teaspoon stevia

Directions:

In the air fryer, add the carrots and rhubarb and cook at 330°F for 20 minutes. Add the stevia and walnuts and cook for 5 minutes. Transfer to a bowl, add the orange zest and orange sections, toss to coat, divide between plates, and serve.

Roasted Broccoli

Preparation time: 10 minutes
Cooking time: 20 minutes
Servings: 4

Ingredients:

- 1 broccoli head, separated into florets
- Juice of ½ lemon
- 1 tablespoon duck fat, heated
- 2 teaspoons paprika
- Salt and ground black pepper, to taste
- 3 garlic cloves, peeled and minced
- 1 tablespoon sesame seeds

Directions:

In a bowl, mix the broccoli with lemon juice, duck fat, paprika, salt, pepper and garlic and toss to coat. Transfer to the air fryer's basket, cook at 360°F G for 15 minutes, sprinkle with sesame seeds, cook for 5 minutes, and divide between plates.

Zucchini, Squash, and Carrot Medley

Preparation time: 10 minutes
Cooking time: 35 minutes
Servings: 4

Ingredients:

- 6 teaspoons olive oil
- 1 pound zucchini, cut in half moons
- ½ pound carrots, peeled and cubed
- 1 yellow squash, cut into chunks
- Salt and white pepper, to taste
- 1 tablespoon fresh tarragon, chopped

Directions:

In a bowl, mix the carrot with 2 teaspoons oil and toss to coat. Place them in the air fryer's basket and cook at 400°F for 5 minutes. In another bowl, mix the zucchini and yellow squash pieces, salt, pepper and the rest of the oil, and toss to coat. Add them to the air fryer and cook for 30 minutes. Transfer the vegetables to a bowl, add the tarragon, toss to coat, and divide between plates.

Roasted Bell Peppers

Preparation time: 10 minutes
Cooking time: 25 minutes
Servings: 12

Ingredients:

- 12 colored bell peppers, seedless and sliced
- 1 tablespoon olive oil
- 1 yellow onion, peeled and sliced
- Liquid smoke
- Salt and ground black pepper, to taste

Directions:

Put the oil in a pan that fits the air fryer. Add the liquid, onion, and bell pepper slices. Place the dish in the air fryer and cook at 320°F for 25 minutes. Season with salt and pepper, to taste, transfer to a bowl, and serve.

Crispy Cauliflower

Preparation time: 10 minutes
Cooking time: 20 minutes
Servings: 4

Ingredients:

- 12 cauliflower florets
- Salt and ground black pepper, to taste
- 2 cups water
- ¼ teaspoon turmeric
- 1½ teaspoon chili powder
- 1 tablespoon grated ginger
- 2 teaspoons lemon juice
- 3 tablespoons white flour
- 2 tablespoons water
- Vegetable oil cooking spray
- ½ teaspoon corn flour

Directions:

Put 2 cups of water in a pot, add the salt, bring to a boil, add the cauliflower florets, cook for 10 minutes, drain, pat dry, and put them in a bowl. In a bowl, mix the chili powder with the turmeric, ginger, salt, pepper, lemon juice, white flour, corn flour and 2 tablespoons water. Stir well, add the cauliflower florets and toss to coat. Place them in the air fryer's basket, spray cooking oil on them and cook at 400°F for 10 minutes.

Baked Potatoes

Preparation time: 10 minutes
Cooking time: 40 minutes
Servings: 3

Ingredients:
- 3 baking potatoes
- 1 teaspoon fresh parsley, chopped
- 1 tablespoon garlic, peeled and minced
- Salt and ground black pepper, to taste
- 2 tablespoons olive oil

Directions:
Prick the potatoes with a fork and season with salt and pepper, to taste. Rub with the oil, garlic and parsley, place them in the air fryer's basket and cook at 390°F for 40 minutes. Divide them between plates and serve with sour cream.

Potato Gratin

Preparation time: 10 minutes
Cooking time: 20 minutes
Servings: 4

Ingredients:
- 2 eggs, whisked
- Salt and ground black pepper, to taste
- 1 tablespoon cheddar cheese
- 1 tablespoon flour
- 2 potatoes, thinly sliced
- 3.5 ounces coconut cream

Directions:
Place the potato slices in the air fryer's basket and cook at 360°F for 10 minutes. In a bowl, mix the eggs with the coconut cream, salt, pepper, and flour. Divide the potatoes in 4 ramekins, add the eggs mixture to them, sprinkle cheese on top, and cook in the air fryer at 400°F for 10 minutes.

Green Beans

Preparation time: 10 minutes
Cooking time: 12 minutes
Servings: 4

Ingredients:
- 1 pound green beans, washed and trimmed
- Salt and ground black pepper, to taste
- Juice of 1 lemon
- 1 teaspoon extra virgin olive oil

Directions:
Put the green beans in the air fryer's basket. Add the salt, pepper, oil and lemon juice. Toss to coat and cook at 400°F for 12 minutes. Divide between plates and serve.

Onion Petals

Preparation time: 2 hours
Cooking time: 15 minutes
Servings: 4

Ingredients:

- 1 large white onion
- Salt and ground black pepper, to taste
- 2 eggs
- ¼ cup milk
- ⅓ cup panko bread crumbs
- Olive oil
- 1½ teaspoon paprika
- 1 teaspoon garlic powder
- ½ teaspoon Cajun seasoning

Directions:

In a bowl, mix the bread crumbs with the Cajun seasoning and oil and stir. In another bowl, mix the egg with milk, salt and pepper and stir. Peel the onion, place on a cutting board and make 8 cuts in it all the way around. Place onion in a bowl filled with ice water and set aside for 2 hours. Drain the water, pat the onion dry and place on a tray. Sprinkle the onion with the paprika and garlic powder, dip in the egg mixture, then in the bread crumbs mix, place in the air fryer's basket and cook at 360°F for 10 minutes. Turn the onion and cook at 360°F for 5 minutes. Serve with a dip.

Dessert

Heavy Cream Cake

Prep time: 3 minutes
Cooking time: 20 minutes
Servings: 3

Ingredients:

- 2 cups flour
- 2 tablespoons baking powder
- Salt
- 3 eggs
- 1 cup sugar
- 2 cups milk
- 2 tablespoons vanilla extract2 cups heavy cream
- 14 ounces condensed milk
- 1 cup evaporated milk

Directions:

Add the flour and baking powder into the bowl. Mix the eggs, sugar, milk, vanilla extract, and salt. Pour the batter into the round baking tray. Bake at 300°F for 20 minutes in the air fryer. In another bowl, mix the cream, condensed milk, and evaporated milk. When the cake is ready, cover it with the topping and serve.

Coconut Cake

Prep time: 2 minutes
Cooking time: 15 minutes
Servings: 2

Ingredients:

- 2 tablespoons butter
- 3 cups sugar
- 3 eggs
- 4 tablespoons vanilla extract
- 2 tablespoons almond extract
- 2 cups flour
- 2 tablespoons baking powder
- Salt
- 2 cups milk
- 2 cups shredded coconut
- 2 cups heavy cream
- 2 tablespoons butter

Directions:

Add the butter and 2 cups sugar to a bowl. Mix the eggs, 2 tablespoons vanilla extract, almond extract, flour, baking powder, salt, milk and shredded coconut and mix well. Pour the batter into a round baking tray. Bake at 300°F for 15 minutes in the air fryer. Mix the cream and butter and the remaining vanilla extract and sugar into a bowl and mix well. When the cake is ready, cover it with the frosting and serve.

Peanut Butter Pastry

Prep time: 2 minutes
Cooking time: 15 minutes
Servings: 3

Ingredients:

- 2 tablespoons butter
- 1 cup sugar
- 2 cups creamy peanut butter
- Salt
- 2 cups Chocolate, melted
- 2 cups heavy cream
- 2 cups graham cracker crumbs

Directions:

Add the butter and sugar to a bowl. Add the peanut butter, salt, chocolate, heavy cream, and graham crackers and mix well. Pour the batter into a round baking tray. Bake at 300°F for 15 minutes in the air fryer. Let cool, slice, and serve.

Dulce de Leche Cake

Prep time: 4 minutes
Cooking time: 15 minutes
Servings: 3

Ingredients:

- 2 tablespoons butter
- 1 cup cocoa powder
- 1 cup sugar
- 2 tablespoons vanilla extract
- 3 eggs
- 2 cups Flour
- 15 ounces dulce de leche
- Powdered sugar, for dusting

Directions:

Add the butter and sugar to a bowl. Add the cocoa powder, vanilla extract, eggs, flour and dulce de leche and mix well. Pour the batter into the round baking tray. Bake at 300°F for 15 minutes in the air fryer. When ready, dust with sugar and serve.

Blueberry Pie

Prep time: 3 minutes
Cooking time: 15 minutes
Servings: 3

Ingredients:

- 2 tablespoons butter
- 1 cup plus 2 tablespoons sugar
- 2 cups plus 2 tablespoons flour
- 4 tablespoons ground cinnamon
- Salt
- 1 egg
- 2 tablespoons sugar
- 2 tablespoons lemon juice
- 2 tablespoons cornstarch
- 2 tablespoons vanilla extract
- 2 cups blueberries

Directions:

Add the butter and 1 cup sugar to a bowl. Add 2 cups flour, 2 tablespoons cinnamon, and salt to the bowl and mix well. Pour the crust into the round baking tray. Bake at 300°F for 15 minutes in the air fryer. In another bowl, mix the egg, 2 tablespoons sugar, lemon juice, vanilla extract, 2 tablespoons cinnamon, and blueberries and mix well. When the crust is ready, pour the filling and serve.

Pecan Pie

Prep time: 3 minutes
Cooking time: 15 minutes
Servings: 2

Ingredients:

- 2 cups flour
- 1 cup vegetable shortening
- 4 tablespoons butter
- 2 eggs
- 2 tablespoons white vinegar

- 1 cup sugar – 1 cup
- 1 cup brown sugar
- 2 tablespoons corn syrup
- 2 tablespoons vanilla extract
- 1 cup pecans, chopped

Directions:

Add the flour and vegetable shortening to a bowl. Add 2 tablespoons butter and the egg, and white vinegar and mix well. Pour the batter into a round baking tray. Bake at 300°F for 15 minutes in the air fryer. In another bowl, mix the sugar, brown sugar, vanilla extract, pecans, and the remaining butter and stir well. When the crust is ready, pour the filling and serve.

Red Velvet Cake

Prep time: 2 minutes
Cooking time:
Servings: 2

Ingredients:

- 2 cups flour
- 2 tablespoons sugar
- 1 tablespoon baking soda
- Salt
- 2 tablespoons cocoa powder
- 1 tablespoon oil

- 1 cup buttermilk
- 2 eggs
- Red food coloring
- 2 tablespoons vanilla extract
- Cream cheese, frosting
- 1 cup pecans, chopped

Directions:

Add the flour and sugar into the bowl. Add the baking soda, salt, cocoa powder, oil, buttermilk, eggs, red food color, and vanilla extract and mix well. Pour the batter into the round baking tray. Bake at 300°F for 15 minutes in the air fryer. When ready, cover it with cream cheese frosting. Garnish with pecans, slice and serve.

Golden Apples

Prep time: 4 minutes
Cooking time: 15 minutes
Servings: 3

Ingredients:

- 2 golden apples, sliced
- 2 tablespoons sugar
- 2 tablespoons lemon juice
- 4 cups flour
- 2 tablespoons ground cinnamon
- 1 cup pecans, chopped
- 2 cups flour
- 1 cup rolled oats
- 2 tablespoons brown sugar
- 2 tablespoons butter
- 2 tablespoons vanilla extract

Directions:

Add 2 cups flour and sugar into the bowl. Add the golden apples, lemon juice, and cinnamon and mix well. Pour the batter into a round baking tray. Bake at 300°F for 15 minutes in the air fryer. In another bowl, mix the pecans, 2 cups flour, oats, brown sugar, butter, and vanilla extract and mix well. When ready, pour the mixture on the cake, slice and serve.

Sponge Cake

Prep time: 20 minutes
Cooking time: 25 minutes
Servings: 4

Ingredients:

- 4 egg whites
- 4 egg yolks
- 1 cup flour
- 1 cup sugar
- 1 teaspoon caster sugar
- 2 tablespoons brown sugar
- 1 teaspoon vanilla sugar
- 1 cup cherry jam
- 1 teaspoon butter
- 1 cup heavy cream

Directions:

Add the egg whites to a bowl. Whisk the egg whites until soft peaks form. Add the sugar and continue to whisk the mixture until stiff peaks form. In another bowl, whisk the egg yolks and add them to the egg white mixture by folding them in gently. Sift the flour into the egg mixture in another bowl and stir well. Take the air fryer form and spread it with the butter. Transfer the egg mixture to the air fryer form. Preheat the air fryer to 380°F. Transfer the sponge cake to the air fryer and cook it for 25 minutes. In another bowl, combine the cream with the brown sugar and mix well until fluffy. Add vanilla sugar and stir well. When the sponge cake is cooked, remove it from the air fryer and let it cool briefly. Cut the cake into 2 parts crossways. Spread the one part of the cake with the cherry jam and then add the cream. Cover the sponge cake part with the second part and sprinkle it with the caster sugar. Slice and serve the cake.

Chocolate Soufflé

Prep time: 15 minutes
Cooking time: 15 minutes
Servings: 4

Ingredients:

- 1 cup flour
- 4 tablespoons cocoa
- 1 cup dark chocolate
- 2 eggs
- ½ cup sugar
- 1 teaspoon vanilla sugar
- 1 teaspoon ground cinnamon
- ½ teaspoon cardamom
- 1 egg white
- ½ cup heavy cream

Directions:

Sift the flour into a mixing bowl and mix it with the cocoa, sugar, and cardamom. Combine the eggs and egg white together in another bowl and whisk well. Add the cream and stir well. Combine the flour mixture and the egg mixture together and stir well until smooth. Chop the dark chocolate. Preheat the air fryer to 400°F. Take the small soufflé forms and fill the each form with the batter. Add the chopped chocolate and add 2 tablespoons of the batter on top. Repeat these steps with all the forms. Transfer the soufflés to the air fryer and cook for 15 minutes. Remove the dish from the air fryer and let it cool for at least 5 minutes. Sprinkle them with cinnamon and serve warm.

Almond Cookies

Prep time: 15 minutes
Cooking time: 10 minutes
Servings: 6

Ingredients:

- 1 cup almond flour
- 1 cup wheat flour
- 1 teaspoon baking soda
- ½ cup butter
- ¼ cup milk
- ½ cup almonds
- 1 teaspoon vanilla sugar
- 1 teaspoon stevia extract

Directions:

In a mixing bowl, combine the almond flour and wheat flour. Add the baking soda and vanilla sugar and stir well. Add the butter, stevia extract, and milk and stir. Use a hand mixer and combine until smooth. Preheat the air fryer to 380°F. Roll the dough using a rolling pin and make small circles from the dough. Add one almond to the top of every cookie. Transfer the cooked into the air fryer and cook for 15 minutes. Remove the cookies from the air fryer and let them cool before serving.

Blueberry Muffins

Prep time: 15 minutes
Cooking time: 10 minutes
Servings: 4

Ingredients:

- 1 cup frozen blueberries
- 1 teaspoon baking soda
- 1 cup flour
- 1egg
- ½ cup sour cream
- 1 teaspoon vanilla sugar
- 8 ounces sugar

Directions:

In a mixing bowl, beat the egg. Add the sugar and continue to whisk the mixture for 1 minute. Add flour and sour cream and stir well. Sprinkle the mixture with the vanilla sugar and baking soda. Take a hand mixer and mix until smooth. Add the blueberries and stir the batter gently. Preheat the air fryer to 390°F. Fill the every muffin form with the batter and transfer them in the air fryer. Cook the muffins for 10 minutes. When the muffins are cooked, remove them from the air fryer and let them cool before serving.

Cinnamon Apple Pie

Prep time: 15 minutes
Cooking time: 25 minutes
Servings: 4

Ingredients:

- 1 cup butter
- 4 sweet apples
- 1 cup pomegranate
- 1 cup flour
- ½ cup sugar
- 1 teaspoon vanilla sugar
- 1 teaspoon vegetable oil
- 1 tablespoon ground cinnamon
- ½ cup brown sugar

Directions:

In a mixing bowl, combine the sugar and flour and stir well. Add the vanilla sugar and butter and combines using a hand mixer until smooth. Transfer the dough to the freezer for at least 5 minutes. Peel the apples and chop them. Combine the chopped apples and cinnamon in a bowl and stir well. Take the air fryer form and spray it with the oil inside. Preheat the air fryer to 390°F. Remove the dough from the freezer and grate it. Transfer the dough to the air fryer form. Sprinkle it with the pomegranate and add the chopped apple mixture. Sprinkle the mixture with the brown sugar and add the grated dough again. Transfer it to the air fryer and cook for 25 minutes. Remove the pie from the air fryer and let it cool briefly before serving.

Doughnuts

Prep time: 15 minutes
Cooking time: 10 minutes
Servings: 4

Ingredients:
- 1 cup flour
- 1 cup sugar
- 1 egg
- 1 teaspoon baking powder
- 1 teaspoon vanilla sugar
- 2 tablespoons butter
- ½ cup milk

Directions:

Combine the flour and sugar together in a mixing bowl. Add the vanilla sugar and baking powder and stir. Add the milk, butter, and egg to another bowl and mix until smooth. Add the milk mixture to the flour mixture and mix using a hand mixer. Make the doughnuts from the dough. Preheat the air fryer to 400°F and transfer the doughnuts in the air fryer basket. Cook for 10 minutes. Remove the doughnuts from the air fryer and let them cook before serving.

Pumpkin Pie

Prep time: 15 minutes
Cooking time: 25 minutes
Servings: 4

Ingredients:
- 1 cup flour
- 1 cup butter
- ½ cup sugar
- 2 cups pumpkin
- 1 teaspoon ground cinnamon
- 2 tablespoons starch
- 2 tablespoons whole grain flour
- 1 teaspoon cardamom
- 1 teaspoon sour cream

Directions:

In a mixing bowl, combine flour and sugar. Add the butter and knead the dough. Grate the pumpkin and combine it with the whole grain flour and starch. Sprinkle the mixture with sour cream, cardamom, and cinnamon. Transfer the mixture to the blender and blend well. Take the air fryer form and transfer the dough to it. Add the pumpkin mixture. Preheat the air fryer to 400°F and transfer the pie to the air fryer basket. Cook it for 25 minutes. When the pie is cooked, remove it from the air fryer and let it rest. Cut the pie into slices and serve.

Sweet Cheese Balls

Prep time: 15 minutes
Cooking time: 10 minutes
Servings: 4

Ingredients:

- 1 cup Parmesan cheese
- 2 eggs
- ½ cup milk
- 1 cup granola

- ½ cup caster sugar
- 1 tablespoon butter
- 2 tablespoons flour

Directions:

Grate the Parmesan cheese. In a mixing bowl, beat the eggs. Add the milk and whisk until smooth. Add the butter and flour. Use a hand mixer and mix for 2 minutes. Add the sugar and grated cheese and mix again. Make medium-sized balls from the cheese mixture and dip the balls in the granola. Preheat the air fryer to 380°F and transfer the cheese balls in the air fryer. Cook for 10 minutes. Remove the cheese balls from the air fryer, let them rest briefly before serving.

Sweet Carrots with Cottage Cheese

Prep time: 15 minutes
Cooking time: 25 minutes
Servings: 6

Ingredients:

- 2 cups cottage cheese
- 1 large carrot
- 5 eggs
- 1 cup sugar

- 1 teaspoon vanilla sugar
- 1 teaspoon cardamom
- 2 teaspoons sour cream
- 4 tablespoons butter

Directions:

Peel the carrot and grate it. Transfer the cottage cheese to a blender and blend the ingredients for 1 minute. Add the eggs and sugar. Blend the mixture for 2 minutes. Remove the mixture from the blender, add it to a bowl and add the vanilla sugar, cardamom, butter, and sour cream and stir well. Add the carrot and stir again. Preheat the air fryer to 390°F. Transfer the cottage cheese mixture to the air fryer and cook it for 25 minutes. When the dish is cooked, remove it from the air fryer and let it rest. Cut into sliced and serve.

Banana Puffs

Prep time: 15 minutes
Cooking time: 10 minutes
Servings: 4

Ingredients:

- 12 ounces puff pastry
- 3 bananas
- 1 egg yolk
- 1 tablespoon water
- 1 teaspoon olive oil
- 1 tablespoon brown sugar
- 1 teaspoon lemon juice

Directions:

Take the puff pastry and roll it out using a rolling pin. Peel the bananas and blend them in the blender with lemon juice and brown sugar until smooth. In a bowl, whisk the egg yolk and combine it with the water and stir well. Make the squares from the puff pastry and fill them with the banana mixture to make the puffs. Preheat the air fryer to 390°F. Sprinkle the puffs with the egg yolk mixture and transfer them to the air fryer. Cook for 10 minutes. Remove the puffs from the air fryer and let cool for at least 3 minutes before serving.

Fried Bananas

Prep time: 10 minutes
Cooking time: 5 minutes
Servings: 4

Ingredients:

- 1 cup bread crumbs
- 4 bananas
- 2 tablespoons corn flour
- 2 eggs
- 1 tablespoon sugar
- 1 teaspoon cinnamon

Directions:

Peel the bananas and cut them into two parts. Beat the eggs in the mixing bowl. Add the sugar, cinnamon, and corn flour and stir until smooth. Dip the bananas in the liquid mixture, then dip them into the bread crumbs. Preheat the air fryer to 400°F and transfer the bananas. Cook for 5 minutes. Remove the bananas from the air fryer and let it cool briefly before serving.

Cinnamon Buns

Prep time: 20 minutes
Cooking time: 30 minutes
Servings: 6

Ingredients:

- 1 teaspoon yeast
- 2 cups flour
- ¼ cup milk
- 1 teaspoon vanilla sugar
- ½ cup brown sugar
- 3 tablespoons cinnamon
- 1 teaspoon salt
- 10 ounces butter
- 1 teaspoon vegetable oil
- 1 egg white
- ⅓ cup caster sugar

Directions:

In a mixing bowl, combine yeast, and milk together. Stir the mixture until the yeast is dissolved. Add 1 teaspoon of the brown sugar and stir well. Sprinkle the mixture with salt, add the butter and flour and knead the dough. Combine the vanilla sugar, all brown sugar, and cinnamon in a bowl and stir well. Roll the dough out using a rolling pin and sprinkle it with the cinnamon mixture. Cut the dough into medium-sized buns. Set the buns aside for at least 5 minutes. Preheat the air fryer to 400°F. Spray the air fryer basket with the vegetable oil inside and transfer the buns to the basket. Cook the buns for 30 minutes. Whisk the egg whites until you get soft peaks. Add the caster sugar and stir well until smooth. When the buns are cooked, remove them from air fryer and let them rest. Sprinkle the buns with the icing and serve.

Baked Apples

Prep time: 10 minutes
Cooking time: 7 minutes
Servings: 4

Ingredients:

- 4 sweet-sour apples
- ½ cup walnuts
- ¼ cup raisins
- 3 tablespoons honey
- 1 teaspoon cinnamon
- ½ teaspoon ground white pepper
- 1 tablespoon butter
- ¼ cup dried apricots

Directions:

Wash the apples and remove the flesh from them. Chop the apple flesh and combine it with the raisins. Crush the walnuts and add them to the raisin mixture. Chop the dried apricots and add them to the mixture. Add the raisins and butter. Transfer the mixture to the blender and blend until smooth. Add the pepper and cinnamon and stir well. Fill the apples with the raisin mixture. Preheat the air fryer to 380°F. Transfer the stuffed apples to the air fryer and cook for 7 minutes. Remove the baked apples and let them rest for 2 minutes. Serve warm.

Peach Boards

Prep time: 10 minutes
Cooking time: 25 minutes
Servings: 4

Ingredients:

- 4 fresh peaches
- 2 egg yolks
- 4 tablespoons sugar
- ¼ teaspoon salt
- ¼ teaspoon cinnamon
- 1 teaspoon ground cardamom
- 14 ounces puff pastry
- 3 tablespoons butter

Directions:

Take the puff pastry and roll out using a rolling pin. Take the air fryer small forms and transfer the dough. Combine the butter and salt together and stir well. Sprinkle every puff pastry boat with a tablespoon of sugar. Separate the peaches into 2 parts and slice them. Transfer the peaches to the puff pastry boats. Sprinkle the dish with the cinnamon and cardamom. Add the butter mixture. Whisk the egg yolk and sprinkle the peach boats with it. Preheat the air fryer to 390°F and transfer the peach boats to the air fryer basket. Cook for 25 minutes. Remove the cooked dish from the air fryer and let it rest and serve.

Sweet Lemon Bread

Prep time: 20 minutes
Cooking time: 30 minutes
Servings: 6

Ingredients:

- 1 teaspoon baking soda
- ⅓ teaspoon baking powder
- 2 tablespoons lemon juice
- ⅓ cup lemon zest
- ¼ cup lemon curd
- 1 cup skim milk
- 4 cups flour
- ⅓ teaspoon rosemary
- 1 teaspoon vegetable oil
- 1 cup sugar

Directions:

In a mixing bowl, and sift the flour into the bowl. Add the baking powder and baking soda. Sprinkle the mixture with the lemon juice and stir well. Combine the lemon zest and lemon curd together. Add the skim milk, sugar, and rosemary and stir well. Combine the flour mixture and the skim milk mixture together and knead the dough. Let the dough rest for 10 minutes. Preheat the air fryer to 400°F. Take the air fryer form and spray it with the vegetable oil inside. Transfer the dough to the air fryer form and cook for 30 minutes. Remove the dish from the air fryer and let it rest briefly. Remove the dish from the form and slice it.

Cherry Dumplings

Prep time: 10 minutes
Cooking time: 7 minutes
Servings: 4

Ingredients:

- 3 tablespoons cocoa powder
- 2 cups flour
- 1 teaspoon baking powder
- ½ cup whey
- 1 tablespoon sugar
- 1 tablespoon butter
- 1 cup cherry, pitted
- 1 tablespoon caster sugar
- 1 egg

Directions:

Combine the flour and baking powder together and stir well. Beat the egg in a separate bowl and whisk it. Add the sugar and stir the mixture well. Add the whey and stir it again. Combine the liquid mixture and flour mixture together and knead the dough. Roll it using a rolling pin and make the small circles from the dough. Fill every circle with the pitted cherry and make the small balls. Dip the dumplings in the cocoa powder. Preheat the air fryer to 390°F and toss the butter in the air fryer basket. Transfer the dumplings to the air fryer and cook for 7 minutes. When the dumplings are cooked, remove them from the air fryer and sprinkle them with the caster sugar. Serve warm.

Plum Buns

Prep time: 15 minutes
Cooking time: 30 minutes
Servings: 6

Ingredients:

- 1 tablespoon yeast
- 2 cups warm milk
- 1 teaspoon sugar
- ⅓ teaspoon salt
- ½ cup brown sugar
- 4 cups flour
- 1 cup fresh plums, pitted
- 1 teaspoon cardamom
- 1 tablespoon butter
- 1 egg yolk
- 2 tablespoons water

Directions:

In a mixing bowl, combine the yeast and warm milk. Add the sugar and stir the mixture until the yeast is dissolved. Add the salt and flour and knead the dough and set aside. Add the egg yolk to a bowl and whisk. Add the water and stir well. Roll the dough using a rolling pin and make small buns. Stuff the buns with the pitted plums, cardamom, and brown sugar. Sprinkle the buns with the egg yolk mixture. Preheat the air fryer to 380°F. Add the butter to the air fryer and transfer the plum buns to the air fryer. Cook for 30 minutes. Remove the buns from the air fryer and let them cool briefly and serve.

Caramel Pie

Prep time: 20 minutes
Cooking time: 30 minutes
Servings: 5

Ingredients:

- ⅓ cup cocoa powder
- 1 teaspoon baking soda
- 1 tablespoon apple cider vinegar
- 2 cups flour
- 1 cup hot caramel
- 1 cup sour cream
- 1 cup sugar
- 1 teaspoon thyme
- 1 teaspoon vanilla sugar

Directions:

Combine the cocoa powder and baking soda together. Add the apple cider vinegar, flour, and sugar and stir well. Add the sour cream and thyme. Use a hand mixer and mix until smooth. Sprinkle the mixture with the vanilla sugar and stir again. Preheat the air fryer to 400°F and transfer the mixture to the air fryer. Cook it for 30 minutes. Remove it from the air fryer and let it cool. Cut the chocolate across and cover every part with the hot caramel. Cut into slices and serve.

Cheesecake

Prep time: 10 minutes
Cooking time: 15 minutes
Servings: 4

Ingredients:

- 1 cup cottage cheese
- 3 egg yolks
- 1 cup sponge cookies
- ¼ cup butter
- 1 teaspoon sugar
- ¼ cup brown sugar
- 1 teaspoon stevia
- ½ teaspoon vanilla extract

Directions:

Crush the cookies and combine the mixture with the butter in a bowl. Add the stevia. Stir well until smooth. In another bowl, whisk the egg yolks with sugar and add the vanilla extract. Transfer the cottage cheese to the blender and add the egg yolk mixture. Blend the mixture until smooth. Add the butter and blend it for another minute. Take the air fryer form and transfer the sponge cookie mixture. Add the cottage cheese mixture. Preheat the air fryer to 380°F and transfer the cheesecake to the air fryer. Cook for 15 minutes or the surface browns. Remove the cheesecake from the air fryer and let it rest briefly. Remove the cheesecake from the form, cut it into pieces and serve.

Oatmeal Cookies

Prep time: 10 minutes
Cooking time: 25 minutes
Servings: 6

Ingredients:

- 1 cup rolled oats
- 2 cups whole grain flour
- 2 eggs
- 1 teaspoon ground black pepper
- ⅓ cup sugar
- 1 cup butter
- 2 teaspoons vegetable oil
- ½ teaspoon baking soda
- 1 tablespoon lemon juice
- 3 tablespoons brown sugar

Directions:

In a mixing bowl, combine the rolled oats and whole grain flour together and stir well. Combine the baking soda and lemon juice together and stir well. Add the baking soda mixture to the flour mixture. Add the butter and beat the eggs. Sprinkle it with the ground black pepper. Sprinkle the mixture with the sugar and combine using a hand mixer. Knead the dough. Preheat the air fryer to 380°F and spray the air fryer basket with the oil inside. Make the round cookies from the dough and transfer them in the air fryer. Cook the cookies for 25 minutes. Remove the cookies from the air fryer and let them cool. Sprinkle the cookies with the brown sugar and serve.

Chocolate Muffins

Preparation time: 10 minutes
Cooking time: 15 minutes
Servings: 12

Ingredients:

- 7 ounces flour
- 8 ounces sugar
- 1 tablespoon cocoa powder
- 1 ounce milk chocolate
- 3.5 ounces butter
- 5 tablespoons milk
- 2 eggs
- ½ teaspoon vanilla extract

Directions:

In a bowl, mix flour with cocoa powder and sugar and stir. Add the butter and mix well. In another bowl, mix the eggs with the milk and whisk. Add this to flour mix and stir again. Add the vanilla extract and stir again. Add the milk chocolate and mix everything. Spoon this mix into cupcakes molds. Place the dish in the air fryer and cook at 360°F for 9 minutes and at 350°F for 6 minutes. Arrange on a platter and serve.

Semolina Cake

Preparation time: 10 minutes
Cooking time: 15 minutes
Servings: 6

Ingredients:

- 2½ cups semolina
- 1 cup milk
- 1 cup yogurt
- ½ cup raisins
- 1 cup sugar
- 1½ teaspoon baking powder
- ½ cup vegetable oil
- ½ cup baking soda
- Salt

Directions:

In a bowl, mix the milk with the semolina, sugar, salt, yogurt and oil, stir well and set aside for 10 minutes. Add the baking soda, baking powder and raisins and stir again. Pour this into a greased baking pan. Place the dish in the air fryer and cook at 360°F for 15 minutes. Leave the cake to cool down for 10 minutes, slice, and serve.

Chocolate Cake

Preparation time: 10 minutes
Cooking time: 35 minutes
Servings: 6

Ingredients:

- 3.5 ounces white flour
- 4 ounces brown sugar
- 2 tablespoons cocoa powder
- ¾ teaspoon baking soda
- ¾ teaspoon baking powder
- Salt
- ½ cup milk
- 1 egg
- ¼ cup water
- ½ cup hot water
- 1 teaspoon vanilla extract

Directions:

In a bowl, mix the sugar with the cocoa powder, flour, baking soda, baking powder and a pinch of salt and stir. Add the oil, egg, vanilla extract and milk and stir. Add the hot water, stir again, and pour everything into a greased cake pan that fits the air fryer. Cover the pan with aluminum foil, prick the foil, and place it in the preheated air fryer. Cook at 360°F for 35 minutes. Leave the cake to cool down, slice, arrange on dessert plates, and serve.

Strawberry-iced Donuts

Preparation time: 10 minutes
Cooking time: 15 minutes
Servings: 4

Ingredients:

- 8 ounces flour
- 1 tablespoon brown sugar
- 1 tablespoon white sugar
- 1 egg
- 2½ tablespoons butter
- 4 ounces whole milk
- 1 teaspoon baking powder
- 2 tablespoons butter
- 3.5 ounces icing sugar
- ½ teaspoon pink coloring
- ¼ cup strawberries, chopped
- 1 tablespoon whipped cream

Directions:

In a bowl, mix the butter, 1 tablespoon brown sugar, 1 tablespoon white sugar, and flour and stir. In a second bowl, mix the egg with 1½ tablespoons butter and milk and stir well. Combine the 2 mixtures and stir. Shape donuts from this mix, place them on a greased baking sheet that fits the air fryer and cook at 360°F for 15 minutes. Put 1 tablespoon butter with icing sugar in a bowl and beat using the mixer. Add the food coloring, whipped cream and strawberry puree and stir again. Place the donuts on plates and serve with the icing on top.

Cinnamon Bananas

Preparation time: 10 minutes
Cooking time: 15 minutes
Servings: 4

Ingredients:

- 3 tablespoons butter
- 2 eggs
- 8 bananas, peeled
- ½ cup corn flour
- 3 tablespoons cinnamon sugar
- 1 cup panko bread crumbs

Directions:

Heat up a pan with the butter on medium-high heat, add the bread crumbs, stir, and cook for 4 minutes and then transfer to a bowl. Cut the bananas into halves and roll each in flour, eggs, and panko mix. Arrange the bananas in the air fryer's basket, dust with cinnamon sugar, and cook at 280°F for 10 minutes. Transfer to plates and serve.

Amazing Cake

Preparation time: 10 minutes
Cooking time: 17 minutes
Servings: 6
Ingredients:

- 3.5 ounces butter, melted
- 3 eggs
- 3 ounces sugar
- 1 teaspoon cocoa powder
- 3 ounces flour
- ½ teaspoon lemon juice

Directions:

In a bowl, mix 1 tablespoon butter with cocoa powder and stir until you obtain a paste. In another bowl, mix the rest of the butter with the sugar, eggs and flour and whisk well. Add the lemon juice and stir again. Pour this into a greased cake pan alternating with the cocoa mixture. Place the dish in the air fryer and cook at 360°F for 17 minutes. Leave the cake to cool down before slicing and serving.

Banana Cake

Preparation time: 10 minutes
Cooking time: 30 minutes
Servings: 4

Ingredients:

- 1 tablespoon butter, soft
- 1 egg
- ⅓ cup brown sugar
- 2 tablespoons honey
- 1 banana, mashed
- 1 cup flour
- 1 teaspoon baking powder
- ½ teaspoon ground cinnamon
- Salt
- Vegetable oil cooking spray

Directions:

Spray a cake pan with some cooking spray and set aside. In a bowl, mix the butter with the sugar and stir well. Add the banana, honey and egg and stir again. Add the cinnamon, salt, baking powder, and flour and mix. Pour this into a greased cake pan and cook in the air fryer at 350°F for 30 minutes. Let the cake cool, slice, and serve.

Coffee Cake

Preparation time: 10 minutes
Cooking time: 10 minutes
Servings: 4

Ingredients:

- 4 ounces butter
- 4 ounces dark chocolate, chopped
- Juice from ½ orange
- 1 teaspoon baking powder
- 2 ounces flour
- ½ teaspoon instant coffee
- 2 eggs
- Salt
- 2 ounces sugar

Directions:

Heat up a pan with the butter on medium heat, add the chocolate, stir well, and melt everything. Add the orange juice and stir well. In a bowl, mix the sugar with the coffee and eggs and beat using a mixer. Add the chocolate mix, flour, salt, and baking powder and stir well. Pour this into a greased baking pan. Place the dish in the air fryer and cook at 360°F for 10 minutes. Let the cake cool, slice and serve.

Cheesecake

Preparation time: 10 minutes
Cooking time: 15 minutes
Servings: 15

Ingredients:

- 1 pound cream cheese
- ½ teaspoon vanilla extract
- 2 eggs
- 1 cup graham crackers, crumbled
- 2 tablespoons butter

Directions:

In a bowl, mix the crackers with the butter. Place a parchment paper circle in a baking pan that fits the air fryer. Press the crackers mix on the bottom of the pan. Place the dish in the air fryer and cook at 350°F for 4 minutes. Meanwhile, in a bowl, mix the sugar with the cream cheese and eggs. Whisk well using the mixer and add the vanilla. Stir again and pour everything onto the cracker crust. Cook the cheesecake in the air fryer at 310°F for 15 minutes. Leave the cake in the refrigerator for 3 hours, slice, and serve.

Bread Pudding

Preparation time: 10 minutes
Cooking time: 1 hour
Servings: 4

Ingredients:

- 6 glazed doughnuts
- 1 cup cherries, frozen
- 4 egg yolks
- 1½ cups whipping cream
- ½ cup raisins
- ¼ cup sugar
- ½ cup chocolate chips

Directions:

In a bowl, mix the cherries with the egg yolks and whipping cream and stir well. In another bowl, mix the raisins with the sugar, chocolate chips and doughnuts and stir. Combine the mixtures, transfer everything to a greased pan that fits the air fryer, and cook at 310°F for 1 hour. Chill the pudding before cutting and serving it.

Peach Delight

Preparation time: 10 minutes
Cooking time: 30 minutes
Servings: 4

Ingredients:

- 4 cups peaches, sliced
- 2 tablespoons white flour
- 4 tablespoons sugar
- ¼ cup white flour
- ⅓ cup rolled oats
- 1 teaspoon cinnamon
- 3 tablespoons butter
- 3 tablespoons pecans, chopped

Directions:

In a bowl, mix the peaches with 3 tablespoons sugar, 2 tablespoons flour, and 1 teaspoon cinnamon and stir well. Put this into a baking pan. Place the dish in the air fryer's basket and cook at 300°F for 20 minutes. In another bowl, mix 1 tablespoon sugar with ¼ cup flour, rolled oats, pecans, and butter and stir well. Take the pan out of the air fryer, spread rolled oats mix on the peaches. Place the dish in the air fryer again and cook at 310°F for 10 minutes. Set aside to cool and then serve.

Sugar Dough Dippers with Chocolate Sauce

Preparation time: 10 minutes
Cooking time: 12 minutes
Servings: 12

Ingredients:

- 1 pound bread dough
- 1 cup sugar
- ½ cup butter, melted
- 1 cup heavy cream
- 12 ounces semi-sweet chocolate chips
- 2 tablespoons amaretto liqueur

Directions:

Roll the dough, cut into 20 slices and then cut each slice into halves. Brush the dough pieces with butter, sprinkle them with sugar, and place them in the air fryer's basket after you've brushed it some butter. Cook them at 350°F for 5 minutes, flip them, cook for 3 minutes, and transfer to a platter. Heat up a pan with the cream on medium heat, add the chocolate chips and stir until they melt. Take off heat, add the liqueur, and stir again. Pour into a bowl and serve the dippers with this sauce.

Apple Fries

Preparation time: 10 minutes
Cooking time: 7 minutes
Servings: 8

Ingredients:

- 3 apples, peeled, cored and cut into wedges
- 3 eggs, whisked
- ½ cup flour
- ¼ cup sugar
- 1 cup graham crackers, crumbled
- 8 ounces whipped cream cheese
- ½ cup caramel sauce

Directions:

Put the eggs into a bowl and put the crackers and sugar in another one. Dip the apple wedges in egg, then in crumble mix, and place them in the air fryer's basket after you've brushed them with some butter. Fry at 380°F for 5 minutes, flip, and cook for 2 minutes. Meanwhile, in a bowl, mix the cream cheese with caramel sauce. Serve the apple fries with the caramel sauce on the side.

Cinnamon Rolls

Preparation time: 2 hours
Cooking time: 15 minutes
Servings: 8

Ingredients:

- 1 pound bread dough
- ¾ cup brown sugar
- 1½ tablespoons ground cinnamon
- ¼ cup butter, melted
- 2 tablespoons butter
- 4 ounces cream cheese
- 1¼ cups sugar
- ½ teaspoon vanilla

Directions:

Roll the dough on a floured working surface, shape into a rectangle, brush with ¼ cup butter, and set aside. In a bowl, mix the cinnamon with sugar and stir. Sprinkle this onto dough, roll the dough into a log, seal well, and cut into 8 pieces. Let the rolls rise for 2 hours, then place them in the air fryer's basket and cook at 350°F for 5 minutes. Turn the rolls and cook for 4 minutes, transfer them to a platter, and set aside for now. Put the cream cheese and 2 tablespoons butter in a heatproof bowl and heat up in a microwave for 30 seconds. Add the white sugar and vanilla extract and stir well. Serve the cinnamon rolls with this cream cheese topping.

Chocolate Soufflé

Preparation time: 10 minutes
Cooking time: 14 minutes
Servings: 2

Ingredients:

- 3 ounces semi-sweet chocolate, chopped
- 3 tablespoons sugar
- 2 eggs, egg yolks and egg whites separated
- ¼ cup butter
- 2 tablespoons flour
- ½ teaspoon vanilla extract
- Powdered sugar, for serving
- Heavy cream, for serving

Directions:

Put the chocolate and butter in a bowl, introduce in a microwave and heat up for a few seconds. Stir well and leave aside. In a bowl, beat the egg yolks well, add the vanilla extract and sugar and stir well. Add the chocolate and butter mix and flour and stir well. In another bowl, beat the egg whites well and add them to the chocolate mix. Stir, pour everything into 2 buttered ramekins, place them into the preheated air fryer and cook at 330°F for 14 minutes. Serve with powdered sugar and heavy cream on top.

Banana S'mores

Preparation time: 10 minutes
Cooking time: 6 minutes
Servings: 4

Ingredients:

- 4 bananas sliced lengthwise but not all the way through
- 3 tablespoons chocolate chips
- 3 tablespoons graham crackers, crumbled
- 3 tablespoons mini marshmallows
- 3 tablespoons mini peanut butter chips

Directions:

Fill each banana with chocolate chips, marshmallows, graham crackers, and peanut butter chips. Place them in the air fryer's basket and cook at 400°F for 6 minutes. Arrange on plates and serve.

Pumpkin Pies

Preparation time: 10 minutes
Cooking time: 15 minutes
Servings: 9

Ingredients:

- 3 tablespoons sugar
- 1 tablespoon butter
- Water
- 1 pumpkin pie filling
- 3.5 ounces pumpkin flesh, chopped
- 1 teaspoon mixed spice
- 1 teaspoon nutmeg
- 3.5 ounces water
- 1 egg, whisked
- 1 tablespoon sugar

Directions:

Put the water in a pot, bring to a boil on medium-high heat, add the pumpkin, egg, 1 tablespoon sugar, spice, and nutmeg, and stir. Boil for 20 minutes, take off heat, blend using an immersion blender, and set aside for a few minutes. In a bowl, mix the flour with butter and stir. Add 1 tablespoon sugar and some water and knead the dough well. Grease pastry cases with butter, cut the dough and press into pastry cases, fill them with pumpkin pie filling, place in the air fryer's basket and cook at 360°F for 155 minutes. Arrange them on a platter and serve.

Butter Cake

Preparation time: 10 minutes
Cooking time: 15 minutes
Servings: 2

Ingredients:

- 3.5 ounces butter, soft
- 1 egg
- 7 ounces flour
- 3 tablespoons sugar
- Salt
- 6 tablespoons milk
- Vegetable oil cooking spray

Directions:

In a bowl, mix the butter with sugar and beat well using the mixer. Add the egg, flour, salt and milk and stir again. Pour this into a sprayed cake pan, place in the air fryer's basket and cook at 360°F for 15 minutes. Let the cake cool before slicing and serving it.

Sponge Cake

Preparation time: 10 minutes
Cooking time: 28 minutes
Servings: 8

Ingredients:

- 3 ounces flour
- ½ cup butter
- 3 ounces sugar
- 2 eggs
- Cooking spray
- 2 tablespoons strawberry jam
- 3 ounces icing sugar
- 1 tablespoon whipped cream

Directions:

Grease a cake pan with cooking spray and leave aside for now. In a bowl, mix 3.5 ounces butter with 3.5 ounces sugar and beat using the mixer. Add eggs and flour and stir again well. Pour this into the cake pan, place in the air fryer's basket and cook at 360°F for 15 minutes and at 370°F for 10 minutes. Let the cake cool and slice in the middle. In a bowl, mix 3.5 ounces icing sugar with 2 tablespoons butter and beat using the mixer. Add the whipped cream and jam and stir again. Spread thinly on one-half of the cake, cover with the other half, let aside to cool, slice and serve.

Pear Surprise

Preparation time: 10 minutes
Cooking time: 15 minutes
Servings: 4

Ingredients:
- 4 puff pastry sheets
- 14 ounces vanilla custard
- 2 pears, cut in halves, pits removed
- 1 egg, whisked
- Ground cinnamon
- 2 tablespoons sugar
- Whipped cream, for serving

Directions:
Place the puff pastry slices on a working surface, add a spoonful of vanilla custard in the center of each and top with pear halves. Brush pears with egg, sprinkle with sugar and cinnamon, gather pastry around pear and place them in the air fryer's basket. Cook at 320°F for 15 minutes. Divide the pastries on plates and top them with whipped cream.

Conclusion

Discover that cooking can be both easy and fun. Learn how to make amazing dishes, combine unique flavors, and get ready for the culinary experience of the life.

Air fryers are the future in the kitchen, and you want to be one of many people all around the world who is already using it daily.

You don't need any magical tricks to make wonderful dishes. All you need is the best ingredients and the right tool. So, get everything you need and get the hands on an air fryer. There will be nothing standing in the way of the success in the kitchen!

Prepare the best appetizers, the most amazing breakfast and lunch dishes along with some incredible sides, fish, seafood, poultry, meat, vegetables, and dessert recipes.

This special cooking journal that you've just discovered has everything you need to make it happen. Enjoy using a new cooking style. Smart using the air fryer and this new collection of air fryer recipes and have fun doing so.

Recipe Index

Made in the USA
Middletown, DE
18 January 2018